TEASE

A Memoir by
Brandy Wilde

Copyright © 2015 by Clarice Gillis/Brandy Wilde

All rights reserved. No part of this book may be reproduced in any form or by any means, electronic or mechanical, including photocopying, recording, or by any information storage and retrieval system, without permission in writing from the author. Exception is given in the case of brief quotations embodied in critical articles and reviews.

For information: claricegillis@hotmail.com

ISBN: 978-0692518267

Cover by Barbara Gottlieb
www.gottgraphix.com

Published in Partnership with
Purple Distinctions Self Publishing
www.purpledistinctions.com
Venture, CA 93004

Printed in the United States of America

To Montserrat Fontes
With unending love and gratitude

Acknowledgements

I am forever indebted to the finely honed scholarship and guidance provided by: Memoir Professor/writer and friend Dr. Joe Ryan and the students in his memoir class; mentor and author extraordinaire Katherine V. Forrest; Norine Dresser, author, mentor and friend; Dorothy Flanagan/Dreamy Darnell who led me into dancing; author Paulino Fontes who originally thought I had a good story; Montserrat Fontes who taught, encouraged, and pushed me along to the finish; Michele Gillis McEuen, my patient sister; Abby Travis; Las Escritoras de Los Angeles: Sylvia Chavez, Montserrat Fontes, Maria Martinez, Rose Rodriguez, Elvia Rubacalva, and Loana dP Valencia.

My thanks to LAMBDA Emerging Writers Program which gave me a scholarship to study writing with Professor/Writer Ellery Washington.

Table of Contents

1. Tease is in the Mind: Houston, Texas, July 1961 — 7
2. The Roadshow — 24
3. Deeply Red, Wide Blue and Spikey Pink — 32
4. Lillian's Four Fancy Women — 45
5. The Smile Shield: A Powerful Weapon — 49
6. Short Vincent Street — 62
7. The Big Guns and Murder — 76
8. Toledo Theatre Chase — 92
9. The Freezing North — 105
10. Hollywood Starlets, 1962 — 114
11. The Largo, 1963 — 127
12. Gorgeous Friends — 137
13. Pasadena Playhouse, 1964 — 145
14. Top of the Sunset Strip, 1964-1967 — 151
15. New Possibilities, 1968 — 163
16. New York City, 1968 — 178
17. Zucchini and Pizza: Rome, 1968 — 185
18. The Pretty and the Pigalle — 194
19. The Crazy Horse Saloon in Paris — 209
20. Israel, September 1968 — 220
21. Singapore: The Police and Little Pinches — 234
22. The Women of Desker Road — 249
23. Bangkok, Thailand, January 1969 — 269
24. Katmandu, Nepal — 274
25. The Crazy Horse Saloon: Paris and Munich, 1969 — 286
26. How to Live in Paris — 304
27. Mama and the Man on the Moon — 320
28. Zaboo: The Best Dancer in Paris — 335
29. Dreamy: The Dream Unfulfilled — 344
30. Los Angeles, 1970 — 359
31. A New Act — 366

Afterword — 378
About the Author — 386

A few months before I started to dance.
1961

Chapter One

Tease is in the Mind: Houston, Texas July 1961

Sharp brown eyes measured me thoroughly, from breast size to rear width to leg length, then traveled back up my body. Lillian's eyes did not pause as she made a quick assessment of my face and decided.

"Go home and pack your toothbrush and a slinky dress. Be back in an hour. I'm taking some of the girls on a roadshow tonight. We'll be gone for six days. Dreamy can't come with us, but I'll pay you two hundred dollars and take care of all the expenses. How does that sound?"

I nodded, wide-eyed, but couldn't say a word.

"We'll take care of your show costume and music when you get back."

I left Lillian's house with hot sweat running down my back and wobbly knees. Dorothy, my beautiful, green-eyed lover, five foot six with short dark hair, big bust and tiny waist, took my hand. We had been together for a year. She had been a well-known stripper in the early 1950's using the name Dreamy Darnell. She smiled and winked at me. I had just passed the first big test.

We had arrived in Texas from Los Angeles the day before to see if we could get the famous agent for exotic dancers, Lillian McCardle, to be my representative. I never thought it would happen this fast. She already had about ninety girls in her stable and I worried she might not want me. At twenty I was underage for dancing in clubs and had never even seen a burlesque show, but I was determined to learn everything about them. I needed to learn fast so I could support both Dorothy and me.

I was sure I could learn to do the bumps and grinds that Dorothy had demonstrated in our Hollywood attic apartment. She thought I would be a great stripper.

"Honey, you have something sweet and deliciously innocent that makes you stand out. You won't have to do the rough and nasty stuff to get people to look at you," she said. "I've worked with over a thousand dancers, in the chorus line and then with strippers in clubs. I know the real thing when I see it."

I did have some of the things that were needed, that could not be bought: a young curvaceous body with a small waist and long legs, thick wavy strawberry blonde hair that fell almost to my waist, large round blue eyes and a big smile. That's what I hoped would make Lillian want to take me to her heart and into the group of girls she represented, who were dancing all over the east and mid-west United States.

Shyness was my problem. That's what I was worried about. I had never teased anyone in my life and if I had to learn to talk to people, I was in trouble.

Lillian McCardle had been Dorothy's agent in 1950. Lillian had helped her rise to stardom in the burlesque world at the tender age of seventeen. Sadly Lillian left her alone and without guidance in the dangerous work place that was rampant with beautiful girls who wanted to share their drugs with you, prostitution, and mafia club owners who didn't care what happened to you as long as you did three shows a night and sold enough drinks to cover your salary.

I didn't have to worry about that. Dorothy had already said she would be there to take care of me and I believed her, for a while.

Lillian lived in a four-bedroom, yellow brick house. I could hear a dog barking as we walked up the driveway where a luxurious gold Buick sedan was parked.

The front door was opened by what looked like a teenaged girl with dark hair, dressed in sheer red baby-doll shorty pajamas that almost covered her thin torso and immense breasts. Her feet were tiny and bare as she led us to the kitchen table.

Lillian sat there drinking iced tea, trying to coax a fat Pekinese puppy to come to her by making kissey sounds and waving a liver-spotted hand covered in large diamond and amethyst rings. She had curly blonde hair, the full-blown figure of a woman about sixty who was comfortable with a few extra pounds around her middle, and spoke with a deep rich Texas drawl.

"Well, hi, Dreamy, hi, honey. This is Brava, Brava Tutti. She's here for a few days recovering from her recent kidnapping. She just got out of the hospital, poor little thing. It's nice to have some company after my husband George died. You remember George, Dreamy."

Brava looked tired of repeating the story but took her cue from Lillian and told it quickly.

"I was leaving the club and a girl I was working with calls me over to this car so I went over to see what she wanted. When I got there this guy comes out of nowhere, opens the door, throws me into the back seat, and takes me to a cabin somewhere. They raped me with everything they could get their hands on for eight days before I could get away."

I couldn't think of anything to say. I had never heard anyone speak so frankly about such an awful personal horror. Tears dribbled down my face and landed on my chest. Living a quiet life in Long Beach, California with my mom and dad and little sister had not prepared me to know what to do in this situation. I decided to do something my mother had told me many times: listen hard and say nothing.

Lillian hadn't seen Dorothy in seven years. She seemed happy to have Dorothy there but kept her eyes on me as she was patting Brava's hand. I felt like Lillian was searching me for fault lines. I could feel her trying to see my character through her lens of experience with young women. She was looking to see if I was brave enough to hear the truth and stick with my decision to become a dancer after hearing Brava's story. I sat up straighter and tried to look strong.

I liked hearing Lillian say Dreamy's name - "Dreamy" after the long sleepy-looking green eyes that some people called bedroom eyes. I loved that name for our new life and decided to call her Dreamy too. It was only fair that Dorothy should have a sexy name again. That way people would know that she had been a dancer.

We were back at Lillian's place in an hour, as she had directed, after scrambling around to pack the bare essentials for a six day road trip: toothbrush, capris and a couple of tops for riding in the car, comb and brush, black high heels and a low-cut black-silk-jersey cocktail dress. I also took a light brown eyebrow pencil and a Pond's Rascal Red lipstick, which was all the makeup I owned.

Perhaps I didn't feel as much empathy for Brava and her awful kidnapping as I thought because I sat right there and took it all in. When Lillian said, "Get ready," I did. Having that kind of thing happen to me seemed impossible, unthinkable. I didn't have to worry about someone hurting me. So I did not jump into the faded yellow '53 Ford convertible and go back to Los Angeles as a smarter person might have. I was in Texas to become a stripper, and I was going to go all the way to the top, like Dreamy did.

Ecstatic to have found such a beautiful special woman to love, I told my mother I was a lesbian as soon as I discovered it. My mom, dad and four year-old sister Michele were on vacation in Boston visiting my grandmother but I couldn't wait until they were back in California to tell her about my wonderful girl and all her exciting adventures.

Over the phone I gushed, "Oh, Mama, I have found the most wonderful girlfriend. I love her so much. She used to be a stripper and she is so sweet to me. I'm moving from Eric's parent's house in Long Beach into Los Angeles today so Dorothy and I can live together."

I heard the telephone fall to the floor and people yelling, "Beverly, Beverly, are you alright?"

"Your mother has fainted! She just dropped to her knees and fell over. Call back later," someone told me and hung up the telephone.

Why did she do that? I wondered. She had gay friends when we lived in San Francisco and loved them. She had always told me how the girls were smart and the boys so funny and artistic.

My mother was mysterious about her early childhood years and her background. Even though my dad was a chief in the Navy and we had led what was considered a traditional middle-class life in the 1950's, my mother's childhood was still a mystery.

I knew she liked Eric, my ex-boyfriend who had been drafted into the army and was now in South Korea. He had the classic Nordic look - tall, blond and handsome, and was very good to me. I had been ready to marry him for two years, but now I knew I didn't love him.

The feelings I had for Eric couldn't compare to what I felt for Dreamy. I needed to kiss her everywhere, touch her body, and feel her inside me.

Now I knew I would never marry Eric because all I wanted to do was kiss Dreamy and hold her next to me. I was so happy. I didn't feel any guilt or strangeness about wanting her or leaving Eric. Until I met Dreamy I had been waiting anxiously for Eric's return so we could be married. Now I couldn't figure out why that seemed so important.

Dreamy helped me move a few days after Eric returned to America. Eric had gone out but his sister was there. I am sure she told him a lesbian had come to move me into Hollywood, just as she had called my father and told him the story of my move. My mother called me and was furious my dad had learned about Dreamy that way. She had been waiting to break it to him an easier way.

Dreamy and I had been living together about a year when the doctors and heart specialists we had consulted in Los Angeles told Dreamy she needed complete rest and shouldn't work for at least a year. The ventricles in her heart were enlarged and she needed a quiet life. Loving her as much as I did made me want to take care of her. I had never felt maternal toward an adult and I liked it.

I had been looking for a way to get beyond office work and wanted to change our life too. When I started working right after high school I didn't have any skills other than my voice. I was trained in the acting classes that my mother had enrolled me in at the age of nine. I read credit reports on the telephone at Dun and Bradstreet and was pretty good at it.

Most of the women I worked with would have stabbed me in the back for the fun of it. They loved making fun of the way I looked and dressed, calling me "princess." My high-heels and tight skirts just didn't measure up to their loose slacks and baggy blouses.

I couldn't see my future there. To support both of us I would need to earn a lot more money than I had last year. I wanted to take care of Dreamy so we could be happy together.

We decided to see if we could find an agent in Hollywood and I would try to become an exotic dancer. I hoped living that kind of life would be exciting and glamorous but safe with Dreamy next to me. There were two burlesque theaters downtown on Main Street, and strip clubs were all over Hollywood and the valleys. Dun and Bradstreet was located at 6th and Main, above the bus station, and the best burlesque theater was only half a block north.

The agency we chose had two partners, Bill Klein and Chuck Bradley, who wanted me to start dancing right away and were willing to teach me how to bump and grind. The evening after Dreamy and I had been to their Hollywood office, they sent

Earl, a plump graying middle-aged agent to the large attic room of the old-age home I shared with Dreamy, to teach me the moves. We were the only ones under sixty-five living there as only younger people could climb the narrow stairs up to the third floor.

Earl looked at me objectively, as a doctor might look at an x-ray, and said, "Yeah, that's fine." I had on a baby blue and white gingham bikini with a little white lace over the bosom. My mother had bought it for me.

He put a 45 RPM record on the small phonograph he had carried up to the third floor. I heard *Tequila* by The Champs loud and clear. It actually made me feel like dancing. I had been hoping for a strong beat because I needed the help but I was worried Mrs. Kellogg, the manager, would send up her sixty-five year-old daughter to tell us to "pipe down" as she always did to the few elderly ladies on the second floor who were usually drunk early in the evening. Each one was a solitary drinker.

Earl started making his rear end and hips go around in big circles in time to the music and throwing his pelvis forward so everything bounced. His feet didn't move. I was horrified. I turned my head away from him. I didn't want to look. I didn't want to look like that.

"Yeah, yeah, it's easy. Just give it a try. Come on now," said Earl still moving his hips to the music. "Put all your weight on your right foot, you're right handed, right? Bend the knee and put your left foot straight out in front about twelve or fourteen inches or so it's comfortable. Now, the lower you squat, the easier it is to grind. Keep your back straight! Don't arch like that! Always point that left foot otherwise you look awkward. Yeah, yeah, that's good. Hold in your stomach. Put your arms out in the air, not down at the sides! Rounded, not like broomsticks. Now, start making circles with your hips only. Don't move anything else. Loosen up your ass, for God's sake, girl!! Yeah, yeah, it takes practice."

Taking my hand, he tried to keep me going as he kept time by pumping my hand up and down with his. The music was loud, deep and rumbly with the singer blasting out *Tequila* over and over. My eyes were trying to pop out of my head at the same time I wanted to close them. Dreamy left the room, trying to stop giggling. Earl was patient and friendly, but I didn't think he was the teacher for me. We hadn't even started the bump and I didn't want to imagine what he would look like doing that.

We decided that night it would be a better idea for us to go out of town for a few months.

"Honey you need to get out in the world for a few months to learn the basics and get some practice before coming back to Los Angeles as a star. I had an agent in Houston who helped me get started and could get me great money. We should go see Lillian. Want to go to Houston?" Dreamy said while nodding her head.

I would have followed her anywhere. It took us a few months to save the three hundred dollars for such a long trip so I had time to practice grinding before I was to meet the famous Lillian.

Now we were here in the middle of Houston, Texas, in the center of everything we had been working toward. Closets and chests with shiny long dresses made of gold lame` and silver sequins, drawers of silver, gold, black and white opera length gloves, jewelry boxes too full of rhinestone earrings and bracelets to close, shoes and other little bits of costumes that had been outgrown or disliked, filled a bedroom of Lillian's house that had been converted into a huge closet. All we had to do was dive in.

Dreamy and I looked at and felt everything. I didn't want anything scratchy and Dreamy said it had to look touchable. I tried on the floor length, strapless aurora borealis sequin gown which was a little big in the bust and hips, but was the right length so we took that one. I secretly love pink, but white and pink would not have been my first choice. As a strawberry blonde I had been trained by my mother to choose blues and greens, but this gown fit, was pretty and available.

"A girl can spend a long time teasing with her panel," Dreamy said as she held out the sequined belt meant to ride low on the hips. "See, it has this floor length section of pretty chiffon attached in the front to cover the pussy and in the back to cover your ass. It sways around between your legs, and when it touches your skin, the guy probably wishes he was touching you there. They think they're going to see pussy any second so they don't get bored. Just let the audience see more and then a little bit more of your inner thigh."

We chose bras and pants and a G-string that would complement the gown, then long classic white opera gloves to complete my costume. Lillian was so generous. She gave me a brilliant blue rhinestone ring that fit over the glove for good luck, and I was ready for performance. Almost.

Lillian fluffed her hair up in the back with one hand as if she wanted to cover a thinning spot on her scalp. She said, "Dreamy, get her walking the bride's walk all around the room to this. The other girls will be here in a little while and I want to leave right away. That's what you do, honey. Start with your feet together, step forward with the right, other foot out to the side, lift the hip, and step to the front, out to the other side, lift the hip and step forward again. Do the bride's walk and always smile, smile, smile."

She turned on the Hi-Fi and out came Billy Straihorn's smooth and silky *You Go to My Head* so I could practice my new steps.

"Hold your head up, smile and look proud of what you've got to show off. Yes, like that," Lillian said as she turned to pick up her puppy and leave the room, cooing to the dog she would be missing for several days. "Pearly girl, come on little Pearl."

Suddenly she turned back to look right in my eyes. "Your parents aren't going to come busting in here looking for you are they? I mean, what do they think about their baby-faced girl leaving California with an older lesbian dancer to become a stripper?"

"Well, at first my mother was searching Chinatown for an assassin to kill Dreamy, but now she is calmed down. She didn't want me to live the hard life she had seen some of her friends in San Francisco endure. My mom sees I'm happy now and she's trying to be all right with it. We told her I am doing the bookkeeping for a chorus line and that's why we're traveling," I said with an embarrassed smile.

Lillian seemed satisfied for the moment.

"You can stop for a minute, grind, then start the bride's step again. Try and feel the music through your body. See where it takes you. You might surprise yourself," Dreamy said as she coached me with an objective eye. "Move your hands like this, draw the audience toward you with your fingers. Make them want to get on stage with you. Don't worry, the club bouncers won't let them do it. Keep smiling."

"So what are you going to name her?" Brava murmured to Lillian as she watched me bride-stepping stiffly around the room. "You have to name her something that brings up her hair. I mean, look at it. What? Brandy? Sherry? Cherry? Honey? Torchy? Amber? Peachy? What? Tiger Lily!" Brava laughed at her joke as she answered her own question. "I think it should be Brandy, and for now, she can use the last name Wilde."

"We have enough Honeys and too many Torchys," Lillian said as she paused in the doorway, looking angry for a second. Then she smiled at Brava and pointed two gold-laden fingers at me. "I like Brandy Wilde, Brava. That's it."

I hadn't been asked for my opinion, but I felt lucky because I liked Brandy too. I had been called Candy for ten years so it already felt familiar. Brandy Wilde would be my name for many years.

I said a breathless, watery-eyed and shaky goodbye to Dreamy, trying to keep a rein on my emotions so I would look like a professional. There was no time to hold on to her as tightly or as long as I wanted. The girls and luggage were already settled in the car.

The first two girls had arrived just as I was changing into my black knit pants and pale aqua blouse for traveling. They began loading their costume bags and suitcases into the wide trunk of the car without going into the house to save time. They seemed to know how to pack Lillian's car without instruction.

I studied them while we waited in the driveway for the last dancer to arrive. Other than Brava Tutti in her red see-through pajamas and Dreamy, they were the first real strippers I had seen.

Coushay Curtis looked about nineteen or twenty. Six feet tall and lanky with blondish hair that showed an inch or more of dark roots, she looked at me and smiled. Coushay turned around and around like she didn't know where she was or how she had arrived there. Lillian had told me she didn't have much more experience than I did. Coushay had only worked a couple of afternoon shows at a small club and was learning the business.

"Sit in the back Coushay and try to stay still," Lillian told her.

Debbie Doll, a beautiful busty redhead in her late twenties, with a friendly smile, drove up in a new black Jaguar E Type convertible. Her white baby French poodle was in the front seat. Debbie handed the car keys and the tiny puppy, which was dressed in a pink and silver collar, to Brava. She would take care of them while we were on the road.

Debbie was careful not to spill the bourbon and ice in the clear plastic glass she carried. She had the bottle tucked safely under her arm. Since Texas was a "dry state" she didn't expect to see "package stores" in the small towns we would drive through. Debbie kept her bottle close.

She was wearing a navy blue and white linen pants suit and managed to look crisp in the ninety-five degree evening bloom. Debbie started to sit in the front seat, but Lillian asked her to sit in the back.

Pepper Powers showed up last, throwing herself onto the back seat without a word. She slammed the door, leaving her costumes and suitcase on the street to be packed in the trunk by

Coushay. Tall, dark and sultry, Pepper seemed to be there fresh from a fight. Her fiery expression and deep breathing suggested that, in her head, she was still arguing with someone. She was scary but beautiful. I was sure if I said a word to her she would fire all that anger at me.

On our drive from Los Angeles to Houston, Dreamy had told me to treat each dancer like she was the star of the show, and I would get along fine.

"Strippers are sensitive beings, honey. You just look at one of them like you think her gown is an off-shade of red or her breasts are on the smallish side, or she has a saggy behind, and you will pay for it down the road somewhere. They seldom forgive a slight – real or imagined," Dreamy had said. Even this early in my career, I could see it was good advice.

"Sit in the front with me Brandy. I want to talk with you," Lillian said.

We left Brava and Dreamy holding the puppies, Lola and Pearl, standing in the light of the open doorway.

I didn't know where I was going or what I was going to do when we got there. I had always been shy and had never met any of these people. Feeling like I lived in a different world than theirs, a world of exotic flowers, I had to trust them and was not very good at doing that.

As Lillian drove toward the highway she began to tell us where we were going.

"First stop is going to be Waco, Texas. You'll dance for the Chamber of Commerce's annual fundraiser. You remember them, Debbie. Then we go on to the Millionaires' Club in Hobbs, New Mexico. We'll work El Paso and Corpus Christi then head on home," she said.

Lillian took these trips every few months. Dreamy had told me about the road trips she had been on with Lillian while we were still in Los Angeles. It sounded like fun the way Dreamy talked about it. Lillian always had a big fancy Buick to ferry the girls around in. To the public her girls were all stars. She made sure they arrived at the club dates in style. When Lillian was there, her girls were treated "like ladies," by audiences, hotel and restaurant employees.

Lillian had said she would pay me two hundred dollars for going on the road with them. I would dance fifteen minutes or less at each club on three different nights. She would pay for the food, lodging, gasoline, and do all the driving. Two hundred dollars was more money than I could make in four weeks of eight-hour days at my office job in Los Angeles and had to be more fun.

We drove past the site where Houston was remodeling the sports arena. They were having trouble of all kinds because it was so huge. The air conditioning system, making its own ecosystem in the upper seats, was causing small tornadoes. They called it the Astrodome.

As we drove the 150 miles to Waco, Lillian told me something about her side of the burlesque world. "The hardest parts of being an agent," she said, " are finding good-looking girls that are willing to show some personality while dancing, have a large enough bosom for men to pay to look at and an act that's hot, but not so strong it will bring the police in to close the club down."

Lillian told me a good agent sometimes trains girls to dance sexy enough so that she can find them work, as we had experienced in Hollywood.

"These moves don't come naturally to most girls, you know. Everything has to be exaggerated so it looks like 'just for you, baby' slowed down or speeded up for the best effect. It has to look like you're having a good time up there. There are choreographers available to create special acts with props like Lili St. Cyr and her bath-tub, but it's really the dancer's personality that sells an act," she said as she fluffed her hair up in the back.

There was nothing but black outside the car window. Nothing along the road to look at and the yellow line went straight ahead without a curve. Debbie and Coushay were sleeping but every few minutes I heard a fitful snort from Pepper. I started thinking about my first steps on the way to this road trip.

I had been working in downtown Los Angeles for a year when I returned to Dun and Bradstreet from my first paid vacation in August of 1959 and met Dreamy, our new supervisor. She was a beautiful, almost tough-looking dark-haired woman with gorgeous, emerald-green movie star eyes with long black lashes. My heart fluttered dangerously at the first sight of her. I became extremely aware of myself. How was I standing? I better stand up straight. Did I look pretty? I wondered what she saw as she looked at me, in front of the telephone order board, staring at her.

I was wearing my best blue dress with the tight bodice and full skirt with two extra-full crinoline slips that emphasized my figure, new and shiny black patent leather high heels. My body became a billion tingling nerve endings on maximum alert.

I could tell she was a lesbian. Her style was like the girls my mom had been friends with in San Francisco. She had short dark hair slicked back in a DA, like Elvis Presley's, and she wore socks instead of nylons, at a time when only men and old ladies wore them. I started going to gay bars with my mother when I was ten to hear Blackie O'Farell, a special friend of hers, sing. Blackie always sang "Little Girl" just for me.

Dreamy smiled, a very little smile, her eyes crinkling like a cat kiss. Her gaze rested on me for a moment. I could tell she knew everything there was worth knowing, and I wanted to learn it all… from her.

Lillian continued her lesson while driving about eighty miles an hour, drinking a bottle of 7-Up. "An agent has to choose a photographer that has the special skills needed to shoot girls in costume as well as nude and semi-nude so they appear glamorous and not vulgar. That way the clubs have sexy 8 x 10 glossies to display in their front windows. She soothes the girls' bruised egos and ruffled feathers when they feel, as all artists feel, that they have not been treated with enough respect." She took a quick look at me, squinting as if to see if I was that kind of girl already.

"If a girl isn't pretty, or doesn't have some kind of allure, she has to let them down kindly with a, 'Honey, this business is too rough for a sweet girl like you' or some such line."

Lillian sighed. "It's a big deal when an owner wants a girl enough to pay her two or three hundred a week to work. That's why you have to have good pictures, beautiful costumes and great music. Remember, don't sing along with the lyrics to your music. It takes the audience's attention away from your dancing.

"Most especially, ALWAYS be on time and sober when you get there. It's money, money, money in this business. The boss is thinking: Is she worth the money? Does she have a strong act? Is she a troublemaker? Will she draw customers in and will they come back to see her again?"

She continued, "You know, I used to be a singer."

Lillian fluffed her hair in the back while looking over at me like she wanted to gauge my reaction. I was interested in everything she had to say to me, grasping for anything to make myself more comfortable. I didn't know I would feel this shaky. Feeling more secure with every little attention she paid me, I tried to relax and enjoy the ride.

The other girls slept in the back seat. I'm sure they had heard Lillian's stories about "how to be a good little stripper" before. It only took a few hours to get to Waco.

We went to a motel to hang up our wardrobe then have dinner. Coushay and I shared a room while Debbie and Pepper had the room next to ours. Lillian's room was three doors down the hall. It was close enough if we needed her but still gave her some privacy.

I was surprised how little it cost to eat out in Texas. That morning in Houston, Dreamy and I had paid sixty two cents each for our bacon and eggs with biscuits. Lillian and the girls seemed to enjoy their dinner, but I didn't have an appetite, just a bad case of nerves. I had a glass of water with crushed ice and slept.

The next morning after two hours with comb and brush, more makeup than I had seen outside a drug store, Aqua Net hairspray, tweezers, pink and red finger and toenail polish, and both Tigress perfume and Chantilly eau de cologne, the girls were ready to go to breakfast around ten a.m. On the way to the diner, next door to the motel, Lillian's girls looked like they were "camera ready."

I didn't do much more than wash my face and brush my hair and teeth. No one said anything, but they looked at me with questioning eyes. Lillian didn't let me go with them until I went back in the room and put on some Ponds lipstick, my light brown Maybelline eyebrow pencil and some borrowed rouge, under her direction. I had worn stage makeup in high school plays but I had no idea people wore it during the daytime too.

While the girls were eating their eggs and toast, between bites Lillian gently said, "Brandy, people are going to know who you are when you walk into someplace now. Especially in these small towns where your arrival is going to be the most interesting thing that has happened in a long time.

"There might be people, men and women, who stand around outside your hotel just to see what you look like. You see anyone here that looks interested in this table?"

I looked at the yellow and pale green leatherette booths around us. Everyone there, three cooks, four waitresses and twenty-some customers, faced our table, their eyes wide, ready to catch each movement or word. I started to laugh, and ducked my head, but Lillian reached out and squeezed my hand to silence me.

"They might follow you around town to see what you do," she said quietly. "You can draw customers into the club depending on how you look at breakfast or even buying toothpaste at the drug store, and make the club owner happy that he booked you."

I could feel Debbie and Torchy looking directly at my shadowless, unlined, naked eyelids.

As she slowly sipped her creamy coffee Lillian said, "My girls are stars and they look like stars all the time. You know what I mean, honey?" she said with a gentle gesture toward her two stars at the table. "We'll take care of Coushay this morning."

She had the same proud shine in her eyes looking at Debbie and Torchy as she did when she looked at her dog Pearl. Lillian didn't glance away until I nodded yes. I was embarrassed but grateful that she had told me what to expect.

Chapter Two

The Roadshow

The day was already hot and it was not going to cool off in the evening. We lounged around the little air-conditioned restaurant eating and reading the newspaper. I wasn't hungry so I drank black coffee, no sugar.

Later, the girls had a late lunch but no dinner. Part of Lillian's philosophy of striptease was that a dancer should always eat early. She told me, "The audience can see a pork chop right through a beaded gown."

I believed her.

It seemed like Coushay ate every minute she was out of Lillian's sight. She had walked a couple of blocks to a little market and brought back a hefty sack of Butterfinger and Baby Ruth candy bars and peanuts which she said were for both of us, but she ate it all. I couldn't have eaten a thing anyway. I guessed she was as nervous as I was but I didn't ask. Turned out I was wrong.

"This is so gooood. I never had enough money to buy more than one candy bar at a time and even then I had to share it with my sister. Now I can buy all I want and more for later," Coushay said while chewing happily.

We read, played cards and watched television in our rooms to stay cool until around seven, when we started getting ourselves ready for the evening performance. Lillian had brought an iron and a sewing kit. She was very particular that all costumes were clean, had no wrinkles or dangling sequins.

About nine in the evening, on the way to the 200,000 acre ranch outside of Waco where we would perform, Lillian told us the arrangements.

"Tonight you're going to take it all off for these fellows. You don't have to worry that the police are going to be anywhere around there because the Chief will be in the audience" she said. "Pepper, you're going to go on first, then Coushay, then Debbie, you'll go last."

The girls would strip and except for jewelry and shoes the dancers would be nude, which was against the law. Pepper, Coushay and Debbie, in that order, would dance on a flatbed truck in the middle of a large pasture normally used for grazing cows.

Lillian said, "We're going to arrive at the back door of the large ranch house. Go quickly with the guard to the dressing area. I'm going outside to do a sound check for the music and make sure they have the security in place."

Lillian smiled and said, "Six feet away from the truck there should be a tall barbed wire fence that goes all the way around. In the little gap, where you go up the stairs, there will be a guard to help you and keep everyone else out. These guys may be the Chamber of Commerce here in Waco, but they are wild."

The girls had two adjoining air-conditioned bedrooms to use as dressing rooms and a private bathroom that could not be reached from the hall. The largest room had a fully stocked bar and everything set out for us to help ourselves. While Lillian was driven out to the pasture, I stayed with the dancers.

When she came back Lillian walked directly to me, took my wrist and led me to the bathroom. She locked us inside.

"Brandy, I want you to stay here at the ranch house while the girls are doing the show. I'll be with you," she said seriously. "We'll wait until the men walk out to the field, then go to the patio. It's been set up as a casino so there's some action after the show. There will be the bar, four or five little card tables and a blackjack table. We're going to stay around here for about an hour for the girls to dress and mingle a bit. I'll take a blue scarf out of my purse when I think it's time to leave. As soon as you see it, you come to me right away and we'll all go to the car together.

"When the guys come back from watching the show, be very careful. You stay with the group and don't wander off somewhere. You're going to be the only one they haven't seen nude and they're going to be curious. Some of them are already pretty drunk. Now smile," she trilled, "because you look scared to death. Nothing to worry about," she said as she fluffed her hair and turned to leave me.

I wanted to reassure her so I tried to smile, but I felt wobbly in the knees again. My heart felt like it had started to race around my body. My breathing was fast and I was beginning to feel dizzy. I put a hand on my chest, an old habit that felt protective. Who had ever heard of anyone dancing on a flatbed truck? I couldn't help wondering what the barbed wire was for and what the dancing would look like. I had never seen a burlesque show, just a few enticing steps that Dreamy had shown me in Los Angeles and the bride's walk I had learned the day before. *Breathe and relax*, I told myself. *I'm not dancing tonight*. The second try at smiling was better.

Pepper was dressed in a floor length, slender, silver lamè gown and silver pumps with spike heels. Her panel, bra and G-string were cherry red lamè and silk chiffon. She had on silver earrings that looked like long shiny new construction nails. Lustrous black hair swayed as she walked holding a double shot glass filled with amber liquid as Lillian and I joined the others in the dressing room. In full stage makeup Pepper's dark eyes looked huge while her cheeks had a peachy glow. I hadn't realized her breasts were quite that large.

I tried to peek out the window to see the members of the Chamber of Commerce for Waco, Texas, a town of about 100,000 people as Lillian pulled me back. They had been served barbeque beef right off the spit with all the trimmings and bottles of beer, bourbon or Scotch. These men operated in a culture that urged hard drinking and taking whatever they wanted. They were the local ranch and farm owners, business men and the budding politicians of Texas.

Dressed in light denim or khaki pants, white dress-shirts with rolled up sleeves, bolo ties, Stetsons and cowboy boots, they carried their beers or bottles of whiskey as they made their way out to the field. Some looked like they were still talking business while others were looking around for the dancers. Not everyone had been there before.

At ten o'clock, Pepper was helped into a station wagon and driven out to the field. The bodyguard who had been in front of the bedroom door went with her and was replaced by an older guard who also worked for our host, owner of the ranch, Señor Carlos Montemayor. Don Carlos was a current member, former president, of the Chamber of Commerce.

Lillian and I went to the casino area, leaving Coushay and Debbie to wait their turns. I could see the man guarding the dressing room doors from the blackjack table. Each act would take about fifteen minutes.

Torchy's music started with the drums of *Temptation*, so loud I could hear it all the way to the bar. A few men had stayed to gamble instead of going out to see the show. Lillian's public personality came on like a thousand watt klieg light. She teased those old boys at the same time telling them how rough and rugged they were. She smiled. Her deep, raucous, and infectious laughter blended well with the sensual music behind it.

The truck was about nine hundred feet from the house, but I could hear the rhythmic pounding drum beat of the music and shrill whistling of the crowd. Lillian had told us a generator was out there for the lights and tape recorder for each dancer to turn on, just like last year's party and the one before.

The men were yelling. The music was slowing. There were only thirty-five men, but they managed to make enough noise for a hundred. A drum solo that started slowly and led to a frantic conclusion ended Pepper's act and the thirty-five that had sounded like a hundred now screamed and applauded like two-hundred men who needed relief.

I was glad I wasn't going to dance that night. The noise and sexual tension these macho men exuded was overwhelming. I didn't want to move a foot away from the safety of Lillian's gaze.

Pepper was back in the house. Her hair hung in wet strings. She had taken a short scarlet silk robe to cover herself in the station wagon but the light silk couldn't soak up the continuing sweat. Her hair and body dripped on the tile as she went into the dressing room to shower and dress.

Coushay was on the truck. I could hear the music as she started dancing to *I'm in the Mood for Love* and just a minute or so later I turned toward the field when I heard the roar. "She's down," said Lillian, with a deadpan expression on her face.

Earlier in the day Lillian had told Coushay she should stand up a little longer in her act. "Once you take off your gown and kneel down on the stage, you do the rest of your act on the floor bumping and grinding or you lie on your back and wave your legs around. The audience doesn't see as much of you because you can't move around the stage. Stay on your feet a while longer and get more tips."

Lillian turned to me and said, in what I was coming to recognize as her *I am now training a young stripper* mode, "It's called floor work and can be sexy but it's boring after a few minutes so you save it for the end. How can you get up and continue dancing when you have supposedly already had an orgasm on the floor?" The question was followed by a long silence. Lillian answered herself, "You can't."

When she ran from the car, toward the dressing room, Coushay looked like she had been rolling in mud. Sweat, bits of straw, dust and dirt from the truck bed covered flushed, pale pink flesh. She hadn't been prepared for the drive back to the house or the dirt on the truck as Pepper had.

Debbie Doll was golden with her red hair curled and teased. She wore a skin-tight gold lamè gown with gold opera length gloves, gold leather pumps, huge gold jewelry, gold all over. The guard carried her little golden robe as they left for the truck. Debbie carried her own bourbon. I thought she was so sophisticated and knowledgeable.

The sweet pure saxophone of Duke Ellington's *Prelude to a Kiss* came from the pasture. It shortly drifted into *Saint James Infirmary* which was a down and dirty blues standard with horns that wailed and cried. The Chamber of Commerce, behind the barbed wire, sounded like they were about to tear through.

The car brought Debbie to the house and the guard followed her to the dressing room. She looked hot but still beautiful, red hair wild, totally golden in her tiny robe. Senor Montemayor left two guards at the dressing room doors as he went out to oversee the gambling. Lillian waited with me at the blackjack table for the girls to come out and the men to arrive from the field.

The men came in wet and riled, ready to drink. Those who had not noticed me before, now came toward me. I had never seen men look at me like that. "When are you going to dance for me, *muñequita*?" whispered the stocky, muscular man who was so close to me I could feel his erection and body heat in the warm night. He was going to grab me. I moved away but tried to look like I was holding my ground. I knew I better not look like the trapped animal I felt like. That could spark a riot among these already aroused men.

"Let's see those titties, honey," said the sweaty one next to him as he stretched out a hand toward my breast that was knocked away by the stocky man.

"Where you been hiding little girl?" yelled the short barrel-chested man next to Lillian, as though he felt insulted.

"She's not dancing tonight gentlemen, maybe next time. Now, let's play poker," said Lillian, smiling as she tried to lead them off toward the card tables. When the crowd that had gathered did turn away, she glanced back at me.

"Stay with me or Debbie. Pepper and Coushay will be busy."

I moved back to the blackjack table, in sight of Lillian, who was setting up cards with four of the former howlers from the field. They were serious now, eyes down and half closed.

Blackjack looked like fun. The elderly dealer slightly bowed his head inviting me in. "Miguel Montemayor, father of

Carlos," he said introducing himself while shuffling four decks of cards at the same time. "All the money made at this table tonight will be given to charities in town."

One of the men who had not gone out to see the girls dance gave me five ten-dollar chips and said, "Use these."

I had never gambled before. It took about two minutes to lose all the chips back to the dealer. I made myself a promise right then, never to gamble with my own money. As I found out that night, there are lots of men who will give a girl money to play with.

"Carlos, darlin', thank you for getting that Surprise Pink gel for the spotlight. That was so nice of you," Debbie drawled as she walked up to our host and put her hand on his wide chest in a familiar way.

She had made her appearance in the casino area to flirt like the other girls. All sparkling in short dresses of rhinestones and beads, they were ready to mix and mingle for a little while. Debbie drank bourbon and talked to a group of admirers while Lillian played poker. Coushay and Pepper disappeared.

"Where you gonna stay tonight?" asked a wiry blackjack player in a blue cowboy shirt with pearly buttons.

The two men beside him, wearing identical black Stetsons, looked up expectantly, with hope in their eyes, while the cards waited.

I smiled and said, "Lillian hasn't told us yet."

I had been warned earlier in the day that I would be approached with that question as I looked the youngest, least experienced of the girls. Dark eyes hardened and went back down to the dealer's hands.

We were to slip out quietly and try to leave without being followed by the Chamber of Commerce. Lillian saw Pepper, then Coushay come back to the casino patio around the arranged time, took the blue signal scarf from her evening bag, made sure each girl had seen it, and excused herself from the poker table.

We started walking toward the house, circled around to the back driveway where the car was packed and waiting with the motor running, facing the road. Lillian put a one hundred dollar bill in the guard's hand and we took off for Hobbs, New Mexico as fast as the Buick could move.

Chapter Three

Deeply Red, Wide Blue and Spikey Pink

Lillian knew the girls would fall asleep soon after they got in the car. They had had a few drinks and work was over. I was so stimulated by what I had seen, she knew I would be the perfect companion to talk with while driving across half of Texas in the dark hours. She could see I was nervous so she sang parts of her nightclub act and told me about her career. She sang risqué Sophie Tucker songs and Mae West ditties. Her deep, clear voice was teasing and bawdy just like the Sophie Tucker records I had heard on my mom's records at home.

I fell in love with one song called *I Picked a Pansy from the Garden of Love*, and the suggestive way Lillian sang it. She also sang a Tucker song called *Nobody Loves a Fat Girl, but Oh, How a Fat Girl Can Love*. I was fascinated. I laughed and relaxed listening to her songs and stories as we drove through Texas.

With little traffic to hold us back, we sped through black night to San Angelo and on to Big Spring seeing nothing but the highway ahead. It gave me time to think about the night that we had just lived through. The girls, especially Debbie and Pepper, were just too gorgeous. Even Coushay looked great after her touchup. It was dangerous to be that pretty in the middle of so many men who were unchaperoned by their women.

Where had Pepper and Coushay gone during that hour after they dressed and rejoined the party? I had looked all around for them to ask about their dancing but couldn't find them. We had escaped with our lives and no one seemed to realize it except me. I saw now that Lillian had taken the necessary precautions and had handed out $100 tips to ensure our safety. That was the reason our evening had been successful and next year's trip to Waco would be too.

Although the dancers had slept most of the trip no one seemed rested except Lillian. She had a new audience – me. She was wide awake but I was drooping a little. I kept thinking that tomorrow I would see the other girls dance and would try to be part of the show. Pepper, Debbie and Coushay were grumpy and cross in jeans and last night's makeup.

Hobbs was just over the Texas-New Mexico border. Lillian told us the Millionaires' Club was for men who were making their money in oil.

"There will be about a hundred men to see you tonight, darlin. You'll dance in the large gymnasium where the fluorescent lights will be brutal. No spotlight tonight; no fancy pink gels that make your skin look young and smooth," she said. "These guys, no matter how much money they have, just want to see some beautiful tits and ass."

We went to the motel Lillian normally used in Hobbs. They knew her and what she needed. The rooms had to be ready for us even if we arrived at three or four in the morning so Lillian and the dancers could shower and sleep. There was an ironing board in each room and extra pillows for lounging.

It seemed like dancers did a lot of lounging and waiting while they were on the road. No family. No pets. No friends. We had no one except each other. I realized a stripper better have a good disposition and be easy to get along with when she is on the road with other people.

We spent part of the day driving around the dry southern New Mexico area looking at sand, sage, and cactus. Lillian called it sightseeing. Debbie sat in front with Lillian and I was behind Debbie next to the window. There were oil wells in the distance and farms with crops growing up against the asphalt. Along some roads greenish-blue sage brush stretched toward the hills as far as you could see.

I noticed for the first time how easy and free it felt to breathe the soft clear air. It smelled sweet and luscious, almost like flowers. I leaned back in the car with the window down and opened my lungs fully to the air.

This was so different from Los Angeles, where the brown smoggy air was hard. It felt dangerous to breathe there. You wanted to protect your chest from it.

Lillian and the girls went out for a late lunch, but I didn't want to go. I decided to stay at the motel to take another shower and sit in the shade near the pool. Having been with four strangers for almost two days without a moment alone, I needed some privacy. Coushay brought me some iced tea with lemon from the coffee shop and patted my back softly.

I didn't have a book. That was unusual as I almost always had one somewhere close to me. I went to the motel manager to see if anyone had left something I could read. She gave me a science fiction pocket book by Robert Heinlein called *Tunnel In The Sky*. It felt like she had saved my life. I could escape from the present.

In just a few hours I would dance nude in front of a hundred or more men. The only thing I would keep on was a pair of pink high-heels and some small net panties that almost matched my skin. I needed to put my mind somewhere else for a while so I wouldn't worry about my smallish breasts and almost no idea of how to do what I was about to do.

I had thought about smiling and the bride's step and how to keep my arms up and rounded for what seemed like a very long time. I had gone over how to get out of the gown and use the panel to tease many times. Lillian decided the long gloves would stay on for the entire act. She said my "slender limbs could take the bulk."

Debbie had advised me to smile as it makes a dancer look more confident. She said, "A smile is like a shield. A girl can say anything to a man, even push him away and make him stay back, as long as she is smiling."

Pepper told me not to get too close to the men, especially when I reached for money they would hold up to entice me to come closer. "They will grab you and put their fingers right up inside your cunt if you get too close, Brandy. That's what happened to me on my first roadshow. So be careful. If a mark looks real drunk or weird, don't go near him; move on to the next guy who has money in his hand."

We arrived at the Millionaires' Club, a square squat beige building in the middle of the desert, surrounded by cactus, around nine p.m. There were some exercise rooms full of weights and machines, a kitchen and some offices. The gymnasium with the basketball court was immense with a high ceiling. This evening's show would take place there. We had a real makeup table tonight with lights around it and chairs for all of us in a locker room just off the gym.

We hung our costumes on the rack provided and brought out the makeup, combs and hairspray. Everyone, including Lillian, had started getting ready about seven o'clock. They looked made up to me, but I found out there was more to do.

Full stage makeup has to make your eyes look larger than life as the wrong lighting or no lighting can make the features fade and almost disappear. Earlier in the day the girls had agreed I would wear a medium gray-blue eye shadow to make my eyes look deeper and should draw the black liner out beyond my eyes so they would look longer instead of so round.

Now, Lillian said, "Pepper, teach Brandy to put on these lashes, will you?" as she handed Pepper a clear case with black false eyelashes inside. "Yours always look so great, honey, and Brandy, put some mascara on your bottom lashes. Coushay your hair isn't combed in the back, honey."

The lips were deeply red and the eyes were wide and blue with long black lashes as I looked at the finished me in the mirror. Rouge under my cheekbones gave my face a sculptured appearance. Pepper and Debbie had transformed me into what looked like a feminine mystery, a sexy exotic dancer. There was something about my face that hadn't been there before. I looked older. I loved it. Had it always been there just waiting to be brought out? This must have been the face that Dreamy had seen when she suggested I could become a stripper, but I had never seen it.

Strawberry-blonde waves were pulled back into a high ponytail. The sparkly strapless sequin gown seemed larger than it had in Houston, but I could still hold it up. I wouldn't have it on that long anyway.

I had chosen the pink satin bridesmaid pumps that Lillian had at her house in the shoe section of her costume room. They were just right; size six, had spikey heels and felt like solid support. I thought they looked good with the pink sheen of the aurora borealis sequins on the dress.

Debbie poured three fingers of bourbon into a water glass while I was still looking at myself in the mirror. She walked over and gave the glass to me.

"For luck," she said as she patted my rear end in a comforting way.

I drank it all like it was medicine that would save me. It burned all the way down. I felt much more confident with this new face. It was like a character mask I could hide in. Not even I would recognize me on the street with this face on. I could become any kind of dancer I wanted.

Pepper opened the show. This time I got to watch from behind the door as I was on stage next. Metal folding chairs held men that were mostly balding, grey, or silver-haired with age. There were over a hundred of them. Many were big and heavyset. It didn't look like those little chairs set against the walls would hold them. The shiny wooden floor of the huge gymnasium was our stage. The only way a man could get a closer look was if he held out some money to tempt a girl toward him.

These men were older and looked as if they spent more time in their offices than out in the open like last night's audience. Dressed in grey or beige suits and ties these men looked prosperous and just the kind of marks the girls had been talking about in the car.

"Tonight could be the big money-maker of the trip girls, so don't hold back. Let these boys see whatcha got," Lillian had drawled.

Fluorescent lighting took away color from Pepper's face and shine from her silver gown, though the smile on her face made up for any lost glitter. In the two days I had known her, I hadn't seen Pepper smile even once. Looking at her now changed my thinking completely. She looked like she was having so much fun. She was enjoying each and every man she looked at. I watched her eyes as she looked at them all over, between their legs, their shoulders and hands and right into their eyes. At times she considered them with a smile on her face that said, "Can you handle all this?" Further along in her act she looked at them with expressions that I read as, "This is yours if you want it, and it's fabulous."

Temptation played on. It filled the space as Pepper strode forward in time to the music. She bumped to the right and then to the left, moved her hips in a small grind and bumped twice toward the front. Her waist was small, her hips round and tight. Pepper reached behind her and slid down the zipper of her dress. It came off smoothly. She laid it on the empty chair closest to the door that was set aside for the dancer's costumes.

Pepper danced toward a man who was holding a five-dollar bill over his friend's head, took the money and, to his delight, shook her full firm breasts close to the friend's face. She put the top half of the bill under the sequined part of the panel and into her net pants then danced on to the nearest man who had a ten-dollar bill. Pepper ignored all the single dollars waving in the air.

While bumping and grinding and showing off some complicated dance steps during the pounding and pulsing drum solo, Pepper played up to other men and collected money as she took off her bra, the full red panel and eventually the sequined pants. Her hips were surrounded with money held close by the thin elastic of her net pants, which let the men see everything except the pubic hair and the cleavage between her buttocks.

When no one else was offering to pay for a closer look, Lillian stopped the music. Pepper smiled, took a bow by brushing the fingers of her right hand on her left breast and extending her hand and arm gracefully toward the audience, acknowledging them all. She twirled, grabbed her costume and left the gym to friendly applause.

Feeling braver and warm inside from Debbie's bourbon, I applauded with the rest of the audience from my spot next to the door. I realized I was going out there in ten seconds and straightened my gown which had shifted over to the left. I could feel my heart beating faster. I wasn't embarrassed to show my body – although I never had. It was young and beautiful and nothing to be ashamed of. I was nervous about dancing though, especially after the skillful performance I had just witnessed. I took a step back, swallowed and took a deep shaky breath.

"Gentlemen, I give you Miss Brandy Wilde, in her very first performance in New Mexico," I heard Lillian say into the microphone. An instrumental version of *Embraceable You* came from the tape recorder and I stepped out into the audience's view. I forgot to smile. I was scared to death.

No one had asked me if I could dance, but I knew a few ballroom steps like the waltz and foxtrot and the mambo. I opened my arms, making sure to keep them rounded and tried to waltz-glide forward. The music was sweet and nonthreatening. It drew me toward the middle of the square. I was thinking so hard about what to do next I wasn't too nervous about how I looked.

I smiled, but it didn't last long. I found out it's hard to smile for more than a minute or so without your cheeks quivering and your teeth and lips and gums becoming dry and sticking together. It takes a little while to learn the trick of turning your back to the audience to release the smile and lick your teeth every minute or so. I did try to turn my back to put my gloved finger between my teeth and top lip, but the audience was in a square all around me. I turned toward the door I had entered through, pulling my lip away from my teeth where it had stuck.

I turned, smiled again and took off the dress, dropping it onto the chair.

"That filly's got long legs Bo, just look at that," said a man who was sitting next to the chair I had dropped my dress on.

He had sleek white hair and a piece of bright blue turquoise in his bolo tie as big around as an orange.

A few admiring hoots came from the men sitting around the square and I felt more confident. One of the men held up a five-dollar bill and I waltzed off for it, keeping my arms rounded. Just as I was there he reached out, took me by the waist and tried to pull me between his legs with one hand as the other aimed for my crotch. I remembered what Pepper had told me and was prepared for the move. The strong spike heel of the pink satin shoe sank deeply into his brown leather wing tip as I put all my weight on that foot and bounced down. He let me go with a yelp, swinging his foot in the air to lessen the pain of what I hoped were a couple of broken toes, as I spun away.

The rubber band around my ponytail came off easily. I lifted my hands to my temples and drew gloved fingers through thick hair that fell in bright strawberry blonde waves over my breasts and covered my back.

Men around the square started yelling, holding up money, waving it in front of them or above their friends. I was afraid to go to them now and my smile had disappeared.

"Come on baby, come on over here and let me see that little ass."

"Come see what I got for you, Puss."

I took off the sequined bra to *Love for Sale*, a song with constant, strong, driving tom-tom drums. There was not a lot to see and what was there I had just covered with my hair. That was successful, I thought: I'm teasing.

I had important things to think about and the fact that I was going to take my pants off in public for the first time wasn't one of them. It had to be smooth and look effortless. I had to smile and move around the floor. I had to be close but not too close to the men fluttering dollars in front of them to tempt me nearer. They were teasing too. I tried to copy what Pepper had done with the money given to her and succeeded except for a couple dollars that fell away when the pants came off without a hitch. The cream colored net panties stayed on.

Lillian had said if any money dropped to the floor, "Never bend over to pick it up." She said, "It looks awkward and ungraceful. A star would never show the crack of her ass for a dollar."

I looked around, saw no more money in the air and all my clothes were off, so, after trying to bow like Pepper, I picked up my costume and left the floor to mild applause.

Now, I was dizzy, breathing hard, a little drunk and naked. I was one of them. I was one of "the girls".

A smiling Lillian greeted me behind the door. "You did it honey! How do you feel? Not so bad, was it?"

She seemed more relieved than I was. I didn't want to tell her about that first man. I felt ashamed that he had tried that on me.

Lillian continued. "I've had girls change their mind mid-step just before going on stage. They turned around and ran. So, you never know." Busy with her next performer, she pulled Coushay's dress up a little on her frame so it fit smoothly and added, "I like how you handled that jerk. You looked good out there, for a first time. Go dry off and get dressed."

Lillian started the lead in for *I'm in the Mood for Love* on the tape recorder and introduced, "Coushay Curtis, your own little New Mexican mover and groover." Lillian looked at me and shrugged one shoulder as if to say, "I don't know either." I hadn't thought about an introduction but apparently Coushay had.

Coushay strutted toward the stage in turquoise blue satin, which contrasted dramatically with her blonde hair. At Lillian's request, she and Debbie had spent yesterday morning brightening, trimming and curling which changed Coushay's casual sloppy look to a clean and cared for style.

Coushay walked around the square of men and flirted with her hips. Hands came up with money in them and she wiggled over bumping and doing sideways grinds. Looking through the crack behind the door, I could see she was a better dancer than I had expected.

This time, she stayed on her feet so she could travel from one man to the next. She tucked the balled-up and flat bills loosely into her bra and circled to see where she was going next. Coushay had seen what had happened to me, so she avoided the grabber who was yowling and waving a ten-dollar bill at her.

The dress came off in the first minute of her act and the panel soon after as she roamed the room for cash. She spun in the middle of the basketball floor, opened the little hook and eye that kept the bra attached, pulling the breast cups out to the side, revealing herself. I was surprised to see that her breasts looked like half-filled sacks. We had each been modest and polite in our motel room. Compared to Debbie and Pepper she looked deflated.

The next surprise was seeing the crumpled bills fly out of the bra and fall to the floor around her. Coushay danced around and through the money, trusting that no one would walk to the middle of the gym and take some back. At the end of her act, she nodded her head in thanks for the applause going down on both knees to rake money toward her. When she had it all, Coushay ran off the floor leaving her costume on the chair.

The man with snowy white hair and turquoise bolo tie, who looked about seventy five, picked up the layers of costume and started toward the dressing room. Lillian was on her way to him as he reached the door, thanking him and showing him out at the same time, in less than a second. He looked happy though, as if he had accomplished his plan of seeing the next dancer before his friends.

Debbie Doll, one of Lillian's biggest stars, was ready to be the final act. I dressed and prepared myself to learn something.

Pepper and I both stood at the crack in the door as Lillian started Debbie's introduction.

"Gentlemen, this evening the Millionaires' Club of Hobbs, New Mexico brings you the personification of beauty in motion, Miss Debbie Doll: The Most Beautiful Doll in the World.

The importance and enthusiasm that Lillian gave each word was enough to start a welcoming applause from the audience. The only place I had heard that kind of grand introduction was on the Ed Sullivan Show when Elvis Presley was about to appear.

Debbie stepped out as the applause was just at its peak and stood in the middle of the wide doorway with arms above her head and her face turned at three quarters profile; chin up as if in rapture. She was in a tight gold lamè gown and heavy gold jewelry. The song *The Most Beautiful Girl in the World* began and Debbie lowered her arms to waist high, well rounded, turned her face toward the audience slowly and smiled. She was radiant, as if she were a doll. As if when the music had started, she had come to life.

Debbie's first pass through the audience of captivated males was slinky and sensual with no discernible effort. She danced forward in a traveling step to give them all a good look at her. They saw the thick red hair, the beautiful gown and the full round breasts barely held within.

As she paraded her assets around the floor in the first trailer, her golden-gloved fingers touched her waist and brought our attention to how small it was. Her hips slinked smoothly from side to side while the rest of her was still. A hand slid down over the hip to point out roundness and shapeliness. Her hand caressed the buttock through the gown as if it were pure pleasure.

Debbie Doll removed the gown with her back to the men while grinding in small circles allowing them to see the movement of the golden zipper as she pulled it slowly, ever so slowly down. The gold zipper split to her waist, revealing soft, touchable flesh. It made its way down, toward her thighs, and gave way there as if by its own desire. She threw her gown on the empty chair.

The second trailer, *Prelude to a Kiss*, began and the money held high was collected with grinds performed toward favored baldies with twenties, winks, smiles and bumps given in the direction of the grey and silver heads with tens and close, but not too close, double grinds for those with fifties.

With fingers on the clasp of her bra she looked at the audience as if to see if anyone wanted her to take it off. "No?" she said, as she batted her eyelashes. No one offered her anything special to remove the bra. Then a bill was raised by the youngest and best looking man there. He was tall with a square jaw, clear blue eyes, and a bit of silver in his wavy black hair. The kind of man a girl might wish she could know. The men yelled their encouragement. Debbie moved forward with little grinds and took a one hundred dollar bill from his hand. Off came the bra for a hundred dollar bill. She looked at him and raised an eyebrow. The panel came off for another one hundred dollars. She smiled, twirled so he could see all sides of her, and danced away.

Debbie laughed and lifted damp hair from her neck with both hands as if it was so pleasurable she wanted to share its deliciousness. She danced to tease and enlighten us how wonderful every part of her body could be for the lucky one to touch her.

St. James Infirmary, the third and final trailer, started with horns and moans. Debbie began to dance like a lover with the insistent goal of orgasm. No more thoughts of money in mind, she danced in bumps and grinds and moved around the dance floor as she looked at each man, especially Mr. Wavy Hair, as if asking, "Are you the one who can give it to me? Are you?"

She twirled away from them as she removed the breakaway pants and reached the door just as the music ended. It seemed like the pants had disappeared but they were on top of the costume chair. Debbie was in the middle of the doorway where she had started. Her hands stretched toward the men, palms up, spread out to encompass them all. Her smile became relaxed and friendly. She giggled as she bowed, waved goodbye, then exited.

Lillian was there to retrieve Debbie's costume and brought it to her at the dressing room table. As our acknowledged star Debbie did not have to pick up her own clothing. Lillian had said it wouldn't look professional. Debbie cooled off while drinking bourbon on the rocks, wiping down her sweaty body and repairing runny makeup. It would be a few minutes before she could dress.

I was relieved my dance was over and I hadn't done too badly. I had not fallen, I got everything off in time to the music and I had not disappointed Dreamy or Lillian. I even made forty-three dollars. Pepper and Coushay were excited about their extra money and they agreed that Debbie had earned about a thousand dollars.

"All the bumping and grinding I did out there and I made three hundred dollars," Pepper said with good humor as she brushed her hair. "I need to learn how to twitch my eyebrows."

Lillian went out to make sure the car was packed. There would be no mixing or mingling tonight. We were off to the Texas-Mexico border.

Chapter Four

Lillian's Four Fancy Women

We drove from Hobbs, New Mexico, over the Rocky Mountains, back into El Paso, Texas for another show. I sat in back and Debbie was in the front seat. The girls talked about the last show for a while. Lillian sang a few songs but Debbie fell asleep so most of the trip was quiet. We arrived at El Paso in the early morning and fell into bed.

Debbie Doll and I shared a room that night. There was only one bed. When Debbie drew me toward her and kissed my lips, my ears and my breast. I wanted her to go further, but couldn't let her. I thought she was gorgeous and sexier than any woman I had known but I didn't want be dishonest with Dreamy. Girlfriends always find out about something like that. It did make me realize that even feminine beautiful women could want me and I was more attracted to them too. She did let me cuddle up to her though and I felt comforted.

I forced myself to get up a little before ten. After the usual two-hour preparation to leave the rooms, the girls ate breakfast. I had a glass of milk but it made my stomach ache.

"What's wrong Brandy? Why aren't you eating anything?" Lillian drawled as she stirred cream into her coffee. "I've never seen anyone eat less than you. At first I thought it was just nerves but now it doesn't seem right."

That word "right" seemed to go on forever. All four of them were looking at me over their first bites of syrupy French toast and pancakes.

"I know, I was real nervous," I admitted with what I hoped was a reassuring smile. "But now I'm fine -- just not hungry," I lied with a smile.

I kept my face serene while thinking, how could they not see how scared I was? Didn't they remember how they felt when they first started? That man had grabbed me, tried to invade my body and had half way succeeded before I jammed my sharp high heel into his foot. Men, groups of men, are thinking about trying to bust into my hotel room while I'm asleep and others are trying to pet me and feel me and rub themselves all over me while I'm just standing there not doing anything to them. What does she mean, why am I not eating? Aren't they terrified too? Who can ever become used to this constant feeling of being in danger?

Lillian and Coushay humphed at the same time and let the subject drop as the bacon, ham, eggs, hashed browned potatoes and grits arrived and coffee cups were refilled.

"Does anybody want to go over the border into Juarez today?" asked Lillian.

"Yeah!" we screamed.

We all wanted to go. We had nothing else to do all day except lounge.

In Mexico we looked like what we were as we walked down the rows of stalls selling everything a tourist might need from armadillo claw key rings to red and yellow embroidered shawls: four young women with fancy makeup and bright hair in pink and red skin tight pants and thin blouses rolled up to the midriff and tied under the breasts, clattering along in silver and gold spike heels, following an older blonde businesswoman in a black silk pant suit. Every head turned our way. People stopped talking. Dark eyes blinked as if stunned by the brightness. We probably looked to some as though we were selling something too, but we were not.

Lillian drove us back to Houston after the shows in El Paso and Corpus Christi but I have no memory of it. I must have been reliving the first two nights of the trip and was not ready to start thinking about anything else or maybe I was dazed from hunger.

Dreamy was outside waiting for us when Lillian pulled the Buick into her driveway in Houston, the morning after our show in Corpus. I had slept almost all the way back and so had the other girls. Poor Lillian was left with an exhausted crew, and her "new audience" out like a light.

As I got out of the car Dreamy gasped and screamed, "What did you do to her?! What happened?!"

Lillian and Debbie looked at me to see what was wrong. Coushay and Pepper looked over from the trunk of the car to see what was going on. Wardrobe in hand Pepper said goodbye to Lillian, waved at the rest of us and took off to finish or forgive the fight she was in the middle of when she had left Houston.

I looked to see if I had torn my blouse, touched my mouth to feel if I had drooled on myself while I was asleep. What was wrong with me? I couldn't see anything different.

"She's so skinnnnny!" Dreamy cried. Tears gathered in her eyes as she put her arms around me and held me close, as if to protect me from Lillian.

"What's wrong with Brandy?" demanded Brava Tutti as she ran out of the house toward us. She stopped and whispered "Oh, my God! You look like you lost twenty-five pounds this week. You don't look very well, honey. Come on in."

"We couldn't get her to eat a thing while we were gone. I don't know why. We kept telling her to eat but she is a stubborn little thing. I saw her eat some refried beans once. She drank a glass of milk the other day but that's all I can remember," Lillian told Dreamy.

Brava took my hand and dragged me to the big blue and yellow bathroom connected to Lillian's guest room. The others came along.

"Brandy, take off your shoes and things, get on the scale. Let's look at you," said Brava.

I undressed to black panties and bra to step on the floor scale. Before I left Los Angeles I weighed one-fourteen. Now the scale pointed to ninety-seven. It didn't seem possible I had lost seventeen pounds in the last six days.

Looking at myself in the long mirror on the bathroom door, I saw Dreamy, Lillian, Coushay and Debbie behind me in the little room or out in the hall. Something had happened to me, and it had happened all at once. I was not slender now. I was quite thin. My cheekbones were noticeable and a gap existed between my thighs that had never been there before. It didn't look bad, but I wasn't as curvy as I had been in Los Angeles.

I looked drained. I didn't have makeup on like the other girls, just a bit of pencil on my eyebrows and a touch of color on my lips. Could I still be a stripper? Did I still want to be a stripper? I just knew I was exhausted and we could pay the rent now.

I could see Dreamy was proud of me as Lillian told her all about the trip and what a "good sport" I had turned out to be.

"So clean too," she said. "Four showers a day, and nice to everyone," Lillian said.

Dreamy looked at me, her eyes shiny with unshed tears of pride. The corners of her mouth turned up just a little. Her eyes closed in the tiny cat kiss way she had. That look said she understood my fears and knew I had overcome them for her.

Chapter Five

The Smile Shield: A Powerful Weapon

The Shamrock Hotel in Houston hosted an amateur strippers' evening on Wednesday nights in the small lounge bar. It was similar to an open mic set for stand-up comedians. A few days after the roadshow Lillian arranged for me to dance there to get more experience.

My first thoughts were, "Wow, I get to be on the program with the INK SPOTS! I hope I get to hear them sing. What are they doing here? They're so famous!" They were my favorite singing group from the 1930's, 40's and 50's. Their song *Whispering Grass* was the prettiest song I had ever heard, after *Stardust,* of course. They were the only group with their unique sound and exceptional harmony. The Ink Spots had voices that ranged from highest falsetto to deep clear bass who sounded like heaven had sent their voices to pierce my heart.

It was the hotel's policy that amateurs performed during the break between the headliners' sets, about ten o'clock. This was a big step up for me and I was self-conscious although Pepper and Debbie had taught me how to apply makeup to make my features look best and how to put on the false eyelashes we all had to wear.

There was an actual stage with lights and real musicians. The black cocktail dress was loose around my hips and even my shoes felt larger than usual. What if a pasty fell off? What if I couldn't do it right this time? I wanted to order a drink to relax but everyone was busy. Dreamy would be there to see me dance on stage for the first time and I didn't want to disappoint her. I would be the only amateur appearing that Wednesday. I was alone but not as afraid this time. There were women in the audience.

The charming Master of Ceremonies, who was also the comedian in the show introduced me. "Ladies and gentlemen, we have only one amateur exotic dancer this evening. Her name is Brandy and she is all the way from California. Let's give her a warm Texas welcome."

I had stolen the lilting, sweet *Prelude to a Kiss* from Debbie Doll for my first trailer and the pounding, pulsing *Temptation* from Pepper for my second. The beat on those two songs would lead my way. I had seen the steps to that music three times on the road and now I could try to copy them. *Take the A Train* was my third and final song because it was faster, more upbeat.

The band, which was on their own small stage near the bar, had three musicians in black suits and green ties: a serious young black man with a baritone saxophone, a drummer with steady black eyes surrounded by two full sets of drums, and an older Chinese piano player. They looked like they had played for the best acts around so I could depend on them to try and make me look good.

My music began as I was sitting at a table in the small dark bar. A solitary, wooden, straight back chair was on the stage when I walked up the two stairs from the audience. I was already into the character of the stripper. It helped me to think of this new person, Brandy Wilde, playing a part in a musical play. Pink lights made my hair glow red and it swirled around me as I turned to face the audience. I smiled.

Trying to glide around the stage as I felt the music called for, letting the small audience look at me, went well. The dress came off without a hitch at the end of the first song. Now I had on a little French black lace bra and garter belt with black nylons and small silk panties that Dreamy and I had shopped for a couple of hours ago. Since I was an "amateur" I had to wear the kind of underwear that women actually use when they want to feel especially sexy.

Temptation did not call for me to glide. I attempted to stride the stage as Pepper had on the roadshow, stopping to look into the audience and throw some bumps and grinds while making sure I kept time with the music. That was the main thing. I had to keep time and that took concentration, but dancing to live musicians was the best part of the evening.

There were about twenty men, old and young, some with dressed up women, who had stayed when the Ink Spots act was over. The couples mostly talked among themselves while others watched the band. A few people looked at me. Dreamy was in the dark, next to the back wall and I was relieved I didn't have to watch her watching me.

The band had decided they wanted to play it jazzy so I had to go along. When I first bumped to the side and the drummer hit a rim shot on the cymbal, my movement seemed huge instead of the timid bump it had actually been. It was so pronounced; I had to bump to the other side so everything was even. I like things to be symmetrical and it seemed the drummer did too.

"*Oh, this is how you do it. This is how it feels right,*" I thought. Feeling like I had crested a mountain, I relaxed some and started to enjoy dancing with "the guys".

The nylons and garter belt came off while I was sitting on the chair I had pulled toward the front of the stage. I took the stockings off slowly and teased as Dreamy had coached me, keeping my face up toward the audience, not becoming hidden in my hair as had happened in rehearsal.

A redheaded man, who seemed like he had been drinking by himself too long, grabbed for a nylon stocking as I held it at the top trying to let the bottom spring off my toe and back into my hand as Dreamy had taught me. He whipped it out of my hand mid-spring, draped it around his neck, and looked satisfied. From that I learned to keep playful drunks out of reach, no matter how cute they are.

The drummer used brushes on the snare drum for the grinds and sticks on the cymbal for the bumps keeping an even tempo for the other musicians to follow, along with all the special effects he played for me. *The A Train* started going a little faster toward a big finish and wound up with a flourish of drums and loud sweet saxophone. There was a little applause and I think it was for the drummer. He deserved it. I had felt sexy, a little juicy and had so much fun doing it right. He was a good teacher.

I had heard from Pepper about a blonde and feisty dancer named Candy Barr who had her own drummer, George Jenkins. George had traveled with her, knew all her steps and could follow her runs up the wall and the backward flips that landed her back on the stage. He played all her shows. Now I knew how a drummer could inspire a dancer and make every movement look larger, more dramatic and so much fun, I wanted to have my own drummer too when I became a star.

Candy was in prison in Texas. She had received a fifteen-year sentence for possession of two marijuana cigarettes and had already served a few years.

It was August, prickly hot and wet in Houston. While I was on the road Dreamy had been taken into the daily lives of Gladys and Mike, our landlords. Gladys, who was almost child-sized and never seen without her apron, had made vats of what she called her famous garlic pickles. The place smelled of garlic and dill days later.

Dreamy had become their official pickle-taster. There were now six jars of official Summer Garlic Pickles in our small kitchen cabinet. Mike had never tasted Gladys's pickles; he had eaten the same thing every day for fifty-five years and refused to taste anything else. He ate only orange food, all orange fruits and vegetables. I had hoped Dreamy would fine more interesting things to do than hang around with the landlords.

Dreamy and I couldn't cool off in our room and either went to the movies or hung around Lillian's house to stay comfortable in the air conditioning while waiting for another job. There were usually a few other girls there as well as Brava Tutti, who was feeling better and almost ready to go back to dancing.

I did work a lunch show at a small club for twenty five dollars. There were no stage lights, no stage, a jukebox instead of a band, hardly an audience but it was a good chance to practice parading, bumping and grinding to different music. *It's Cherry Pink and Apple Blossom White* was on the jukebox. I played it three times and ran the small audience out of there.

Lillian was arranging for us to go to Cleveland, Ohio on a week-to-week contract for two hundred twenty five dollars. That meant I would be making about nine hundred dollars a month before Lillian's commission and hotel costs were subtracted. This seemed like an enormous amount of money. Lillian was setting us up in a hotel where two of her other girls lived who worked the same club. Dancers worked three shows a night from nine at night to three in the morning, six days a week, with Sunday off.

Lillian explained, "The laws are very strict in Cleveland. Not only do you have to wear pasties and full pants, you absolutely must keep your navel covered. Most girls paste a large rhinestone over their belly button."

"Oh, no Lillian! My belly button?" I laughed and laughed as she nodded seriously.

I needed to have costumes made and music charts for my act before we left Houston. Dreamy knew the man named Steve who now made costumes; he had been the choreographer for the chorus line she had starred in. Lillian used him for all her girls now, as he was settled in Houston. His designs were lovely and he would let her dancers pay in weekly installments even when they were on the road.

Lillian said, "Steve's work is beautiful and he doesn't try to get the girls in bed. He has good manners for a straight guy working with young naked women because he has seen them all his life. His mom was one of my girls a long time ago."

Dreamy and I went to see what I could buy on short notice that was not too expensive. Steve, who was about fifty, short and wiry, emanated masculine electricity and tension. As he opened the door he looked at Dreamy with a shocked smile and held out his arms to embrace her. His large dark eyes under heavy brows took in the whole picture.

"It's been a long time baby, and you sure have changed. A little weight there, huh. Where is that little seventeen-year-old girl I saw last? You and that composer's granddaughter, Violetta Puccini, ran off to join the circus, remember? And then we never heard from you again. Whatever happened to her? How are you? Come in, come in. I'm sorry about the heat but Charmaine and I belong to a religion that will not tolerate air conditioning."

Dreamy and I exchanged surprised looks but didn't say a word. The three-bedroom brick house that Steve and his wife, former dancer, Charmaine, "The Champagne Blonde," later said they had purchased for ten thousand dollars was hot as a pistol.

Steve led us up to his tightly packed studio on the second floor of the house. It felt like we had walked into a double rainbow. We were surrounded by bolts of purple, red, black and lavender velvet, silver, blue, gold and pink satin, and sheerest silk in all possible flesh tones. One wall was made of more than two hundred built-in boxes with small name tags titled: size six pink rhinestones, fancy black lace, gold sequin trim, G-strings, and bras. Long, full feather boas in jewel colors, hung to the floor from two coat racks in a corner and a huge white ostrich plume fan Steve had been working on covered a table. There were three sewing machines on a built-in counter top that had three chairs under it. Another wall was one huge walk-in closet, from which he brought several half-made items on padded hangers.

Steve said, "I started using this beautiful pale turquoise satin for a girl a few months ago but the slut changed her mind, so I can take it in a little and it will be great for you. This color will look good under all kinds of lighting and not change to grey the way green does under certain pinks and orange. Look what it does for your hair. Pretty, huh? Although why someone would put an orange light on a performer, I don't know. But, they do. You have to be careful what they light you with." He sighed as if he knew all the dangers to costumes and dancers that were caused by poor lighting. "I've got this white silk peau de soie with silver sequin trim and it won't take long either. It shows up real well on stage. When do you leave? You want to start fitting them now?"

Steve sent Dreamy downstairs to visit with the still blonde and bountiful Charmaine, who had been her inspiration and teacher in the world of 1949 burlesque. While we were on the way to Houston, Dreamy had talked about how much this couple had helped her.

"They showed me how to dance and do beautiful fan work on stage, things I never thought I could do. They wouldn't even let me walk across the stage when I first started working for them. They put me on top of a stage pillar. All I had to do was wear a tiny outfit and move my black cane in time to the music. I fell off naturally, right onto two dancers, in the middle of a show. But they were patient and kinder to me than anyone I had known," she had said. I was prepared to like and admire them before Steve answered the door.

Dreamy told me she had been a jewelry model when Steve had first taught her how to walk on stage with grace and poise in her first high heels. He also taught her to make a "grand entrance," and work with ostrich feather fans that were almost as tall as she was.

Charmaine had taught Dreamy how to shimmy, giving her ideas for acts centered on what she called "shake dancing." Dreamy Darnell became an "overnight sensation" fronting their chorus line of twelve girls when she was sixteen years old.

I stepped onto an eight inch high, round wooden dais, dressed in only beige net pants and silver spike pumps I had bought that morning. Steve placed me in front of the three large mirrors angled so I could see all parts of myself, front and back, at the same time. This was exciting.

Steve started measuring me, writing notes under my name and the date in a red hardbound book. He measured the distance from the knuckle nearest my palm to my wrist and from wrist to elbow and the length of each finger, "in case I make gloves for an outfit someday in the future," he said. He studied the distance from the tip of my earlobe to the top of my shoulder in case capes were ever needed and recorded it. The circumference and protrusion of my nipples were set down for pasties that Steve would make that day. He regarded, calculated and wrote down the space between my legs that had to be covered with silk and satin and must lie smoothly.

"The last thing you want is to look "crinkly in the crotch," he said.

I was having so much fun. Standing among the vibrant colors and rich textures was so sweet it was almost like eating candy and all the materials felt delicious.

"The pants have to be cut as low as possible in front to be enticing but let no pubic hair show and must ride high on the hip to make the legs look longer. All these items have to come off easily, without visible effort from the dancer. It must look magical," Steve said in a lilting voice while his fingers fluttered over buttock and under breast.

He was teaching me how to put the garments on as well as how to remove them with ease as he measured my body and fitted the partially made pieces. "And for God's sakes, don't look down at the snaps and hooks unless you have a good reason. It dispels the mystery you're trying to build."

G-strings had to be large enough to cover all the necessaries and small enough to look like they were not there. Steve's hands were strong and sinewy but his touch was so light I hardly felt them passing over my nipples or moving between my thighs. All possibilities were measured and noted in the red book.

"Girls call me to design costumes for them all the time when they are on the road. I make whatever they need and send it on to them. So don't go and gain weight on me," Steve said as if that had happened more times than he wanted to mention. "Every piece has to look like you were poured into it but still comfortable enough for you to dance in. This gown," he said as he held up the white silk, "has to hang smoothly over your hips and rear end and look alluring even though it covers a full panel and two pair of pants – the jeweled and the nets." He pinned the heavy silk together on my body.

"Costumes should do everything to flatter you and nothing to detract from your form or profile. Keep that in mind when you order other costumes or even buy street clothing. They should be opulent and luxurious. Don't ever skimp on yourself," Steve said, "because it's the first thing an audience will notice."

We left after Dreamy and Charmaine had given their approval of the gown designs, all the underwear, shoes and jewelry. Steve took a one-hundred dollar deposit and the promise that we would send the remaining two-hundred seventy-five dollars in eleven weekly payments from Cleveland or wherever we were. There would be another fitting in a few days and then, hopefully, we could drive to Ohio.

Sitting around the kitchen table drinking iced tea, while Pearl licked her little feet, Lillian talked to us about Cleveland and what we should expect the working conditions to be like.

"The girls mix in Ohio. Do you know what that means, Brandy," Lillian asked as she fluffed her hair up.

I told her I did know what mixing was and she nodded. It looked like she had expected Dreamy to tell me about that part. She knew that Dreamy had mixed in Chicago and it had cost all of her front teeth as some angry mark had knocked them out for her.

"Girls can make a lot of money mixing if they do it right," Lillian said. "The club pays you for drinking with a mark and the more drinks he buys for you the more money you make. Most clubs have the bartender give you a swizzle stick or a chip for each drink you sell and they pay you fifty cents or so for each one you have at the end of the night. You only get a stick for the drinks a guy buys for you though. If a mark buys champagne you get more money, usually five dollars, so most girls try to get them to buy a bottle. A good mixer can make hundreds of dollars a week if she stays sober."

Lillian said, "I have some pictures of a girl who died in Las Vegas that looks just like you, so I sent them to Fuzzy the club owner of Mickey's Showbar in Cleveland."

"How did she die?" Dreamy asked.

"Suicide. She was deep into the Las Vegas life style. I don't know if it was the gambling, prostitution or drugs but I guess she didn't think she could make it out," said Lillian sadly.

"Oh no!" I gasped. Superstitious as hell and scared to death I said, "I'll have pictures taken in Cleveland as soon as we get there. I'll send them to you right away. Please don't send out any more of that girl's pictures saying they're me."

Lillian arranged for me to do a club date with Debbie Doll just before we left Houston. I was to receive fifty dollars from Lillian for about ten minutes work. That sounded like a lot of money.

Someone from a fraternity of students studying to be dentists at a local university had called Lillian to book two dancers for a party. Debbie and I were to meet at Lillian's house and drive there together in the little black Jaguar. I would go on first, wait for Debbie to dress after her act, and leave with her immediately.

Debbie and I met at Lillian's and left about nine in the evening. A few minutes later we arrived at the address, which turned out to be a motel.

I did not like the idea of dancing in a motel room but as we got out of the car Debbie said, "This isn't unusual. I've danced in rooms like this before and it's been fine. No hassles. Just don't wander off somewhere by yourself or with any of the guys."

I still didn't want to go but she shoved my shoulder forward and we walked up the stairs into the motel suite through a few dozen white men, between twenty and thirty years old, who were holding sweaty brown bottles of Pearl beer. Most looked as though they might play in the high school band or be in the ROTC. They could have been poster boys for their university. Dressed in a prep school sort of way with ties and brightly colored dress shirts, they looked like their mothers took good care of them and had given them a hearty breakfast that morning.

Debbie and I were welcomed with whistles and yells of "Yahoo, it's party time in Texas," "Give 'em a beer," "Two redheads, could it get any better?" and "Where are the damn blondes?" We went toward the bedroom that would be used as a dressing room and dropped our travel cases and costumes on the bed. I had the sequined gown Lillian let me wear on the roadshow.

Debbie smiled, "Be just a few minutes darlin's. You put this in the tape recorder honey," she said to a boy who looked paralyzed in the doorway.

The frat boys, who had promised to have a tape recorder, couldn't get it to work. It seemed broken. Debbie and I didn't have a tape recorder with us so we didn't know what to do. Lillian was out for the evening and we didn't know how to find Dreamy either.

After about ten minutes of wrestling with the recorder, the guys decided they would hum and clap their hands as we stripped. That sounded awful. Even if they could sing I didn't want to do it. I couldn't dance to humming yet.

"Let's just be nice, take our clothes off as quick as we can and get out of here, come on," Debbie said as she tried to soothe me and make the best of things while in the bedroom we had made into a dressing room.

Forty faces turned toward me as I opened the door. Men started humming a deep and fractured *Yellow Rose of Texas* as I stepped into the front room. I did not smile. I didn't know what I was doing and I was afraid. I felt like crying.

I started to do the bride step around the room, where there was space. Men were sitting on the couch, on the floor, in the chairs, on top of the desk and standing two deep against the walls. The bedroom door was closed and Debbie was dressing.

They yelled, "Smile, why don't cha'?" and "Aren't ya' having a good time, pussy? Smile." They sounded mean and coarse. My eyes opened wide with fright and my jaw hung loose.

The blond boy just in front of me with the baby face and pink scalp didn't seem like he was having a good time either. His mouth was screwed up tight yet his tongue was forcing its way out. His eyes were squinched closed and he looked about to throw up. I moved a few feet away in case he was a projectile vomiter.

I tried to smile, but the humming and the heckling continued as the boy was retching and vomiting. Young men climbed over each other to get out of his way. I couldn't make myself dance. One after another they stopped humming and started yelling at me.

"Who is this cunt anyway?" "When's she gonna do something?" "Do something, stupid!"

As I turned toward the dressing room someone stretched out a leg and kicked the back of my knee, tripping me. I fell flat on my stomach in the middle of them. A large foot in a hard shoe was instantly on my neck. Some future dentists roared approval and others shouted, "Noooo!"

I tried to scream and roll away from the foot that was pressing down so hard. I couldn't move but I could yell now.

"Debbie! Debbie! Help!"

Two more feet were pressed on my back and another under my chest tried to turn me over as others held me down. My legs were free. I tried to use them to help me turn over and stand up but I could not force the weight of the heavy feet off of me. Then more feet were on my thighs. A foot forced its way between my legs. It moved from side to side between my legs like it was grinding out a cigarette.

Debbie Doll came out of the dressing room, wearing a long hot pink satin gown and matching picture hat with black feathers, in response to the unusual noise and stepped into the center of the fray.

"Get off that girl! Move away from her! What do you think you're doing?" she yelled. Debbie pushed men out of the way with both arms and used her elbows to sharply nudge others to move and pounded them on the back.

A blue-eyed monster, perhaps the one who had made me fall, with fair hair and long black trousered legs stepped off my neck and shoulder where he had been standing. Debbie took my hand to help me stand up and I looked at him. I was looking at pure evil. He smiled like he was happy to have been part of the show, but his shoulders had slumped, as if disappointed that it was over.

We were both dressed to dance but Debbie walked toward the dressing room, quickly picked up her traveling case and street clothes.

"Get your stuff now!" she said. She never stopped yelling at them as if her voice was the wall of safety between them and us. We walked away from the future dentists of America, and drove toward Lillian's house to wait for her.

I was stunned. My chest and arms were red, my back scratched and bruised. My stomach and hip were scraped and swollen. I realized that Debbie Doll had saved me from rape, broken bones and maybe even death if the guy who had been standing on my neck had decided to bounce before stepping off of me. Debbie was brave and strong and a true hero to me. I never did another fraternity show in Texas or anywhere else.

Debbie said, "I will slice Lillian into little pieces before I go on another date like that," as the Jag squealed while turning a corner. "It was partly your fault too Brandy. We told you in New Mexico about having to keep your 'smile shield' up so they can't see that you're scared. Never let a mark see you're afraid. It brings out the worst in 'em."

I knew I would never trust a man again, in any situation. I had seen that look in their eyes, a look of hate, willing to do anything to be amused. I didn't know if I could go back to being mildly indifferent to men now that I had seen how they could hurt women for the fun of it.

Chapter Six

Short Vincent Street

The day we arrived in Cleveland the newspaper headline read CHAMPAGNE FOR LOVE. The newsstand in front of the hotel had four papers left and we took two. The exposé of strip clubs and how they operated to relieve men of their money covered the front page and the story continued inside.

"Look at this. Oh, my God!" Dreamy whispered as she scanned the paper. She inhaled deeply and explained to me. " It's a hell of a time to start in a new city with this going on. The vice squad and every other kind of cop are going to be hanging around the strip clubs. The marks will be a lot more careful now. You have to read this right away. It'll let you know what to expect when you open tonight."

The gleaming white columned façade, wide white marble stairway and lobby let us know the Colonnade Hotel had been built when this neighborhood was more fashionable. We registered for the room that Lillian had arranged for us to live in during our stay while ignoring the interested expressions of the bellmen and desk clerk.

The huge room was almost an apartment, with four tall windows that were each six feet wide and looked out to the busy street below. It had an "L" shaped kitchenette in a corner and a round wooden table with four matching chairs next to the pale yellow and white tile countertops.

A double bed in one corner and an upholstered navy blue and white couch and two chairs in another completed the layout which was airy and comfortable.

The bathroom floor was black and white marble squares, like a checkerboard, and one wall was covered by a deeply beveled art deco mirror.

We were paying the "entertainer's rate" so this great room was affordable at fifty dollars a week. We could actually afford the rent.

We hurried the bellman out so we could sit at the table, drink our warm 7 Up, smoke Kents and read the newspaper. The Cleveland Plain Dealer said the city had "corralled" most of its striptease clubs onto Short Vincent Street. There were a few restaurants on the street and a jazz club opening soon that promised to feature big name performers.

The story went on to say that dancers, and women called B-girls who were hired especially to drink with customers, "are allowing men to fondle them above and below the waist" and they are "caressing the men's bodies in return for drinks and champagne."

Dreamy took a look at my panicked expression again and explained patiently, "Don't worry, honey. You look so sweet and innocent they won't expect you to do much mixing for a while. They will teach you how to do it, but by the time they see you're not going to be a good mixer, we'll be ready to get out of here and on to the next gig. Just be sure when you get to the club you don't take another dancer's costume space in the wardrobe closet or her place at the makeup table. We don't know how many girls work there yet, so try to take up as little space as possible at first. The girls are used to new dancers coming and going so they know how it works even if you don't. Call me or come right back if you don't think you can work there. I'll be here waiting for you."

I decided to arrive at the club an hour early the first evening so I could meet the manager, take my costumes in, and get instructions well before the other dancers were supposed to show up. I left the hotel at 7:30. The all-seeing doorman whistled up a taxi before I reached him and instructed the driver "Mickey's" with a toss of his head toward me. I guessed he knew I was headed there because my grey silky costume bag was over my arm and the fine red leather makeup and accessory case Dreamy had bought me was similar to what she said other girls carried back and forth to the clubs each evening.

The thought that he might know I was a stripper because I was wearing a revealing evening gown and full stage makeup with long false eyelashes plus rhinestone earrings that rested on my shoulders did not enter my mind.

The ride took about ten minutes and I was let out onto a narrow street in downtown Cleveland. Short Vincent Street was one long block, a row of one and two story buildings aglow with red, hot pink, green, purple, yellow and blue flashing, popping and blinking neon signs. The whole block jiggled and bounced with names like Mickey's Show Bar, Blues Body Shop, The Pink Tickle, and The Bon Bon Box.

I stepped into Mickey's and was met by the manager who introduced himself as Racehorse Dick. In the darkness he looked thin and sinister, in his late thirties. If I had seen him in another place I know I would have thought he was tall, dark and handsome. He laughed at his nickname and looked like he expected me to laugh too. I was so nervous I could only offer a little smile but he seemed satisfied.

"I got that name running against a racehorse down the main street of Columbus," he said. "We ended up dead even after two blocks."

He looked at me carefully.

"Say, how old are you? Let me see your identification."

Lillian had given me a copy of my California birth certificate with a new birth date on it before we left Houston. She had said I would have to give it to the club manager so I had brought it with me. I handed it to him hoping he would just give it a quick glance.

He read it slowly and looked at me again.

"If I ever tell you to go across the street and get something to eat, go right away. Don't get a coat or anything, just go. Have dinner and wait for me to come get you. The Alcohol Beverage

Commission comes around once in a while and they don't like the dancers being underage. You look too young even if this thing says you're twenty two." He kept holding the paper and I held my breath while waiting for him to give it back. He finally folded it, smiled grimly under his mustache and returned it to me.

"Remember what I said."

The club had a long narrow bar that curved toward the back wall at both ends. There were about forty dark red and chrome bar stools but no tables or chairs. The stage was the same height as the bar, about fifty feet long and six feet wide. The drum set, a chair for the sax player and one for the girls to put their wardrobe were on stage near the dressing room side where the steps were, so it was a little crowded getting on and off. The old upright piano was next to the bar on the other side, near the entrance and the jukebox.

Racehorse Dick led me down the long aisle behind the bar stools, past the bathrooms, the small storeroom and into the dressing room. The walls of the small square room were mirrored from the ceiling to about waist high on three sides where there were wide wooden shelves for the girls to put their make-up cases. A metal rack against one wall held costumes, wardrobe bags and boas that were left out to stay fluffy. There was lots of light here, but no bathroom.

I couldn't tell where one dancer's costumes ended and another one's started. I kept hearing Dreamy's voice saying, "Keep yourself small in the dressing room" but there was no space on the clothing rack for one extra hanger much less my gowns. There were no chairs for me to get in trouble with, but where could I put my wardrobe?

"There ain't no chairs. You ain't here to sit," Racehorse said as he squinted at me. "You dress to go on stage and when your act is finished, you change into something slinky as fast as you can and get out to the bar and make some mark buy you a drink. Champagne. You ever done spit-back?" he asked gruffly.

I just looked at him. What was he talking about?

Racehorse Dick took my costume bag and flung it on the rack.

"Drop your case and come out to the bar, now."

I tucked my beautiful, new red case under the makeup table and followed Racehorse out to the main room.

"This is G, our bouncer, the guy ya go to if ya have any trouble when I'm not here," said Racehorse.

G looked up from behind the bar and nodded. A black snub-nosed revolver in each hand was pointed at me. He had taken them out of his pants pockets and was laying them on the workstation where he sat at the bar near the stairs leading to the stage.

G noticed I was looking at his guns with fascination and shock. I had never been that close to a revolver before. My back started to sweat. G laughed gently.

"Yeah, they're so heavy my sister has to sew in new pockets for me 'bout every six weeks. Good guns though," he said affectionately as he started cleaning one with an oily cloth he had drawn from its hidey-hole under the bar top. "Don't worry 'bout nothin', you're okay here," he said softly.

I immediately trusted him although everything told me I shouldn't. Short and squarely built, about fifty years old, G looked at me with a clear, open gaze. His face was calm with the knowledge of his own physical strength. Wavy black, graying hair and heavy jowls set off his warm brown eyes. I believed he would be there at the stairs and not let anyone near them while I was on, and would make sure no one followed me to the dressing room when I left the stage.

As Racehorse Dick turned away, G adjusted his long shirt sleeve. A leather blackjack, held onto his wrist by a thin strap, used for hitting offending customers in the head, fell into view. He winked and nodded.

"Always there and ready," said G.

"This is Joyce, our singing bartender," said Racehorse Dick as he introduced an older pudgy blonde. "You're going to be close to Joyce here, so pay attention to what she says." He took a deep breath and started his well-worn spit-back patter.

"With every drink a mark buys ya, Joyce will give ya a swizzle stick. Ya keep all those sticks and at the end of the night turn them in to me, no one else. End of every week ya get fifty cents for each one. Ya keep count too, cuz I don't want no questions about my arithmetic."

"What Joyce is gonna give ya is forty-two proof vodka. That means twenty-one percent alcohol. The marks can only buy doubles for ya. Don't drink it. Ya got three or four shows to do and the other girls won't like it if they have to cover your time and you're sprawled on the floor somewhere. We charge four-fifty for every drink ya have."

He picked up two glasses and told me, "This little one is a double shot glass. See how the bottom is real thick so ya don't get as much liquor? This larger one is a chaser glass and holds water. Joyce will fill it half way and when ya take a drink from the shot glass ya take the chaser glass and spit the vodka back into it. The thing is, ya don't want to let the marks see ya do it. They won't notice when the amount goes up unless there are lots of spit bubbles. That's the thing. Don't let 'em see the bubbles. Got it? Joyce will change the glass when it looks like it's getting full. Remember to have the mark tip her because she'll be the closest one to see if you're having trouble and signal G. Ya gotta sell at least fifty of these a week so ya can make your salary. Girl can't sell, she's gone. Understand?"

As I was trying to figure out if I did understand, two beautiful smiling girls came in holding hands, makeup cases swinging. Racehorse Dick frowned when he saw them and they let go of each other and stuck their tongues out at him. The tall blonde laughed and crinkled her nose, but the dark-haired beauty gave him a look filled with poison.

"Pixie Lynn and Torchy Blair, this is Brandy Wilde," said Racehorse. "They're some of Lillian's girls too. I don't know why all Lillian's girls are queer. I hear you got a rooster with ya, too."

My mouth dropped open but I couldn't say a word. I felt so insulted my eyes started to well with angry tears as both girls grabbed me, and between them walked me back to the dressing room.

Torchy put a Kleenex in my hand. "For your make-up. It's starting to run."

"That your garment bag?" asked Pixie. "I'd move it over here if I were you. If Alicia comes in and sees your hangers on her new boa, she'll slit your throat. Just kidding – but move it before she gets here."

I wondered what the next hour would bring. Would I be sent home right away? Would the girls accept me?

At one minute before nine Lorna Love arrived in jeans, without makeup, her long brown hair in a ponytail, with loose costumes over one arm, and two small suitcases under the other. She was exactly on time if you already worked there, but late if it was your first night.

When Racehorse Dick's eye hit Lorna coming in the door, he raised a dark brow and stopped showing me how to wave a champagne bottle around while giggling, looking tipsy and available, how to spill champagne all over the floor and into the ice bucket to get marks to buy another bottle quickly. He rose to capture Lorna.

She looked dizzy and frazzled, as she closed her eyes for a second, adjusting to the dark. Turning from side to side as if trying to decide whether to stay or go out the door, she whimpered as Racehorse Dick grabbed her arm and hustled her back toward the little dressing room.

"Oh, help," she whispered, as she passed me and I saw her eyes roll up into her forehead.

I sat frozen on the maroon leather barstool looking after her and hoped the other girls who were already in the dressing room would be a buffer between the new girl and this angry man. Lorna and I had met at Lillian's house so maybe she knew Pixie and Torchy too.

Three men in dark suits entered the room from a hall that was a continuation of the aisle behind the bar stools. The older man, grey-haired with a big stomach, had a saxophone tucked under his arm and all three walked toward the stage.

Just like me, the skinny man walking to the piano didn't look old enough to be in there, but the man who sat at the seven-piece drum set looked just like I had imagined a strip club drummer should. He was about six feet tall, seemed muscular and his furrowed face looked like he had seen everything there was to see as he sat across the bar looking into the audience six hours a night - his face, pale in the bright stage light; his dark hair fell over his high forehead and rested on his eyelashes. I hoped he would play like the drummer at the Shamrock Hotel in Houston and be my friend on stage.

Racehorse Dick had taken my music charts for the band to read while playing for my act. I had chosen the songs, but I had no idea what they would sound like with this trio. Lillian had warned me that musicians sometimes read the title of the song and play it the way they always had.

Joyce, who was also looking toward the dressing room said, "Don't worry about her. He's not really mean. He just needs to look like it. He has to get her in line tonight though, or she won't last another day. We have eight girls in the show. That's too many for one to show up looking like she slept on the sidewalk. She could have been scheduled to go on first and look at her."

"There's a schedule? Where is it? When do I go on?" I wailed as I ran back toward the dressing room where she had pointed.

Running down the short hall I heard the band start playing a few fast bars of *There's No Business Like Show Business*, then Joyce on the microphone introducing the first dancer of the evening.

"Welcome to Mickey's Showbar. For our first act this evening we present the faaaabulous 'Peaches Delight'."

I turned to look as Peaches, a tiny blonde with huge breasts who looked about twenty, walked up the six little stairs, holding her dress up so she wouldn't trip. She would be my fourth stripper and I was anxious to see what I could learn from her act, sitting in the audience instead of backstage.

Our trio played *Sweet and Lovely* and she started walking back and forth along the narrow stage. There were no customers yet and she didn't put too much effort into her dancing, though she did look beautiful in her strapless, white, fluffy ankle length gown with pink flower trim. Peaches looked like she was on her way to the high school prom, but had lost her way, as she walked back and forth down the long stage.

Racehorse Dick came down the hall talking to me.

"You're on fourth" he said in a flat tone. "Be sure you're ready early. We don't have any pauses between acts."

I knew each girl would be on stage about twelve to fifteen minutes so I had time to watch Peaches. She had no audience so she played to the bartender and to me, throwing us sudden bumps and sly "come hither" gestures. The wall behind the stools was mirrored from the height of the bar to the ceiling so Peaches could flirt with herself too. This was going to be perfect for me.

By the middle of Peaches' act, more dancers had come in to sit at the bar. A woman with long blue-black hair, dressed in a dark red gown that allowed nearly all of her breast to spill out, rested on a stool near the door and looked out to the street as if willing men to enter. She looked much older than the others and I couldn't figure out why she was here. Was she a B-girl?

Racehorse Dick had explained that the show was continuous.

"If a customer sticks his head in to see what the show looks like, there has to be a dancer on stage."

Torchy and Pixie sat together talking, waiting for their turns to dance. There was an elusive connection between them; you knew they were up to something. They were either planning a bank robbery right there at the bar or talking about what they would do to each other when they got home that morning.

I went to dress for my first show as a professional stripper in a real club. All that had gone before had been practice for this night. Dreamy was at the hotel and there was no Lillian or Debbie Doll around in case I needed them. G might be ready and even looking forward to protecting me, but I was on my own now.

My back was covered with sweat that trickled down in little cold streams as I put on the high cut turquoise satin pants and matching bra. The dressing room looked like a tail wind had followed Lorna's flight in. The floor was covered with her open bags and costumes as she squatted above them trying to figure out how to hang them up.

I realized now that Steve had forgotten to alter my bra. The cup size was much too big for me. It was still the size of the original dancer who ordered the gown and then did not pay for it. Now I was going to go out there and when I took off my bra, there would be a big difference between what had been promised and what really was under the stiff satin and sequin bra.

I wanted to die. I couldn't bear to think about the inevitable snickers and laughter from the audience, much less the other dancers who were the ones that mattered to me. How was I going to get through this? I moaned to myself as I looked in the mirror and open and closed the bra a couple of times. The Big Bra choreography would have to go like this: smile, turn to face the back of the stage, take off the bra, face the audience and tease for a while hiding myself with the panel until they might almost forget how big the bra was and then let them see my breasts, smile. That would have to do for tonight.

I finally finished dressing, repaired my makeup, and pulled on the second white glove as the dressing room filled up with women in clingy long gowns. Peaches had rushed in, thrown on a long orange gown and run out again to sit at the bar as a customer had come through the door. Lollie Lake was on stage dancing to *Fever*.

The girl now closest to me was a short thin-faced blonde who looked about forty and was dressed in a red satin and fringe gown, ready to go on stage. She had tired little brown eyes and heavy chalky makeup. She must have been around clubs like this for a long time because every move was quick and efficient. She looked at Lorna and casually threw Lorna's gowns to the floor again.

"Hi honey," she said to me. "Where are you from? I'm Alicia Christie, this is Glory Dawn."

Alicia was on before me. She left the room before I could get out an answer.

Glory Dawn was the woman in dark red who had been sitting at the end of the bar. I realized now that Glory was a dancer too, but in the harsh fluorescent light of the dressing room I could envision her as someone's grandmother. The skin of her neck and between her breasts was loose and wrinkled and even the heavy makeup could not disguise the firm set of her mouth and the furrows across her brow. Right then, I swore to myself I would never stay in the business that far past my prime.

I smiled at Glory and walked out to the little hall so I could watch Alicia dance and still remain hidden. There were a few more men in the audience and Joyce was mixing their drinks. Glory passed me in the hall and sat at the bar next to one of the new arrivals.

Down the bar, a few seats from the front door, sat a lady of about fifty or more who was alone. She had on a too short dark brown mink stole and a little black hat with a net that covered her eyes. A small purse sat on her lap and I noticed she didn't have a drink.

Alicia smiled on stage but she still looked sad to me. I wondered how long she had been a dancer and when she had started at Mickey's Showbar. She obviously thought she owned the place.

A short man, with lots of dark curly hair that sprang straight up out of his head came into the club just before I was to start my show. He looked at me appraisingly as he passed and walked into the back office. This must be the "Mayor" the newspaper had written about, I thought. This must be Fuzzy Lakis, the owner of Mickey's coming in to see what his new girls look like.

I walked up the stairs to the first four bars of *Body and Soul* and the sweet silky strains of the tenor saxophone. This was a true love song.

Even a few weeks later I loved dancing on this stage. With the mirror behind the bar and the mirrored wall facing the bar my best audience was me. All the girls danced mostly to themselves in the mirror unless they had a good spender waiting for them at the bar. This was the time to check out my technique and style, my smile for authenticity, the turn of an ankle to make the longest leg line.

I had copied and perfected a little step that Peaches did and watched Torchy for every sexy signal she sent out to the audience and practiced them at home. I saw how Pixie tried to draw the customers into the good spirit of her cowgirl act and make them happier. All of this and more I learned from the girls and would take it away from Mickey's and on to other clubs with me.

The time off stage was not so much fun. The pressure from Racehorse Dick for me to mix increased nightly.

"Ya otta know how to do this. Ya been watching Glory and Alicia. Haven't ya learned anything?" railed Racehorse.

I had been watching them. I had seen how they drank the first seven or eight vodkas straight down without picking up the spit-back glass. After a few more drinks, they would let the mark do anything to them if he would buy them a bottle of champagne. Their gowns were split up the sides and they sat on the front edge of the bar stool to give the customer easy access to what was between their legs.

A bottle of champagne cost the mark a hundred dollars and the dancer was paid five dollars commission on every one. But, the important part was, with that one bottle, the dancer had made the club about half her weekly salary. In the last two weeks I had seen both Alicia and Glory get suckers to buy them four or five bottles a night. That was called job security.

"Where da ya go anyway? I look for ya and you're never around," Racehorse said.

I couldn't tell him I was hiding next to Mr. Trinkle's legs, under the piano keys. I hoped no one knew I was there except for young Mr. Trinkle, the piano player, and one time G saw me, but pretended he hadn't.

I loved my co-conspirators.

The first publicity pictures of Brandy in Cleveland. 1961.

Chapter Seven

The Big Guns and Murder

It was October. I had been at Mickey's Showbar for eight weeks and was trying to mix a little more to keep the job but without getting caught up in it like most of the dancers were or were sliding toward. The money was tempting and it mounted up fast.

I knew that if I had been a lover of men instead of women it would be easy to stay here. I could let a woman touch my thigh, maybe even let her hand wander a bit if I liked her, but I could not let a man do it. The last few weeks I had made fifty or sixty dollars in tips given to me secretly, sometimes much more, and about twenty-five a week for mixing.

To sell fifty drinks a week and receive fifty cents commission for each one was the hardest work I did. I usually only got one drink from a guy before he realized the buddy next to him was getting some hand action under the bar and he wasn't. Lillian didn't get any commission from my tips or mixing money and the government took no income tax since I was an independent contractor like all the dancers were.

Dreamy had said, "You keep all the mixing money aside and use it as you want and we'll put the tip money in the bank. I don't want to use it for living expenses. You start relying on it and it's hard to stop working clubs like this."

Dreamy had worked mixing clubs in Calumet City just outside of Chicago. In two years she had made more than $150,000 in Cal City, which was a fortune for an eighteen year-old girl in 1952. She spent it on having fried oysters and hominy flown in from New Orleans and chili from Texas; and in newly discovered gay bars. Then drugs had entered her life and she wasn't as good looking or as reliable as she had been. She had started living in drag and only dressing like a woman when on stage. The Mafia club owners who had thought she was such a great moneymaker wouldn't let her work for them anymore. It was hard for me to imagine Dreamy like that.

"Calumet City was called Sin City by the Chicago girls. It was funny though. No matter how much they pushed the girls to mix, the club owners told us never to hustle a guy in military uniform. It was during the Korean War and the syndicate was very patriotic," Dreamy said. "You could drink with them but you couldn't work 'em so they would spend every penny they had."

In September, wearing only a long pink mixing dress and silver high heels, Lorna Love had run out of Mickey's one Thursday night and never returned to the club or her hotel. She had left her costumes at the club and the luggage in her room. We kept waiting but no one ever heard from her again, including Lillian, who was her agent.

Lorna had been acting strange for a few weeks. Lollie Lake was on stage one night when Lorna sat down at the bar next to me. She laughed as she watched Lollie's thrashing side bumps.

"My pussy is growing teeth," she said with excitement and a wide smile. "I love to think of being able to bite off dicks with it. Doesn't that sound like fun?"

The smile dropped off my face. I was speechless.

The week before I had seen her on stage dancing in front of a guy she had been sitting with at the bar. He kneeled on the stool and leaned over empty space toward her, trying to touch her leg. With a strong high kick in a silver spike heel shoe, Lorna spread his nose across his face in perfect time to *Love Potion Number Nine*.

The poor guy was screaming and bleeding all over his white shirt as G went over to try and help him. Racehorse and G put him into a taxi.

"What da ya think you're doin' tryin' to grab my girls when they're on stage?" Racehorse Dick yelled at the back of the mark's head. "Get the hell out of here!"

I sent Lorna's costumes and suitcases to Lillian in Houston. I never heard if Lorna had picked them up.

"The big guns are coming in from Vegas on Friday. We gotta get this place in shape. Don't even think of missing a night," Racehorse Dick warned us.

He looked at me to make sure I understood. Somehow he knew about Bren, one of the marks, who told me he owned a diamond mine in South Africa. Bren said he was a regular customer at Mickey's when he was in town so Racehorse must have heard that story. I knew Bren wanted me to ask him for a diamond so he could play the "you want something and I want something" game. I never asked, but he came in once a week and gave me a hundred dollars each time so I could say I was sick and stay home the next night.

By Friday evening, Mickey's was clean. The floor had been waxed and the mirrors sparkled, while the ever changing color wheel went round and round making the stage red, green, blue and orange, living up to Steve's greatest fears for his costumes. Racehorse Dick stood at the far end of the bar with G and waited breathlessly. Fuzzy Lakis was in his office waiting for the buzzer on his desk to signal the "Big Guns" had arrived.

A little after midnight, Fuzzy left his office and stood in the hall as four men in dark suits entered the club. Three of them walked toward the back. Standing in the hall waiting to go on stage, I could see that none of them looked at the dancer for more than an instant. Fuzzy hugged each one in a respectful way, right arm around the shoulders with three pats on the back while the left arm lay lightly on the lower back. They followed him into his office.

The fourth man who, from a distance, was a dead ringer for Tony Curtis, sat at the bar next to the piano near the entrance. He watched the street traffic.

A moment later two more men in dark suits came in, sat close to the middle of the bar and ordered beer. By now I could almost always tell when police were in the club and these two looked familiar. Their stiff necks, straight backs and constantly roving gazes to catch anything suspicious were my main clues. They didn't watch the show with interest stare into their drinks, or occasionally peek up as customers did.

Alicia left the stage and I went on with *You Stepped Out of a Dream* for my first trailer.

A song like that makes you feel really good dancing. It can give you a little boost of sexiness if you need it, like I did right then. I checked to make sure the large rhinestone covering my navel was in place. No sense getting arrested for that while everybody was on alert.

We were all curious about these men from Nevada and why they would travel so far to meet with Fuzzy. He was called the "Mayor of Short Vincent Street" so maybe that was more than a nickname. I started to ask Glory but she wouldn't listen to me once it became clear to her what I wanted to know.

"In this business, you learn to keep your mind on your act and your good health, otherwise you don't stay healthy very long. Know what I mean, honey?" she asked.

I knew she was being kind and giving me good advice but I wanted to know everything as usual.

While on stage I could see the girls mixing in a big crowd of guys, laughing loudly. Joyce was changing spit-back glasses as fast as she could. Smoke and music enveloped me as I glided across stage. Lots of practice in front of this mirror to perfect the "Debbie Doll glide" had worked wonders for my act. I felt good on stage and my smile was natural and inviting – no matter what I was feeling. A champagne bottle, knocked over by Lollie to let her current mark see it was empty, dropped to the floor near the cops and G bounced over there to soothe the customers and retrieve the heavy glass container.

There were no empty seats at the bar. Lone men were lined up with their backs against the mirrored wall. Many tried to look like they weren't interested in the show but were there for the great drinks and to do some deep thinking. It was a typical night considering the syndicate big boys from Las Vegas were there and the cops were sitting front and center trying to look like they were watching the show and not waiting for a mob meeting to end so they could follow them again.

Torchy Blair went on after me to the pounding drive of the theme from the television show *Peter Gunn*. Her proud, powerful stride and tremendous sense of rhythm enhanced the mood of the music. She was gorgeous with young smooth skin, long, shapely, strong legs and flat stomach. The men could not help themselves. They had to look at her and she gave them a show worth watching. Even the musicians looked at her and seemed to play better for her than for anyone else. I was halfway in love with her too, just because she was Torchy.

I dressed quickly in a black slinky gown that showed all the cleavage I had to offer and went down the bar to stand near, but not next to, the Tony Curtis look-alike. I didn't want him to think I was trying to hustle him. I just wanted a closer look.

He had a wide, glittery white smile and dimples to go with it. What a knock out! His hair was dark and curled softly. He was as pretty as any of the girls on stage.

"Hi...liked your show. I'm Specks. Would you join me?" He spoke so I could hear him over the music but not too loudly. He must be older than I thought. I knew now it took quite a while to learn how to do that.

Joyce looked at us to see if she should ask me what I was drinking and Specks nodded to her to come over.

"Ten for the pretty girl," he said sweetly as he put a fifty on the bar.

Joyce swept up the money and went off to bring ten double shot glasses full of the watered-down fortytwo proof vodka to sit in front of me. She only brought one spit-back glass because we all knew I was not going to drink any of that awful stuff. In this setting it was a gesture of courtesy from one professional to another. I noticed Millie, our one B-girl, was alone at her usual place near the end of the bar and had four drinks in front of her and no spit-back glass. She smiled at me through her net veil and signaled with a circling finger and a movement of her head toward Specks that we were sharing the same mark. This cutie was a real nice guy.

"Are you from Cleveland?" I asked Specks.

"No, just in from Vegas for a meet and greet. Ever been to the Stardust?" he asked.

Specks laughed when I told him I had never been to Las Vegas and had a strange superstition about it. I had started telling him about the pictures of the dead dancer Lillian had sent saying they were me, when Fuzzy opened his office door.

The bright light reflected in the mirror. Specks looked toward the street then stood and while looking down the hall toward his boss said, "Come visit if you're ever in Vegas. The Stardust."

I saw the spectacular smile one last time, and then they were gone. The two men seated at the center of the bar followed them out to the street. Looking out the window I saw three black cars leaving in the same direction. It looked like the heavy hitters, their bodyguards and the police were all together. Maybe the police were bodyguards too.

The meeting was over and the "Big Guns" were gone. I wondered what had happened but none of the dancers ever heard more about it.

Every morning at three a.m. after the jukebox played *Hit the Road Jack* by Ray Charles, and all the suckers were gone or walking away, uniformed Cleveland police officers stood outside to guard and escort each of the ten dancers to a waiting taxicab. After a full shift of promising marks everything they wanted so they would pay for our watered-down hooch, we needed guarding. The drivers knew they might have trouble on their hands as drunk and irate customers sometimes tried to sneak back and block dancers from entering the taxi or follow them to their hotels.

Mixing could be a dangerous business. Night after night men who had been drinking, and spending their hard earned money on promises of blowjobs and more, waited for girls to leave the nine strip clubs up and down Short Vincent Street. When no one showed up to relieve the pressure, and maybe even give back some of the money they now regretted spending, the marks would roar forward from around corners and the dark doorways of nearby buildings.

"I spent four hundred dollars on the bitch and now she's gone!" they would scream to the police guarding exit doors.

That's a real sucker. The police were on the payroll of the clubs. The big newspaper articles Dreamy and I had read explaining all the evils available on the street had acted like a magnet drawing more men toward Short Vincent. More girls, more bartenders, more taxis and police had to be hired to accommodate them. I was still trying to figure out which dancers were my friends and who were my enemies.

Mickey's now had ten girls in the show. Glory Dawn was still the last act on the schedule and she was real popular with the guys. She twirled tassels on her breasts and on her rear end. She had shown me how all tassel tossing begins with vibrating one foot against the floor and working that movement up the body.

The last three minutes of her act were all in black light so everything that was white showed up bright purple. The color wheel was turned off and the bar became even darker. During those three minutes some promises were fulfilled: I learned that was called "zipper mixing."

It was cold by mid-November and the city changed. The trees were naked and the chilly wind off Lake Erie raked Short Vincent Street and blasted through the open door. Millie, our B-girl still sat there, with the short mink stole around her shoulders and little purse on her lap, waiting for a john to buy her a drink. Our show was back down to eight girls, and it looked like I was about to leave too.

Lillian called me at the hotel to let me know Racehorse Dick had complained again because I had not yet become a "money maker." Dreamy and I knew this was the call to tell us it was time to move on and that was all right with us both.

I had learned so much there by watching the other dancers night after night for eleven weeks. I learned to be ready early in case a dancer fell down and broke her ankle, which had happened when Peaches had been drinking with a mark. My smile came naturally and my makeup and false eyelashes were always perfectly applied. Some borrowed dance steps and sexy gestures were part of my act and I had my own style.

"Yes, he's right. I admit I don't do it very well. Last night a guy gave me a little bottle full of beautiful opals in the rough and a polished one about the size of a fifty-cent piece, but he wouldn't buy me one drink. We need to move to warmer weather anyway. Remember we're California girls. We were thinking about going home for Christmas."

"You don't have to stay, Brandy. I've heard good things about your act and I can book you somewhere else with no trouble," Lillian said. "There's a nice theater in Toledo for two weeks if you want to go there. Four shows a day but it pays a little better because the hours are longer. You might have to be a talking woman for a skit or two, but I don't think you'd mind doing that, would you?"

"Yes, that sounds good to me, Lillian. I think I'm ready now to go out and make you proud," I said as I laughed with relief. "Watching the girls every night and trying some of their steps in the mirror when I'm on stage has really helped my act, you'd be surprised, and a theater sounds like fun. No mixing either, right?"

At the club that evening I was so relaxed. I didn't feel the pressure to mix, as I had ever since arriving in Cleveland. After my first show, thinking about Toledo, I wandered out of the dressing room and sat down at the bar next to a single mark about forty wearing a dark grey suit.

"Would you like some company?" I asked with a smile.

"Would you like to go fuck yourself?" he responded as he raised his arm and poured his highball over my head.

I froze for a moment. My legs were so wobbly I didn't think I would be able to stand. I could hear my heart beat and feel my eardrums fluttering. I was hot and confused. I slid off the bar stool without looking at the mark and did the only thing I knew how to do. I went to get dressed for a show even though I had just left the stage and would not go on again for over an hour.

With each piece of clothing I put on I became angrier. Adrenaline pulsed through my every vein and capillary making me aware of things in the dressing room I had not noticed before, like the small hole in the ceiling with Kleenex stuffed into it. The anger grew until I finally knew what to do with it.

My heartbeat grew quiet and the tension went out of my shoulders. My cheeks were pulled in toward my tongue. My eyes were large and still as I looked in the mirror. I had never lost my temper in my entire life, but this was the moment. The frustration of a lifetime and especially the last eight or nine weeks came out.

I drew on the last glove and walked purposefully out to the bar. Reaching for an empty champagne bottle in passing, I failed to break it on the bar where I hit it twice, but walked steadily toward the mark intent on killing him with it.

As I drew my arm back and aimed the bottle toward the back of the mark's head, G was suddenly there grabbing it from me. He picked me up, threw me on top of the bar so I was sitting on it, and turned to the man in the dark grey suit, who sat with an irritated look on his face, like he didn't know what the commotion was all about.

The blackjack dropped into G's right hand as the left one took hold of the sucker in grey and threw him onto the floor. G hit the man over and over on and around his head while the guy writhed and screamed trying to protect himself. When he stopped moving and looked unconscious, a small man appeared out of nowhere to help G. Each took one of the beaten man's arms, pulled him past the other bar stools, down the hall, past Fuzzy's office, and out an open door into the back alley. I saw them empty the mark's pockets of keys and a wallet. The small man started pulling him away from the door and down the alley. G reentered the club and left them in the cold. He shut and locked the hidden door and slid a mirrored panel over it.

Pixie Lynn in her little white cowgirl outfit, white leather fringe boots, and mother-of-pearl cap guns, who was on stage during this ruckus, danced on as she watched us. The band didn't miss a beat of *Ghost Riders in the Sky*. No one had tried to help this guy and no one said a word to me about trying to hit him. G came and lifted me off the bar and set me on my feet.

"Take a minute to calm yourself and put on another dress, then come sit by me," he said gently. He wasn't even breathing hard and he had a serene little closed-lip smile.

As I walked toward the dressing room I tried to focus on what had just happened. I was trembling and had to hold onto the wall to walk in a straight line. Where was Racehorse Dick? Who had opened the alley door and why did they take the man's wallet and keys? Where were they taking the guy? What would happen to him?

I was afraid G might have been extra hard on the jerk. Racehorse had told me in the ten years he had worked with G that I was the only stripper he had ever asked to his sister Roselyn's house for lunch. Dreamy and I had gone to Shaker Heights, the nicest residential area in Cleveland, to meet Roselyn and see her beautiful gardens.

G lived there with his younger sister and her husband who was at work while we were lunching. We talked about California, gardens, her needlepoint and other ladylike topics. I could tell that G was happy with the way our visit had progressed. He wanted his sister's approval and could see that he had received it.

That day G also took us to his auto mechanic so we could get our '53 Ford tuned- up. The mechanic worked on the car that afternoon and G took us back to pick it up. As he drove, and was away from his innocent sister, he reminisced about Cleveland.

"You know, things have changed a lot since I started. My first job was running guns when I was fifteen. Always loved guns. That was so long ago, the cars we used still had candles where the headlights are now."

I didn't know whether to believe him or not. I had never heard of cars like that. He said he had never married because he didn't want "to bring a nice girl into this life." G liked me and I knew he was glad I wasn't a "good money maker."

It was my last week at Mickey's Showbar and I was happy we were moving on to Toledo. It had been ten and a half exhausting weeks for me, and Dreamy was bored to death. She hadn't done much while I was gone in the evenings other than watch television and cook for me and Pixie and Torchy. After work they often came to breakfast in our room. Being Southern Texas girls, they loved the pepper steak, barbequed pork chops, red beans and rice with Iberia peppers, and all the other wonderful southern dishes that Dreamy cooked for us.

My costumes and pictures were paid for, and we started saving money to help us in Los Angeles where I wanted to take some college classes. I had decided I didn't want to be on the road much longer. There had to be strip clubs in Hollywood and I could just as easily work there and have days free to go out on auditions for movies and television shows and take classes at Los Angeles City College.

There would be tougher competition for work in Los Angeles because the most beautiful women in the world are there to get into the movies. Tens of thousands of them were there to be discovered and more arrived every day; not all of them were strippers.

My grandmother Rose, a buxom four-feet-ten inches tall beauty, had been among the first young women who poured into Hollywood. She had been a music-hall singer near Covent Garden and moved from London to Los Angeles in 1910. At twenty-three she had already abandoned three husbands and one small son, to get into the new "moving picture" industry.

Rose never became a movie star. The closest she came to show business in Hollywood was working as a cook for Sam Marx, a cousin of the Marx Brothers whose job it was to invest and take care of all the money rolling in.

Friday night, almost my last night in Cleveland, I was feeling jazzed after my second show. Things were going great and the night was almost over. A little before one a.m. two powerful looking men came in the door. The slender one, who wore an expensive looking camelhair overcoat and a cream-colored silk scarf at his neck, nodded at Millie as he passed her. He was welcomed by Racehorse Dick and G as a long lost brother might be greeted. The other man, who had to be six-foot-seven or more and was wide enough to fill a doorway, was not greeted as wildly but simply acknowledged with polite nods.

In three minutes money was strewn all along the bar where Lollie Lake and I were sitting.

"Girls, this is Tony Boots. Tony Boots!" exclaimed Racehorse Dick acting like this was the greatest event since the big race when he got his name. "Sit down, relax. This is Brandy and our little Lollie Lake. So, what da' ya' want?" Racehorse asked expansively, his arms spread wide as if ready to lay down the world before Tony.

"Ten drinks for each girl including that one on stage and Millie there too," said Tony Boots as he sat between Lollie and me.

"Quite a name you got, Lollie. Cute."

Lollie tried to snuggle up to Tony's shoulder, looked up at him with big eyes and said, "Just like a lollypop, you can suck all day."

I had been looking straight ahead at the scene in the mirror and I saw Tony Boots sneer at Lollie and felt him draw back as if from a bad smell. He turned his back on Lollie and didn't talk to her again, but he kept the drinks coming. Tony drank his scotch slowly while his bodyguard did not have a glass. About every fifteen minutes he ordered another round of ten for each dancer and Millie, then he made sure to spill as many as he could so he could order again. There were thousands of dollars on the bar – mostly hundred dollar bills, all wet and sticky. Vodka was all over my dress, dripping from Lollie's hair and running down the bar. It was chaos.

Dusty Starr and Alicia joined us and almost knocked me off the bar stool trying to cuddle as close to Tony Boots as possible. Tony reached over to steady me, took Alicia by the arm and moved her over to his other side. Lollie refused to be moved off her stool by Alicia's forceful rear end so Alicia stood facing Tony, with her elbow on the bar, effectively hiding Lollie from Tony's sight.

I had been around a few big spenders in the last weeks but not like this one. Every round cost him more than four hundred dollars and he was giving Joyce fifty-dollar tips. Lollie and I looked at each other trying to signal, "Who is this guy?" He sure knew the game that was being played here. I thought if he isn't careful, he'll have four or five girls following him home.

Tony looked at the show once in a while which was very sweet considering all the action he was getting on one side with three girls each trying to find and pet his penis. He didn't receive any petting or stroking from my side, but he talked to me a little, asking me questions about myself.

"So how old are ya honey? Where ya from? Ya got a big family,?" he asked. I answered softly, thinking he wasn't really interested in the answers.

"I'm leavin' for Brazil tonight. Got a plane waitin' at the airport for me right now," Tony said.

"Wow! I never heard of such a thing. How wonderful," I gushed. A real gush, a genuine gush of happiness for this stranger with a private plane and an exotic destination.

Lollie was on stage when Alicia moved away from the barstool she had appropriated. She had to dress to go on stage and her place was taken immediately by Glory Dawn. A few minutes later I followed Alicia to the dressing room as I was on after her.

As I was leaving, I heard Tony say to his bodyguard, "Poot, keep this one for Brandy. I'm gonna talk to Racehorse Dick for a minute."

The huge man who had accompanied Tony Boots into the club never did sit down, but stood directly behind Tony as if protecting his back from assault. Now, Poot protected the two empty bar stools from predators as he kept an eye on Tony and the money that was left on the bar.

Tony Boots and Racehorse Dick looked at my act from the end of the bar. That seemed strange. Racehorse was only interested in a girl's show if she was staggering or she wasn't wiggling some part of herself while on stage. Tony applauded between songs and that made Poot applaud. Then Racehorse Dick took the hint and clapped along with Tony after my last number, which inspired a couple of the girls to clap too. What was going on?

After my show I had to put on the same soggy black dress again. It was still wet from the vodka, but I hoped that wouldn't show in the dark. I walked out to the bar and sat on the only empty stool, which was next to Tony Boots.

"You're gorgeous up there, doll. I like your show now, but we'll get special choreographers when we get back and that'll make it even better. I'll rename my club in East St. Louis after ya' like I did with the other wives and you 'll be the biggest star ya' ever hearda. Wha' da'ya' think a that?" he said. "Go get your stuff. We're leavin'."

I looked at Racehorse Dick. He was standing behind the bar, beaming down on the new couple with pride.

G was at his place at the end of the bar. He looked upset while waiting for Torchy to end her act and Dusty Starr to begin hers. He kept his eyes down and seemed frozen at his station. G wanted to help me but I could see that he was afraid to take something away from this obviously high level mobster.

"No."

"We'll get married in Rio when we get there. Don't worry honey. It's all legit with me. You'll see," he said to reassure me.

"No, sir," I said.

"Poot," Tony Boots said in a commanding voice as he lifted his chin to motion toward the door and the street beyond.

Poot circled me with massive arms, shook me hard and lifted me high off the floor to throw me over his left shoulder. I landed there with a thump as he gently but firmly took hold of my hair to keep me still and turned to the door. Tony Boots headed down the aisle, leading the party toward the door when Millie stood up, stopping him with a whack, using her little purse to hit him on the chest.

"Stop it, Tony. Stop it! She's just a baby. Look at her," Millie cried.

I could tell she thought this was really serious.

We continued toward the door and out onto the street with Millie hitting Tony and shouting at him the few yards to the big black Cadillac waiting at the curb.

"No, I don't want to go. Why are you doing this? Let me down!" I yelled over and over with every bit of strength I had as Poot pulled my hair harder with his right hand to try and quiet me. He pressed my thighs to his shoulder with his left hand and forearm. I was terrified but I could feel that Poot was trying to be respectful while he was squeezing me just in case I did wind up as Tony's wife.

Millie stopped hitting Tony Boots. She looked at him seriously now as she blocked the open car door. She looked up at me hanging over Poot's shoulder and quietly asked, "Can't you see she doesn't want to go, Tony? She can't be over seventeen. She's just a baby."

Held firmly in place, my face and torso hung over Poots shoulder, I was level with Tony's eyes. Now that Millie had subtly brought up the law against transporting minors over state lines or taking them out of the country, he looked straight at me, with his brow furrowed in disbelief, and said, "You don' wanna to go to Brazil wit me? How come?"

"I want to go home to California. I don't know you and I miss my mother," I sobbed, taking my cue from Millie.

Tony shook his head and signaled Poot to put me down. He reached into a pocket inside the lining of his coat and without looking at it gave Millie an immense wad of bills.

"For your trip home. Be a good girl," he said to me as he got into the car.

Poot lowered me to the sidewalk and backed away from me, executed a precise right turn and entered the back seat of the car with Tony Boots who looked straight ahead. The driver closed the door and they sped out of Short Vincent Street.

As I entered the club Millie sat at her usual place, straightening her little hat, and patted the seat next to her. I slumped onto the stool and put my head on the bar. Pixie and Torchy walked down the bar to see how I was and Glory Dawn patted my back.

"Do you know who that is?" Millie asked me.

"No, how could I know who he is? I've never seen him before. He was just introduced as Tony Boots. How come you know him so well?' I asked as I lifted my head off the bar and looked at the little grandmother type lady in the moth-eaten mink stole I had become friendly with as she sat waiting each night for men to buy her drinks.

"I used to work for him at his club in East Saint Louis," Millie said. "I was there for five years through two wife changes. He has had six and you could have been lucky number seven." She smiled at me and opened her little black velvet purse to reveal four fat rolls of quarters, nothing else. The velvet purse was a heavy hitting tool that she held on her lap every evening. "He wasn't kidding. He likes to get married. Been in the Mafia all his life you could say. He's Lucky's nephew and a more serious mob guy you will never meet, even though this scene tonight didn't look like it. I don't know. I guess you just got to him."

She gave me the wad of money without looking at it. I split the two-inch thick pile of hundred dollar bills in half and gave her the top.

Goodbye, Cleveland. Hello, Toledo.

Chapter Eight

Toledo Theater Chase

Friday, at exactly one p.m. on November 24, 1961 I opened in Toledo, Ohio. It felt like a hard winter was on the way. I had worried and fretted all the way from Cleveland. Would an audience come out in the cold to see us at the Town Hall Theatre? What would the girls be like? Who was the headliner? I hoped she wouldn't be another redhead, like me. Would my costumes look as brilliant, as beautiful and sexy as the other dancers'? How much money was the star making? When would I make that much? How could I improve and be a terrific stripper by the time we arrived in Los Angeles? I pestered Dreamy with these questions and musings and more as she kept laughing, driving and turning the radio volume higher.

Lillian called to tell me about the contract for three-fifty a week for four shows a day and how to reach the rooming house where we would live. She also told me there would be two comedians on the bill and to stay far away from them.

"Burlesque comedians bite, you know. They will do anything to get a laugh on or off the stage. They will eat anything like bouquets of roses or live insects, they will pee on you if they think it's funny at the moment, try to put a hand up your skirt and down your blouse at the same time and even injure themselves by doing pratfalls over and over again. They are absolutely driven. You might have to do a skit with them as a talking woman, so be careful," she warned, knowing I had no experience with comedians of any sort.

Lillian prepared me for the owner of the theatre with a very earnest voice.

"Don't ever get caught alone in a room with Rose, and keep Dreamy right by you. Rose is like most of the men who own theatres. My God, the calls I've had from girls who have been mauled by her. But she pays good and always on time," Lillian said.

The Town Hall was owned by Rose La Rose, a retired "Burlesque Queen" called Cooze La Cooze by many in the business. Her lewd dancing had closed more clubs and theatres in the 1930s and '40s than anyone else in show business.

While the law stated that all dancers must wear net bras with pasties underneath and net pants, she made four or five inch long cuts in the crotch of her pants. For the highlight of her act, she sat on a straight-backed chair with her legs spread wide apart, leaned back and switched her weight from side to side. She acted as though she had no idea the pants had been cut.

"I don't know why you're taking me down to the police station, officer. One of the other dancers must have cut my pants. They're all jealous of me. You could see that for yourself," she had been heard to say.

When Rose stopped dancing in 1958, she bought a theatre in Toledo and it was rumored that she had married a high-ranking police official there. This enabled her to bring burlesque to the small city with few questions from the up-standing citizens. She looked about fifty and was still beautiful, with thick, shoulder length dark hair, pouty lips, large brown eyes and a sultry facial expression that was permanently affixed.

Rose was with the backstage doorman as Dreamy and I entered the stage door and she greeted me with a practiced smile and an assessing competitive stare. It felt like a knife point entering my chest. I introduced myself and Dreamy, but Rose's eyes never looked toward Dreamy or acknowledged her presence.

"Brandy Wilde, well, you are fresh and lovely, just as Lillian said. Your dressing room is back there. I'll come by later," Rose said slowly and half closed her eyes in what she probably thought was a romantic expression. She pointed toward backstage right.

The Town Hall Burlesque Theatre, at St. Clare and Orange, was huge and dark as Dreamy and I walked in to study the stage, find the dressing rooms, deliver my costumes and give the music charts to the six-piece group. There was an organ, drums, and four horns: tenor saxophone, clarinet, trombone and trumpet. It would be true luxury to have more than three live musicians play for me.

A runway cupped the orchestra pit and spread to the front of the box seats on each side of the stage. The main floor sat six hundred and fifty people and there was even a small balcony.

Tinker Bell, the "Star of Stars" as she was billed on the marquee outside, had her own large, well lit dressing room with makeup table and chair, a couch, and a steel wardrobe rack behind a four part wooden screen that had been painted baby blue. As we passed, the tiny blonde who was wearing a short red silk robe open to the waist, moved away from her makeup table and shut the door quickly.

As the "Added Attraction" I had a smaller private dressing room with the same kind of furnishings as Tinker's, just pushed closer together. The five stock girls, dancers who lived in Toledo and worked there often, were squeezed into one long dressing room with five small makeup tables and two costume racks. Someone had placed a big vase of yellow chrysanthemums on the table nearest the door which helped to brighten the dingy space.

We would be there about twelve hours a day. The first show started at one p.m. and the last one at eleven p.m., except on Saturday when we started at three p.m. and there was a midnight show. Ladies' fares were half- price on Wednesdays.

"Oh, are you still here?" said Rose as she entered my dressing room, looking directly at Dreamy now and frowning.

"Yes, and I intend to stay. I'm Dreamy Darnell, Brandy's manager. I've headlined at some of the same clubs you have Rose."

Dreamy smiled slightly and remained seated on the couch, staring back at Rose.

"Yes, I... recognize the name. Shake dancer, right? Well, let's get on with this. Here is your contract Brandy, and we need you to do one skit each show as a talking woman. See Roger, the straight man, about that. Lighting and music rehearsal start in five minutes. If you have any problems, talk to Jim at the stage door," Rose said as she left.

Dreamy smiled and shook her head as she drawled, "That's a tough old broad, honey. No wonder little Tinker jumped up to close her door. She had a reputation for chasing girls all over Chicago. I guess her mother isn't with her today."

"Her mother?" I asked as I tried to stifle a laugh.

"Yes," said Dreamy, drawing out the word so it had three parts. "Mom La Rose traveled for eighteen years on the burlesque circuit taking care of her little girl. When mom got sick Rose decided to settle down here in Toledo."

The skits between acts were performed center stage, with sparse sets of doctors' offices, court rooms and street corners to help set the mood. When I found the comedians, Roger Clark and Tuggems Pardee, in their dark dressing area backstage left, they were pushing raw potato wedges into a machine and catching the freshly squeezed potato juice that looked like dirty water, in paper cups.

"You must be Honey Harlow's little sister. Didn't know she had one. Welcome, welcome. How's Honey? Where's Lenny?" Tuggems spurted in a quick lyrical phrase.

"I'm Brandy and my six year old sister's name is Michele. Who is Honey?" I said, as I laughed at the whole setup before me.

Tuggems Pardee had curly red hair, just the same color as mine, pale skin and big blue eyes. He could have been my grandfather. His Irish lilt was funny and musical as it slid up and down the scale. Dressed in grey pants and jacket, he looked like a dust ball and fit nicely in the under-stair space that was their dressing area.

The Acme juicer was as big as a bucket with a hole on top to force the fruit and vegetables through and a spout below to catch the final product. Red net sacks of unpeeled potatoes and carrots were under and around the low table the machine was placed upon.

"This stuff keeps my pecker up," said Tuggems as his eyebrows danced up and down his forehead. "Have you never seen a juicer before?"

I couldn't help laughing. He was so funny, yet serious as a senator.

"I'm supposed to see you about a bit as a talking woman," I said turning to Roger. "What would you like me to do?"

Roger Clark looked crisp and refined in his finely tailored black suit and white shirt, his dark hair brushed back neatly. He spoke with what could pass for an upper class English accent that was perfect for a straight man. Much taller than Tuggems and me, Roger seemed to look down on us vocally as well as physically. He was to introduce each dancer before the curtains parted. I could hear that his voice would infuse the large auditorium with elegance.

An eight-by-ten glossy picture of a beautiful brunette with a pistol in her hand was pinned to the wall. It was signed "To Roger, my loving husband, Misty Marlowe." It was as obvious as a brand mark on his forehead that this picture was meant for the other girls to see and keep their hands off her property.

"When Diana, Goddess of the Moon, comes off stage, the theatre will go black and when the lights come up the audience will see a doctor's office center stage. I will be the doctor, Tuggems the patient, and you will be the nurse in this uniform and cap. When I yell, 'Nurse,' you walk up to me, from stage right, with an exaggerated wiggle. You face the audience and hysterically scream 'Doctor' three times while doing a forward bump each time and then wiggle off stage the same way you came on. Got it? Okay then, see you on stage. Here's the uniform. Don't button the top four," Roger said.

"Ah, little girlie, are you nervous?" Tuggems asked, scanning my face. "Don't be nervous now -- nothing to it. Put your hands behind your neck when you bump," and he modeled what he meant. "Doctor, Doctor, Doctor," he hollered as he did three huge bumps with his feet wide apart, toes facing front, knees bent, hands clasped lightly behind his neck, elbows sticking out around his ears and blue eyes bugged. "Just remember, as the nurse you are very serious. Then it's funny. And Honey is Honey Harlow. Hell of a dancer, and she used to be Lenny Bruce's wife."

"Hi, you look beautiful. Roger will like that," Diana said in a friendly way while we were waiting in the wings. "I'm Diana, Goddess of the Moon. Can you tell?" she asked uncertainly while biting at her thumbnail.

The show opened a few minutes after one with Diana Goddess of the Moon on first. She was about five foot six and had a pretty smile. Her long brown hair had a head-dress made of tin foil in the shape of a new moon stuck into it. Dressed in flowing wrinkled white chiffon and silver sandals with short heels, she looked like she was trying to float over the stage and around the runway.

Diana had been the first dancer to welcome me to the Town Hall and she was as sweet as she could be. A former teachers aide, she had worked there about six months and was a former runner-up in one of the amateur striptease talent shows Rose held twice a year. You could see local girls there trying to find out if they could take their clothes off to the music. Men living in the area loved watching the waitress down the street or a neighbor's daughter half-naked.

Those shows drew performers and audiences from as far as Bowling Green and Sandusky, Ohio. Some even crossed state lines and came from as far as Tecumseh, Michigan. Occasionally, one of the winners would go on to become a professional exotic dancer.

The audience loved Diana. Fifty or more men welcomed her with whistles and roars and then sat back to enjoy the show. Waiting in the wings to do my nurse bit, I watched her act and paid attention to the audience as they filtered in.

It was early Friday afternoon, so there were mostly men in their fifties and sixties who came in alone and sat up front. The first fifteen or twenty had scrambled for chairs in the box seats on either side of the stage. Each box fit four chairs and were the closest seats to the dancers. These were the regulars who were first in line, the connoisseurs, who came to see the first show of each new week. Admission was five dollars, but on Thursday only, you could see two shows for the price of one.

Diana tried to float while doing bumps and grinds and, although to my now trained eyes, she looked a little awkward, the sweet smile and her good-natured teasing pleased the growing crowd. She might wink at someone who had caught her eye or lick her thumb discretely. She was not trying to be a "sex goddess" who was above them all. Diana was a "goddess" who was one of them.

The audience gave me a big laugh as the nurse. I wiggled off stage as happy as if I had done something great.

I went back to my dressing room to prepare for my first show. I could hear someone running backstage and a woman's desperate voice wailing "Wait! Wait!" I looked out the door and saw Rose moving fast, fingers reaching out for Busty Block, trying to grab hold of her robe as Busty cut around a corner.

Misty Marlowe, the dancer just before me, did a detective act in a bright silver trench coat and "sky high" four inch heels. Her pistol was silver and so was the little costume under the crotch length coat. A large cherry-red fedora hat and matching gloves completed her outfit. The long gloves stayed on for the entire act. That pistol went almost everywhere. She opened with *Peter Gunn* which was a natural choice for her and ended the act by singing a few phrases of an upbeat version of *Blues in the Night*. She was one of the few strippers around who could belt out a song as she emphasized every bump with a pistol shot.

The audience had grown to about two hundred men and a few boys who were probably playing hooky from their last class of the day. I could still hear Busty and Rose running around backstage.

With the spotlight in my eyes I was terrified of that runway. It was narrow and high. I was afraid I would fall into the lap of some mark who was busy under his newspaper – though it turned out that the runway was the best part.

Working across the orchestra pit made the audience seem so far away and they could feel the distance too. This was a real theatre with a wide middle aisle and two side aisles. No drinks were served so the only people with access to alcohol were the dancers who drank secretly in our dressing rooms. Dreamy and I drank a little wine most evenings.

After dancing on Mickey's narrow platform for three months with the musicians at my side, this stage was wonderful. The proscenium arch was more than fifteen feet high, and about seventy feet across. Sets for the comedian's blackout scenes hung backstage, high in the flies. I had worked in theatres like this as a child actress at The Globe Theatre in San Diego, where my dad was stationed, but there were always other people on stage with me. This time it was mine alone and I loved it.

The audience howled when they could see you were about to go out to them on the runway. I tried to spend at least half of my twelve minute act somewhere along the curved strip of stage that brought me within an arm's reach of the already teased, tantalized, taunted and titillated crowd of aroused and semi-aroused men.

What is this Thing Called Love? was my first number and I tried to make every audience member think I was asking him this question by looking into his eyes sincerely while still smiling. In reality I was looking at the middle of his forehead. Most of the time those eyes held something feverish and furtive that I did not want to see. Women got the truly sincere look, when there were any in the audience but that made my hands shake a little because I cared about what they thought of me. Keeping alert for any quick grabbing movement from the orchestra seats, I twirled in the turquoise satin gown, with the new rhinestone pants and bra ready to be shown for the first time, and felt like a million bucks.

The musicians were very talented. Even though they must have played *Night Train* and all the stock striptease songs for years, they filled the Town Hall with music that was so hot and sexy it made my case of opening day nerves disappear and instead I felt juicy, playful and relaxed.

I had time to grab my wardrobe from the pole where Jim, the stage doorman, and number one "catcher" had hung it, and dash to my dressing room to pick up a short green silk robe and return to the wings with Dreamy, to see Tinkerbell, our star of stars on stage. She was going to portray her "Sins of Cleopatra" act which was billed as "Incomparable and Unforgettable." Tinker advertised herself as the "Most Talented and Exciting

Star in Burlesque today," so this would be something special to see.

Standing in the wings with Dreamy and me were all the other dancers on the bill for this week. We could see Tinkerbell being rolled up in a small peach and blue silk carpet and left on stage alone in the dark. Jim attached the edge of the rug farthest from the orchestra to an almost invisible slim rod that he carried off stage with him.

The music began. Deep red velvet curtains parted and the audience could see a little carpet on the stage. Tinker's head, covered with a black wig, showed on one side and her feet which were bare, cuddled each other on the opposite end. The back edge of the carpet slowly rose and little Tinkerbell rolled out onto the rounded apron of the stage.

She had on red and gold chiffon Turkish harem pants and a midriff top probably meant to look Egyptian. Average little bumps and grinds went on for ten minutes and her show was over. She did not go out onto the runway, she did not give her audience any attention, did not smile and her movements were small.

I felt cheated and by the lack of applause I think the audience felt that way too. Tinker was so tiny on stage and her movements were so modest I wondered if most of the audience had seen her at all.

That show taught me more than if it had been spectacular and lived up to its publicity. Some girls can make a simple grind look like a total sex act. I had seen girls dance like that for the last three months at Mickey's and had learned as much as I could from them. Tinkerbell showed me what not to do and how not to do it. Small movements, eyes down, solemn and far away looks will not make an appreciative audience. Tinker didn't look happy with their almost nonexistent applause.

The rest of the week I only saw Tinkerbell when she was on stage. She stayed in her dressing room and seemed to emerge only to do her shows. There were three different costumes with special music to match each one but it was basically the same act each time, with and without the rug.

My shows were the same also. I made it up as I went along as did most of the girls. Now I could see why Dreamy insisted we find a good choreographer when we arrived in Los Angeles.

This was Busty Block's last week at the Town Hall and she was anxious to get away. We found out Rose was chasing her all over the theatre trying to make her sign a personal management contract. By Monday everyone could hear Rose imploring Busty to sign.

"Busty, that sixty inch chest on you could be a real draw if you just lost a little weight and colored your hair and took a few dancing lessons from me. I could make you a star, Busty. Think about that. I could get you a thousand dollars a week on the road. Honey, think how you could help your mama with that kind of money," Rose pleaded.

That was low. We all knew by now that Busty came from a poor family and her mother was ill. Busty wanted nothing more than to get out of Toledo and go back home to Oak Harbor, a town of about three thousand people. She was a small town girl and very shy. How she ever got on stage to show off that sixty inch bust line was a mystery to everyone but Rose. But even Rose couldn't keep her there for long.

Billed as "Sexquisette," Gail Winds came into town and took over the star position on Friday. She was a classic blonde old-time stripper who gave the audience everything she had. Gail was almost forty and she was about to retire in Colorado. Her husband Troy, who traveled with her, was a tall body builder with huge muscles and dark curly hair. He said they only traveled a few months of the year as they owned a place called "The Oldest Bar in Denver."

Troy decided I needed a good workout program and between shows took Dreamy and me up to the hotel room he and Gail shared. Down I squatted, up I stood, over and over, lifting the bar bell on and off my shoulders with twenty pound weights on each end. Then he had me lifting the ten pound hand weights for about fifteen minutes. Troy said that would be a "good start."

When I couldn't walk the next day I decided they were trying to kill me. I had to do my shows because all contracts are "play or pay". If I didn't go on stage and perform, I would have to pay Rose to find another dancer to cover for me. Each step was agony and stepping off the curb when walking to the car took several seconds that included groans and squeals. I was mad at myself and everyone in Ohio. By then I could see it had been a clear case of professional sabotage.

Hopefully, only Dreamy could see I was in pain. Somehow, once I was on stage, with the sensual music, the warm pink lights and the expectation of the audience, pride and a new sense of professionalism took over and I could move without wincing. When I closed the door of the dressing room after each act I fell onto the couch moaning again.

By Tuesday, I could walk more comfortably, and before we went to the theatre Dreamy and I went to buy coats for the next engagement. A one week contract at the Crystal Palace in Duluth, Minnesota had arrived and the newspaper reported the weather there had been five degrees below zero for the last few days. The ground was covered with snow.

Dreamy said, "Your father's Norwegian genes will help you there. I am the one who should be nervous. I'm one-hundred-percent from Louisiana where we shiver when it hits a low of eighty degrees."

Walking downtown we tried to figure out why Lillian had sent us there at this time of year. It was not that much closer to Los Angeles because we had to go so far north.

As we entered Lord and Taylor's Dreamy said "Lillian must be pretty mad that we want to go back to California. You're a good property. I'm sure she thought you would be around for more than five months."

Looking in the mirror while modeling the heavy black cashmere trench coat I hoped would keep me warm in Minnesota, I could see the pale, young salesman squinting at me.

Knowing that he had been caught leering at me, he said, "You're the new stripper in town."

"I am. How did you know?" I asked.

It was 1961 and I was dressed in long, black, flesh molding pants, silver spike high heels, no bra, a tight peacock blue sweater that left no question unanswered and had a waist length, wavy red ponytail set high on my head. I had never been recognized as a dancer in public and I couldn't figure out how he knew who I was without my stage makeup. He smiled as he rang up our coats and looked happy to have made himself a man of mystery.

Toledo was a friendly little town. My fondest memories are the people who were so nice to us and the great butter burgers at the little White Tower restaurants. Looking forward to arriving in Los Angeles soon, we left Ohio and drove north.

Chapter Nine

The Freezing North

The yellow '53 Ford convertible was warm enough with the heater on inside, but after six hours of driving the motor froze in the twenty degree below zero weather. We pulled off the road as the car gave out; we huddled there, under the trees in the early dusk, trying to stay warm. No motor meant no heater. It was snowing lightly. Although the road had been cleared, we thought about how the low temperature and swirling wind chill might kill us if we left the car and started walking.

"Brandy, we can't stay here. The convertible top is letting in all the cold and wind. We have to do something," Dreamy said.

"It's only four o'clock so there should be people using this road. This is the major highway into town. Where is everybody?" I said as I jumped out of the car and started jogging up and down the road a few feet from the car to warm up. The new cashmere coat helped keep some of my body heat near, but in seconds my black leather high heels were covered in wet and freezing snow. I wished I had worn slacks; the short skirt offered no defense against the weather.

I tried to protect my face and nose from the chill with the large soft collar of the coat but could not warm the searing cold air enough to breathe easily. My lungs burned with each intake of breath. I jogged, trying to keep my eyes closed to slits so the moisture around my eyeballs would not freeze solid.

I had never imagined such weather and we were in no way prepared for it. Not dressed right and not ready for the possible dangers, my mind wandered off to a familiar series of conversations I'd had with my mother recently.

"California is becoming more populated every day. The damned Rose Parade shows everyone in Minnesota and Wisconsin what a heavenly life they could live if only they moved to Southern California," she had complained.

Well, of course they wanted to go to California. I wanted to be home too. It was probably seventy degrees in Hollywood today.

I remembered my mom's threat to find an assassin in San Francisco's Chinatown to kill Dreamy and wondered if it was really safe for us to go home yet.

"We'll flag someone down, don't worry. We just have to be ready when we see them," I called to Dreamy.

I wanted to be ready to wave and shout when the first car came by. Needing to do something to keep my mind off the cold and misery I started to sing anything that came into my head.

Mama's little baby, Mama's little baby
she's my baby
Oh, God protect us, Oh, God please protect us.

I ran faster and faster. I sang faster. Tired and about ready to give Dreamy a chance to run back and forth, I saw lights, then a large dark blue sedan coming our way. It was heading toward Duluth. A man and woman who looked like they were in their eighties slowed their car to look at us.

The lady had thin white curls that lightly covered her pink scalp, and was wrapped in a red and brown striped blanket. She lowered the passenger window an inch and said, "There's a police station down a ways. Oh, yaaa. We'll stop and tell them you're up here. Yaaa. They'll be by soon. Stay in the car now."

The window went up and they rolled on. Our life line was leaving us there. Although we needed them to go, I worried no one would return. I wished they had taken us with them. We stayed in the car and had to trust that strangers in an unknown landscape would help.

True to her word, the lady had told the police about us and they in turn sent a tow truck that arrived about thirty minutes later. This was every-day work for the Auto Club heroes who seemed like knights in shining armor to us. They did not seem surprised or bothered. Our car was taken to an auto shop not far from the hotel Lillian had arranged for us.

With help from passing motorists, policemen, tow truck drivers, mechanics, hotel desk clerks, and a cab driver, I was thankful as I arrived at the Crystal Palace at eight o'clock ready to start the week. I was in time to meet the band and Marie, the lady band leader. She was a hefty natural blonde who looked like she had probably been a pretty little girl but life had gone wrong for her along the way. Her expression was one of disgust, disdain and bitterness.

The club was like a drafty old barn with a high beamed ceiling and a little stage in the back. Mirrors etched with snowflakes and several mismatched crystal chandeliers completed the décor and helped make the room look frosty.

The stage was filled with the piano, drum set and horn stand with a chair so there was not much room to dance. I wondered how my *Cherry Pink and Apple Blossom White* mambo number would fit on this stage. The new dress had a full white tulle skirt with neon pink accents that would take up most of the dancing space. How did I ever get talked into a dress like that, I asked myself again.

The bartender was at least six-foot-four and looked like a woodsman in his red and black checked shirt, under a fleece lined brown leather jacket. He introduced himself as Bill, and hung my costumes in the almost empty supply closet which was also the dressing room. At first I could not understand what he was saying. I couldn't find his mouth. The full brown beard covered his face from the top of his cheeks to the bottom of his neck where it met the curly chest hairs. Having walked and prayed on the Duluth highway earlier that day I understood his need for the massive beard.

I was to dress with the paper napkins and mops, and the liquor bottles that were locked away in a special cabinet. Bill set my bag on the only chair and gave me a sad consoling wink.

"You can sit in here or with the customers if you want to. Sure. Yaaa. You may not even have to stay here the whole week. Yaaa. Lou is going broke and can't even turn on the heat for the customers," sighed Bill. "Hell, the whole town's going broke. Even the movie house is only open one day a week. Yaaa." He sighed once more leaving me to think about how angry Lillian was at our returning to Los Angeles.

I was relieved that Lillian had put it in my contract that I was to be paid every night before I left the club. It came to fifty-four dollars each evening and at the end of the week Lou would send Lillian thirty-five dollars. It was not bad money for a regular gig but this was above and beyond the call of duty. Why had Lillian sent us here if not to punish us? I could tell we would leave most of my salary in town after buying clothes to keep us warm for the next few days.

Marie, the bandleader, came into the dressing room and took my music sheets but would not look at me. She looked at everything in the closet/dressing room, except me. Marie must have seen my puzzled expression when I caught her sneaking a tiny peek at me. Maybe she could tell I was trying to figure out what else was wrong here.

"I may have to work here now, and play for you bunch of whores that come and go, but I don't have to look at you," she said as she departed, her backside looking as broad as a bench.

Bill hung his head and looked sorrowful.

"The minister at her church won't let her play for Sunday services anymore because she works here. Her husband is unemployed, and she has a couple of kids. This is the only job she could get after the dentist she used to work for packed up and left town."

Bill understood and forgave her, but could I? There wasn't much I could do to change her mind about me and other dancers who would come after me. I had to smile and not let her know I thought she was a hypocrite. She works in a place she thinks is sinful and she condemns the dancers who work there before she has even met them. I felt she was un-Christian as well as hypocritical. She might have faith but where did hope and charity go?

I knew if she had any idea what I thought of her she would go wild. She would ruin my performances for the whole week. She could make me look awkward and stupid by changing the tempo, volume or arrangement of my music. She could spread rumors about me and have club customers pounding on my hotel door for sex at all hours of the night with just a few words. Joyce, the bartender at Mickey's in Cleveland, had done that to a couple of dancers who hadn't made the marks tip her. The girls showed up the next day looking haggard from lack of sleep.

There were four people in the audience when I went on stage. They were drinking beer, bundled up in heavy jackets and thick lace up boots.

When I made my first turn on the stage I saw that each member of the three-piece band was wearing an overcoat and a hat. Marie had gloves with the fingertips cut off so she could feel the piano keys and the horn player's gloves were the same. Their eyes were down and hooded by their hat brims. I could see there would be no heat in the music or warmth of friendship from the musicians this week.   Marie might consider that a sin and she was their leader.

At that moment, I realized I was going to strip down to jeweled panties, pasties and silver high heels in the chill of unfriendliness and below zero temperature inside the club and I had to look happy about it. I had to look thrilled to be there in front of this sad little group of men so lonely they would face the harsh weather to be with others of their sort. I could do that now.

My biological father's gift of Norwegian genes must have kicked in because from what I could see in the mirrors around the stage, I didn't look like I was freezing. My arms were able to rise away from my body and make come-hither gestures instead of hugging myself for warmth. My teeth did not chatter and although the breath did come out of my mouth in puffy clouds, I could smile and ignore it. However, that night I did start counting the number of shows left before we could leave Duluth. I had one show down and seventeen to go.

Two days later, covered in long bulky green quilted down coats over the cashmere coats and dressed in long underwear, Levis, heavy socks and sweaters, boots, neck scarves, sunglasses to protect our eyes, fluffy ear muffs and snow caps, elastic cords pulled in tightly against the twenty-seven degrees below zero wind and snow, Dreamy and I stood on the corner looking for the restaurant the hotel desk clerk had recommended. Just eyes, noses, and mouths were exposed to the weather. Our bodies looked huge and formless. My face was without makeup and chapped. Half an inch of the widow's peak in my hairline showed bright red.

A man who was engulfed in the same type of clothing we were wearing walked up to us and said, "You're the new stripper in town."

"I am. How did you know?" I asked.

"I was at the Crystal last night," he said. "My last name is Wilde too, so I come out to see ya. The wife is expecting next month. When we saw your picture in front of the club, we decided if we have a girl we would name her Brandy, if your dance wasn't dirty."

"How did I do? Did I pass muster?" I chuckled as I asked him, as if it was a regular thing for us to hang out on the corner in twenty seven below zero weather and chat.

"Oh, yaa. Nice and decent. Cute, too. The wife and I like it that you travel with your mother," he said as the wind pushed him and he turned to walk away.

I looked at Dreamy and she just nodded and shrugged a shoulder as if it didn't matter. This was not the first time someone had said they thought she was my mother. Dreamy was only six years older than me, but the Chicago and Calumet City years had been hard and it showed on her face. She had learned caution and distrust from working in Mafia run clubs where you keep your mouth closed and your eyes open for trouble with the customers. Dreamy's eyes were the color of fresh spring leaves, with long dark curly lashes. They held a world of experience and knowledge that can only come with age or pain.

For days we could not find a decent meal in our hotel or any nearby restaurant. We tried the dining room in the best hotel in town and neither of us could swallow the grey food we were served. They had no green salads or fresh vegetables on the menu. I was losing weight and what breasts I did have were disappearing again. Dreamy went on a search and discovered a small "Fancy Food" grocery store a few blocks from the club where we bought feta and goat cheese, garlicky green olives, rosy apples and several kinds of nuts and crackers.

We ate our remaining meals in Duluth inside our tiny room, which barely held a chair and a desk with a small black and white television set and the bed. Two windows faced the street and were covered by heavy gray drapes. The small green glass bottles of 7 UP which we placed next to the window to stay cold had an inch of iced soda on top when we opened them.

Every other small store along Main St. was closed, with signs in the windows that advertised space for lease. Shops with mud-stained carpeting or linoleum, walls in need of paint and half-filled shelves were the norm. The shopkeepers looked like we were intruding on their misery. Even the hearts of the people had closed down.

This was our lowest point in the five months I had been a stripper. Only the hotel desk clerks and the restaurant servers would talk to us during the daytime. We couldn't walk around and see the town because of the cold and wind. A customer told me we were near the shore of Lake Superior but I never saw it.

Dreamy must have guessed that I was blue because she tried to console me. "I think when we find a place in Los Angeles we should stay there a while, honey. This is not the way stripping usually is. Remember what fun you had with Lillian and her girls and in Cleveland with G and the Mafia guys and all the other girls around? We'll be able to find an agent in Los Angeles. You have experience now and you're good. You're a polished dancer. You know the ropes, your costumes are beautiful and you look gorgeous on stage."

My Dreamy. She knew what I wanted to hear and she was right. I loved dancing now that I knew how to do it. Working with other girls was fun and I had learned so much from them. How could you not love them? The few that were not friendly I didn't worry about. They considered me competition for tips and tricks and I knew I wasn't.

If I had been alone and the tricks had been women, I admit I probably would have been interested, but that's not the way the world works. Everyone knew many of the dancers turned tricks on the side and that was an accepted part of the business. If you did, it was all right and if you didn't that was okay too, as long as it didn't affect the club or your show.

No one called me "beauty queen" now, with a snide inflection and turned up nose as if I should put a bag over my head. I found dancers to be more honest and generous, more interesting and more sincere in their friendships, and less likely to gossip and bad mouth you than office clerks.

This job was a good fit for me. It made me feel beautiful and sexy. I loved the applause and the money was great. It wouldn't last forever but I didn't intend to be a dancer all my life.

On Friday morning we filled the Ford's gas tank for four bucks and put more antifreeze in the radiator. We could hardly wait to leave Duluth. No one would replace me at the Crystal Palace that night. It was too close to Christmas for people to come out in the wintery evening to an empty club. The owner decided to close for the rest of the harsh winter season. Duluth was a broken town and its people were sad and down-hearted. It was uncomfortable and unwelcoming.

California, of the golden sun and blue ocean, of tall palm trees waving in the warm winter breezes during the Rose Parade, we are on our way home to you.

Chapter Ten

Hollywood Starlets, 1962

The Zamba Club on Ventura Boulevard needed a stripper right away, so on the 24th of December I was there bumping and grinding for the absent April Hart. The well-known agent, Coralee Jr., had told me she would represent me if I could start at the Zamba right away. As all dancers knew, you needed an agent if you wanted to work in Los Angeles. The competition was ferocious.

The streets of Hollywood looked as if all the pretty girls in the world had come here to become movie stars. Most ended up taking other jobs and waited for their big break to come along. Until then they went out to be seen by any passing director or producer, dressed in their high heels, sexiest short skirts and tight sweaters. Gorgeous girls walked their poodles, pugs and Rhodesian ridgebacks along Sunset and Hollywood Boulevard. Groups of beautiful blondes and brunettes sat at tiny tables in the outdoor cafes, like the Old World, along the Sunset Strip, at the corner of Holloway, sipping coffee, attracting attention with their stunning good looks and artful poses.

The trip back to Los Angeles had been tough. Dreamy drove for six days and the little Ford only broke down once, but that could have been deadly. From Duluth we went to Chicago, and then all the way to California by Route 66, through St. Louis, Oklahoma City, to Amarillo, and Albuquerque, past Flagstaff, Arizona and finally over the California border.

On a long empty stretch of desert the radiator sprung a leak and we drove until the engine temperature gauge passed red and could go no higher. We could not go on without water. There we were on the side of the road once again waiting for help. Even in December, the area around the Arizona – California border, before you get to Needles, was blistering hot with no shade.

Flat and sandy brown desert stretched for miles in all directions. Cars passed us going both ways, and though most slowed down to look at two women waving for help, no one stopped. We were afraid and at the mercy of a pitiless sun.

When the little family of three, going east in the red Ford truck, circled around and came back to us, we knew they had figured out a way to help. They were towing a big dusty sedan. The gentleman got out of the truck, while his wife and little girl sheltered inside. He walked slowly, giving us plenty of time to see he was not carrying a gun or some other kind of weapon.

"The wife says you girls might need water and she's usually right about these things. Do you need water?" he asked, his brow furrowed with concern.

"We sure do. We drove until I thought the engine might catch on fire but there's no-where to buy water," Dreamy said in a deep sigh.

"You see that blue Cadillac we're towing? It's got a radiator full a water and I got some duct tape in the truck to patch a leak or maybe a blown up hose. Just be a minute."

The words thank you and grateful didn't come near expressing what Dreamy and I felt for this wonderful family. Brad and Sara and their little girl, Cathy, were leaving California and driving back home to Mississippi.

"It's too brown out here. I can't wait to get back to Natchez where it's green all the time. You breathe in that air and it's like honey," Sara sighed. She smiled and her dark brown eyes danced just thinking about it.

In a few minutes, Brad had drained the Cadillac and put water into our Ford and the duct tape looked like it might hold until we got somewhere we could buy a new hose. They had done everything for us but there was nothing we could do for them. Sara wouldn't take any money and we didn't have anything else to offer. We just had to be grateful, wave goodbye to these kind strangers and go on our way. We knew that without them, we could have died out there in the desert.

We stayed with Berylynn, Dreamy's mother, for two days until we found a one bedroom apartment on Normandy, near Franklin, in Hollywood. The rent was seventy-five dollars a month, with utilities included, about average for that area. It was a shotgun type apartment and you had to walk through the bedroom to get to the kitchen. That became a problem. But I definitely wanted to live in Hollywood. We weren't worried about money. I had made enough while we were on the road to last several months in Los Angeles.

Coralie Jr. was my agent now. Tall and busty with flowing blonde hair, she had started acting in the Our Gang movies when she was an adorable three-year-old with white-blonde curls, a rosebud mouth and expressive face. Coralie had been in show business ever since, which was about forty years. I thought I could trust a woman with that much experience. She discovered young that she didn't want to act and became an agent for a variety of performers including tumblers, singers, exotic dancers, comics, musicians and actors.

With her strictly business attitude I couldn't see a funny little girl in her anywhere. I was to discover that she kept a close watch on how I was doing. I didn't think of her as being nosey, I figured she was taking care of business. I was her business.

"Charlie says you're knocking 'em dead at the Zamba, Brandy. Whatever you're doing keep it up. I haven't been there in a while, how are the musicians?"

A few weeks into January the owner of the Zamba Club came into the tight little dressing room around midnight. I had just finished my second show and he seemed pretty excited.

"Brandy, change fast and come meet a couple of friends of mine. They're waiting for you in the kitchen. Hurry!"

That was the only place we could sit with guests and even then Charlie worried. This time he was thrilled.

I walked in and there was Michael Rennie, so regal, so slender, so cool and sophisticated. He was the star of my favorite science fiction movie when he played the alien Klaatu in *The Day the Earth Stood Still.* He was waiting for me. Sitting at the green and white oilcloth covered kitchen table, with a plump friend or maybe agent, he looked comfortable even in this environment. He should have been in a palace or a penthouse at the very least.

"Would you like to go to Michael's house tonight and dangle your feet in his swimming pool?" his friend asked after the introductions were made and drinks were ordered.

Michael just sat there looking cool and gorgeous but interested in the answer.

"If you were a Kim Novak or a Debbie Reynolds I would probably say yes, but a Michael, no. I love you, but only in the movies," I said with a smile.

I wanted to be friendly but not that friendly. Michael understood what I meant and didn't look too rejected but the other guy would not take no for an answer.

"What? You're not a lesbian, are you? Charlie, you got lesbos in your club? A guy can't come in and find a blowjob here anymore? Everybody a lesbo here, Charlie?"

Charlie wasn't happy about my answer either. All the excitement in his expression was gone and he looked very depressed. I knew my time at the Zamba was at an end. The good thing about it was most of the other clubs were closer to Hollywood and there were lots of them.

Hollywood and Vine is a very busy and famous intersection. The club was on prestigious real estate and the black marble front almost looked chic. Inside, it was just another small rat hole, long and narrow with a tiny stage at the far end that almost had enough room for the dancer and the huge drum set George needed.

"How do you like working on Hollywood Boulevard, Brandy?" Coralie asked when I was in her office one day just to say hello and hang around with the other acts in the waiting room.

"It's not so bad. It's wonderful in a way," I said. "Working with George Jenkins is teaching me so much and he is such a nice man. I can understand why Candy Bar didn't want to work with any other drummer. When she was put in prison for those two joints, which George said were really Pixie Lynn's, it was bad for him too. He told me her drum solo was five minutes long and she would run up walls and do back flips. I would love to have seen that. Also, there is this mark who comes in every week, gives me a hundred dollar bill and asks if he can please watch me put it in my back pocket. Cute, isn't he?"

It was so funny dancing in California. The police and the club owners said there was no mixing allowed, but if you didn't sit down in the showroom and just stood around, the dancers could meet anyone they wanted to in almost all of the clubs.

There was a petite brunette dancer named Lulu Blue working at the club who had one of the first boob jobs in California.

"Show Brandy what you can do with your tits Lulu. This is so funny," said Pookie Wold, another dancer with a flat chest.

Lulu could mold her breasts into any shape she wanted. She could make them look like marshmallows or ice cream cones or squares and they would stay like that until she squashed them into a different shape.

I never did find out what she had in there but it couldn't have been healthy. We were too young to be thinking about health though. We wanted our bodies to look as luscious and desirable as possible.

With no comic to act as Master of Ceremonies our drummer George was also the M.C. He was the first one to introduce me as "The Million Dollar Smile" which I thought was great. I felt like I never danced better than when I was with him, but of course, it was all George. He even made the audience think it was me. Any bounce of fringe, toss of hair or hand gesture was included into my act by the percussion, exaggerated and ready for me to do it again as George finessed my act to make me look sexier and more professional on stage.

I think he must have been bored and it was his kind of fun to find some way to change us for the better. Our acts were not at all challenging for him but his heroin habit had reduced him to playing at this unglamorous, seedy little bar in what had become a run- down part of Hollywood.

In 1962 people that lived in other parts of the country, and had never been to Los Angeles, sometimes were not quite sure what Hollywood was. When I was on the road, bar customers asked questions like: "Is Hollywood a great big building where all the movies are made?" and, "If I go to Hollywood will I see movie stars walking down the street?" I was always sorry to spoil their fantasies.

Hollywood Boulevard was full of little shops selling souvenir mugs, postcards and key rings. There were a few nice clothing stores on the boulevard including the small department store Lucy's which was owned by an older Swiss couple I had become friends with, and Mandel's Shoes where all the girls bought their silver and gold four-inch "skyscrapers" for the stage.

Fredericks of Hollywood, which opened in 1946, was famous all over the country for its catalog of fancy and risqué underwear, but there was only one store where you could actually touch, smell and rub up against the bras and panties. Mannequins dressed in black and red lace bras with holes to expose the nipples and backless edible panties were there for all to see in the wide windows. Feathers and sequins of all colors adorned the nightgowns with necklines down to the pubic hair were on display when no other store would carry such merchandise –much less advertise it.

A month after leaving the Zamba, I was working at Sixth and Main in downtown Los Angeles at the Follies Burlesque theatre which felt familiar. I had worked on that street my first year after high school. Dreamy and I had met while I was working for Dunn and Bradstreet and now I was back, just half a block away. I was earning more in one week than I did in a whole month, just one year ago and loving it most of the time.

Dreamy and I went to see the last show with Sunny Dare as the star, before I started at the theatre. I only saw her perform once but knew I would remember her always. She was exactly the kind of dancer I wanted to be. Smooth, sleek, sensual, classy and sophisticated, hard-to-get but worth the trouble, all described Sunny. That's exactly what I wanted audiences to feel about me.

Satana was our star the first week I was there. Dark and fiery, half Native American and half Chinese, she looked exotic and dangerous. Extremely strong and very athletic on stage, she incorporated into her dance martial arts moves and fighting techniques that most of the audience had never seen. She used the black straight pony tail that hung below her waist as a weapon to beat the person she was supposedly fighting and having sex with while on stage. None of the girls bothered to speak to her as she never answered a greeting or a question. She entered the theatre, performed, and exited without addressing anyone.

My contract was for two weeks so I figured I could stand just about anything for that long. An incident backstage made me change my mind and the two weeks seem like two months.

One night, Tina, a quiet girl who kept to herself, was looking around for Kleenex. No one had any. Then Bip, a dwarf salesman who stood crotch-high, made nightly rounds spreading gossip and selling creams, paper goods, stationery, aspirins, nylons and an occasional piece of jewelry, came backstage.

"Gimme that Kleenex, Bip" Tina said.

"That'll be a quarter."

"Lemme give it to you tomorrow. You know I'm good for it," Tina cajoled in her flat voice.

"You know the rules. No credit," he said in his singsong way.

Tina reached over, took the hand of some strange guy standing around back stage and led him out of sight. In thirty seconds they were back. The unknown guy was breathless, hustling to zip up his pants. Tina flipped a quarter to Bip, picked up the box of Kleenex with a poison stare directed toward him and went toward the dressing rooms. She left the three of us rooted to the spot.

I told Dreamy about it that night and she said, "That had to be one of the fastest professional blow jobs in history."

The Tina incident worried me. How did a person allow herself to get there? She was not bad-looking and a fairly good dancer, but something had hurt her so much she thought nothing of herself. I felt an emptiness from her, a blank where no feeling resided behind the façade. I took that as a warning that I had to take care of myself. What happened to Tina could happen to lots of girls.

A few months later on Hollywood Boulevard, at an unfashionable east Hollywood address, in a second floor two-room suite, my agent Coralie Jr. presided in all her glory. She had a large reception room filled with an assortment of chairs, a comfy brown sofa, and one wall displayed 8 x 10 black and white glossy photos of all the handsome men and luscious women she represented.

Her office was about the same size and full to bursting with a desk, which was covered with publicity pictures and three telephones, the large chair she inhabited and several file cabinets holding client pictures and resumes snuggled around the walls. She sent pictures out to casting directors and anyone else she could get to take a look at her talent. She had no secretary or assistant; Coralie Jr. Agency was strictly a one-woman operation.

When Dreamy and I went in to Coralie's office on August 6th of 1962, we joined nine red-eyed platinum blonde girls already clustered in the waiting room; all were crying, sniffing and holding each other while wiping runny black mascara off their cheeks. It looked like we were all there for the same reason. Marilyn Monroe had just died and we rushed to Coralie for comfort. Our role model and hero had killed herself. Everything would be different now. Who would we look up to?

Beautiful girls blew their noses while crying in profound pain. "Why, why would she do it?" "I loved her so much." "No, no, no." "It can't be true."

There was only one Marilyn, although many of the girls tried to look like her or copy her mannerisms in their acts. Would they have to change their shows for a while, or forever? It wouldn't be right to do an imitation of her anymore. Would it?

When I finally got into her office, always thinking of business first, Coralie asked, "How was your first week at the York Club? Quite a change from Hollywood Boulevard, isn't it? Dreamy is still driving you back and forth to work, right? Joe Fine likes you and although it's only one seventy-five a week, you can probably stay there as long as you want to. Just be careful. Any new girls there?"

I saw that she was busy and ready for us to leave so I gushed out as much information as I could in a short time. "Western and Slauson isn't Hollywood but I like the club," I said, still sniffing. "Linda Doll is beautiful. She looks just like Ava Gardner and Holly Parks has a big personality, plus a cute figure. She's just like a little cricket. She's all over the place. There's a real cute new girl named Dana you might want to sign up, long dark hair and sweet too. She doesn't have an agent yet. The stage is bigger than I'm used to in clubs, but the band is still right there in the middle of it with you."

Eventually we saw the girls had been right about the changes. A famous dancer back east, Dixie Evans, whose entire act had been an impersonation of Marilyn, stopped dancing completely. She couldn't get a job anywhere. Other girls changed hair styles and some had new stage gowns made that didn't look so much like the wardrobe Marilyn had worn in *Gentlemen Prefer Blondes*.

Marilyn Monroe was so feminine, gorgeous, and full of tease that many of us couldn't stop trying to act like her or look like her. We had grown up with Marilyn as our model of femininity and grace. She was part of us.

The York Club was a four thousand square - foot dark box, black walls, with a round bar in the middle. The night before, during my act, the sax player motioned me to look at a part of the audience I hadn't paid much attention to for a minute. Leaning back on the bar shaking his chest was a beefy guy who looked like a truck driver. He had on a stuffed white cotton bra under his unbuttoned shirt and was trying to get me to admire it. He was swaying back and forth, kind of dancing, and smiling.

"He comes in all the time, and buys for the whole bar. If you don't pay attention to his little titties he gets really pissed," the sax player told me later.

I would tell Dreamy all about my night as she drove us home. Most of the time she was interested but it was two in the morning and she had to be tired.

There was a short stocky guy named Frank who came in every night. He started bringing me presents. One night it would be a fifth of Chivas Regal scotch, the next a gold chain necklace. Frank swore he had a deadly blood vessel disease. Said they could pop any minute and he would die instantly. I'm a good listener and he liked to tell me about his health.

One evening I arrived at the York Club just as Joe was calling the five dancers and the band together for a meeting before the show started. He looked shaken; his color was ashen.

"I just received a phone call from Dana's husband. He said she was dead when he tried to wake her up this morning. She must have died in her sleep but they don't know what she died of yet."

It was shocking. She was such a sweet girl. Not bitter or jaded yet. A cloud of gloom descended on the club and did not leave for days. Linda, Holly and I cried and tried to comfort Joe and each other. We found out the next day she had died from a combination of alcohol and sleeping pills.

Some people thought Dana had committed suicide but I think it was an accident. She was always cheerful and seemed to be having fun. She didn't look depressed. She was a little high when she left work but most of us usually were.

"She used to take pills to help her sleep, so maybe together with the vodka it was too much. It had to be an accident. Who knew you couldn't drink and take pills together?" Dynamite said. We all agreed.

Dynamite was a tiny redhead from Mexico; about four foot three in her platform high heels. She had huge breasts and did a tassel number, strutting all over the stage and sometimes crawling into the musicians laps. She came in full time to take Dana's place instead of dancing weekends as before. She joked around with the audience in Spanish and English all through her show and they loved her. Little by little the club returned to normal.

Frank gave me a car when the yellow Ford convertible gave out for good. It was a shiny little red Triumph and although it only fit two people it was just great. It was the best present he ever gave me because I really needed it. The girls couldn't believe he gave it to me with no strings attached but he was just that way. When I gave the car back to him the next year because he needed the transportation he cried and never spoke to me again.

1963

"I want you to get me into the Largo, Coralie. It's time now," I told Coralie as I delivered my carefully rehearsed speech in her office. "I've been in Los Angeles for a year and a half and I hear things. It's the best club in town with the best stage, a real follow spotlight and the dressing rooms are great. The money is better, the location on the Sunset Strip is better for me. It's classier, closer to where I live and on the West Side, away from the rough part of town. The band is pretty good and I want to work there. It's time," I stressed by nodding my head emphatically.

"You're right Brandy. This is a good time for you to change clubs and I think he is ready to let someone go. I'll talk to Chuck Landis about you," Coralie responded. She sounded very positive that she could get me in there but had a warning for me too.

"Understand he isn't the easiest person to work for. He's not like Joe Fine, always there and willing to talk to you. Chuck sneaks into his office and won't open his door for anyone if he hasn't called them in. If he sees you on the stairs as you're going down to the stage, he probably won't say hello, even if you do.

"Everything has to go through the club manager, Bernie, who has been there for years. Get on his good side because if you try to go around him with a problem or something, you won't get anywhere with Chuck," Coralie said. "Okay? Good." I could see she was revving herself up, getting ready to make the call.

"By the way, there is no mixing at all at the Largo. All the girls have to stay in the dressing room upstairs and cannot come down for any reason until all the customers have gone. He's had some bad publicity about gangsters, Mickey Cohen and his friends, hanging around to see Candy Barr and now he is very strict about no contact with the audience. That's good for you, right?"

Dreamy and I moved again. We moved this time because Dreamy had a feeling the apartment was going to fall apart during an earthquake. We moved to a nicer apartment at Fountain and Kenmore. The six unit apartment building was owned by a woman who had played the piano at cocktail lounges all over the country for forty years and she was very tolerant of our late hours and lifestyle. We still didn't have much furniture so I decorated the living room with huge red, orange and hot pink pillows to lounge on and colorful posters on the walls. We also had a fiftyish style black and white bar with two black wrought iron stools which had been a present from Frank.

We had lots of liquor. Large bottles of unopened Aquavit, tequila, expensive scotch, vodka and bourbon, fancy bottles of brandy, Grand Marnier and various liqueurs graced our little bar. All were presents from Frank who was working at a liquor store by then.

The apartment directly under us was occupied by a young woman with huge hazel eyes and long dark hair, who had also been a dancer for a short time. When she mentioned her mother had been a dancer in Chicago and what her name was, Dreamy's eyes opened wider and she smiled.

"I worked with your mom on a few club dates," she said. "Hell of a dancer. I never saw such muscle control."

Later Dreamy told me she had known the older dancer pretty well in Chicago and had probably met our neighbor when she was a teenager.

"I never saw anything like it in my life. That woman could smoke with her pussy and blow smoke rings with it -- drove the men at those club dates crazy. Can you imagine what a great lay she must have been with all that muscle control? I didn't want to say anything earlier – didn't want to embarrass our new neighbor in case she didn't know that about her mother."

The Tina Kleenex incident at the theater downtown scared me and I found myself thinking about where and when I was going back to school when I was finished dancing. I didn't know how long I could dance or would want to dance. With a college degree there would be lots of things I could do, but I didn't know what kind of new career I would be interested in. I had to figure out what I wanted to do with the rest of my life. Los Angeles City College was on Vermont, near Melrose and close to my new apartment on Kenmore. I might as well take some lower division classes there. It only cost five dollars a semester.

Chapter Eleven

The Largo, 1963

The dancer steps onto the dark stage through a door frame, stage right, which is covered with a black curtain. Once there, she stands stage center, positions herself, and waits. The Master of Ceremonies announces her name with a brief comment regarding her form or her style to the audience. The band starts to play as a spotlight hits the dark richly red velvet curtain which will rise to reveal a beautiful young girl dressed in brilliant satins and silks, feathers, bright beads, and rhinestones and revealing lots of fresh, dewy flesh. The Club Largo on the Sunset Strip was the top-of-the-line girlie show in Los Angeles.

The showroom held a maximum audience of four hundred. The stage was shaped like a wide triangle, made of highly polished hardwood. It was gorgeous. A shimmering silvery black curtain served as backdrop for the dancers and hid the huge Vogue magazine cover and other props used by the dancers behind it.

On the second floor, stage left, was a curtained platform that held the band plus all their instruments. An organ player, a saxophone man and a drummer played for three shows a night, six days a week and rested during the comedian's two eighteen-minute acts.

With a line-up of a dozen girls from all over the world, the Club Largo boasted a continuous show. Patrons paid a five-dollar cover charge, plus two-drink minimum; a steak dinner was served to those who wanted it. The tables were covered with red cloth and flickering candles in bubble vases of red glass gave the room a romantic atmosphere.

Largo dressing room snapshot. Los Angeles, 1965

But the Largo had competition. The Pink Pussy Cat on Santa Monica Boulevard, set between a market and some small shops, had lines of casually dressed men and a few women in sport clothes waiting to enter its doors. We at the Largo said it was their vulgar name and the glaring hot pink colored building with the bright pink Cadillac parked in front that attracted their crowd. We drew in a quality audience of men attired in suits and ties and women in lovely dresses to our classic black building at the top of the Sunset Strip.

The "Pussys," as we called them, were named after male movie stars: Dina Martin, Toni Curtis, and Geri Lewis. Many of our dancers were authentic beauty queens: Miss Beverly Hills, Miss Hollywood and Miss Albuquerque. Competition between the two clubs was fierce.

The first night I danced there I was nervous and excited riding up the Strip in our newer baby blue Cadillac convertible as Dreamy drove with the top down so we could see everything and everyone could see us. The costume bag and my worn, but polished, red leather makeup case were in the back seat.

Dreamy and I passed The Body Shop, a small club in the less fashionable part of Sunset Strip. It was a little place, operated by a man and wife, and did not advertise their small group of dancers. Farther up, Sneaky Pete's marquee announced a jazz quartet was playing there. Another block west, past the Whisky a Go-Go, at 9069 Sunset Blvd., was The Club Largo.

CHUCK LANDIS
CLUB LARGO
STARRING MISS BEVERLY HILLS
AND 12 AMERICAN BEAUTY ROSES

I had never met Miss Beverly Hills but I was impressed by her billing, and I was inspired. Maybe, someday Miss Brandy Wilde would be up there in lights instead of Beverly's name.

Dreamy looked at the marquee and murmured, "Mmmm mmm mmmmm."

I looked at her, raised my eyebrows and answered, "Mmm huhh !"

Bernie, the club manager, met me at the door and showed me the way up to the dressing rooms. He was thin and small boned but the no nonsense expression on his face showed me he thought only his iron will kept the four matte black walls of the showroom standing. His eyes grew smaller and tighter as he told me 'The Rules' after we had climbed the fourteen steps to the second floor.

"You will be here by seven-thirty in the evening and you will go on first at eight. Give me your music," Bernie said, holding out his hand. "This is the only empty space at the dressing table and your costumes go into that closet. Keep your things together and try not to spread out onto someone else's space. There are ten girls in this room for six hours a night and you won't stay here long if you don't get along. There's a TV in the other room. Some of the girls play cards or Scrabble. Hi, Tiara."

A pretty Latina with huge dark eyes, dressed in a short tightly belted black dress entered the room. She placed her big black and white zebra patterned makeup case on the mirrored shelf that was used as a makeup table. The walls were covered with huge plate glass mirrors that reached the ceiling. Tiara smiled toward us, pulled open the closet doors and walked in.

"You don't come downstairs for anything except to do your show, no matter what. There's the telephone on the wall in case of an emergency, but don't use it. Got it?" Bernie continued.

I looked around at all the things he was pointing out and nodded yes as he looked at the song titles on my charts to make sure no one else in the show was already using one of the same songs. The well- lit closet was as wide as the room and about five feet deep with shelf space above the wooden rod for hats and props and space under the costumes for shoes.

"When the last person in the audience goes out the door, the dancers can leave." Bernie looked at me with what he must have thought was a commanding attitude and said, "Remember, no floor work. Understood?"

I nodded and Bernie left, leaving me about twenty minutes to get ready to go on stage. Placing my makeup bag where he had shown me, I took out the spirit gum to hold on my rhinestone pasties. I had put my makeup on at home and was almost ready to undress. Long, black, false eyelashes, smoky eye shadow and dark eyeliner made my eyes look larger and the bright blush on my cheeks insured I would look rosy on stage no matter what the lighting was like.

"Hi, I'm Tiara. I go on after you tonight so I'll catch for you. There's a hook there but you have to leave the stage for a second to reach it, so we catch the next dancer's stuff and put it on the hook. Just hand it through the black curtain. I'll be there."

Her gaze was casual and cool and took in every part of my anatomy, my cosmetics, my costumes, which were now hanging in the closet, and the bright red hair that still hung to my waist. Tiara had an "I've seen it all before" expression which looked like "Girls will come and girls will go but it's almost always a beautiful show. I guess you'll do."

The dressing room was filling up with gorgeous girls taking off their clothes or starting to apply stage makeup while wearing silky short robes that revealed shapely thighs, bare breasts and long necks. It was close quarters, but possibly because I didn't know anyone and did not know the histories of whatever tensions existed among the dancers, that first night I didn't feel too crowded.

I felt their curious eyes on me and I was anxious to measure up to the high standards these dancers seemed to expect. Every one of them was a true beauty. They would be my most critical audience. I wanted to please them and be accepted as their equal.

Each dancer would instantly measure my appearance and personality on stage; second, and more slowly, would be my costumes and music; and finally, they would judge my dancing and then my entire act.

By the time I got back to the dressing room after my first show, they would all know where to place me in their own constellation of stars. Each one would have gone down the stairs and taken a good look at my performance while they were safely hidden behind the black curtain. I was nervous because this was the club I wanted to work for a long run, maybe several years.

Tommy Russell, the Master of Ceremonies, dressed in a sleek black tuxedo with silver cummerbund and bow tie, microphone in hand, met me at the bottom of the stairs and asked how I wanted to be introduced.

"Well, other M.C.'s have said something about million dollar smile or feminine beauty," I answered.

I was surprised at how fast my heart was beating. I should be used to this by now, I chided myself. Calm down Brandy. I could feel a light perspiration on my nose and cheeks.

"We'll just say Miss Brandy Wilde for now," he said. "I'll watch your act and come up with something for the next show. You let me know if you like it. Your show's about ten minutes long, right?" Hearing the opening music he said, "Okay, let's go."

I stepped on stage and as I took my position behind the red curtain I heard the resonant, satiny smooth voice of Tommy Russell announce me for the first time. "Gentlemen and ladies, good evening and welcome to the Club Largo. To start our show the Club Largo proudly presents the intoxicating loveliness of Miss Brandy Wilde." The saxophone's first strains of *Prelude to a Kiss* filled the showroom as the velvet curtain rose.

I could see several long tables that held large parties of men and there were smaller groups of men with women as well. Once the music started they became quiet and settled down to watch the show.

In a gold lamè trench coat with silvery rhinestones scattered to look like sparkling raindrops on the shoulders, a glittering golden lamè umbrella with the same bright stones dripping from it, matching gold opera length gloves and high heels, I performed my parade number around the Largo stage.

There was so much room, I felt light and bouncy. I smiled and relaxed. After thirty seconds or so, I put the umbrella down on one side toward the back of the stage so the audience could still see the golden circle and it was out of my way. The spotlight, with a beautiful pale pink gel, followed me as I danced and I didn't have to share the stage with anyone. The audience was close and the black walls, which repelled all light and sent it back toward the stage, helped make it feel intimate, dark and sexy.

I couldn't see much beyond the second ring of tables due to the spotlight so I worked to groups of tables specifically and the whole club in general. It didn't make any difference. From the audience it would look like I was making special eye contact even with the far tables and they would feel included in the moment.

Off came the gold rain-coat to reveal a corselet completely covered with rhinestones colored gold, aurora borealis, silver and baby pink and lavender. It zipped up the front and held my breasts up and pushed them out, cinched in the waist, smoothly rounded my hips and was easy to take off when the right time came.

Extremely small, rhinestoned, high-cut breakaway pants fit below. Tightly stretched elasticized side bands sat high on the hip and the pants were taken off by unhooking both sides with the thumbs at the same time, pulling them forward through the thighs and dropping them on the black curtain at the back of the stage. If I did it fast enough, while spinning, the audience could almost be made to think the pants had disappeared.

The second trailer was *Stormy Weather* and the tenor saxophone cried; the drummer produced a mood of thundering, throbbing danger, while the organist played jazz riffs around the melody. I wasn't used to music like this anymore. The charts were simple and had been played without much imagination in other California clubs.

The musicians in the Largo band were experienced, talented and bored. They tried to take every song and maximize its jazz potential. That meant they didn't follow the dancers' movements as they should have, to make the dancer look good, but the musicians sure sounded great.

I moved around the stage including bumps and grinds with the rest of the dance steps and flirting with different ones in the audience while keeping up with the music. With a huge flourish, the corselet came off at the end of *Stormy Weather* leaving only the rhinestone pants and a pair of baby pink rhinestone pasties that covered my nipples.

The surprise pink gel in the spotlight slot was meant to make my skin look alive and touchable and cover up the pressure marks from the tight corselet that had squeezed my torso for over twenty minutes. I could see it was working. The gel made my hair look fiery red as the waves and curls caressed parts of my body or flowed away when I spun.

The audience had been dazzled by the golden brilliance of the costume and I could see they liked what was under it too. They looked like they were having fun and I was glad. That meant Bernie, the manager, and Chuck Landis, the owner, would be happy too.

The band segued into *Tequila*, my third trailer, and played it as loudly and with as much enthusiasm as a three-piece group could. As I danced toward the umbrella I twirled and the little breakaway pants came off with a flick of my thumbs and dropped to the edge of the back curtain. I pulled at the pale net panties that had been underneath the breakaways so they stretched over my rear end and were almost invisible as I flipped up the umbrella by the top of the circle and tossed it to the other hand so I could hold it in front of me by the handle while flirting with the audience. I hoped I had done all that so quickly that they had not seen too much of me. I could use the umbrella like other dancers used large bubbles or huge ostrich feather fans to hide themselves, and tease the audience after they were nude.

The front part of the net pants was reinforced by cotton material of the same pale color and was sprinkled with a few pink rhinestones. The idea was to look as bare as possible, still sparkly gorgeous and just within the decency and public behavior laws.

A nice round of applause came from the audience as my act climaxed with the umbrella held straight, high above my head and figure fully exposed, the other golden gloved arm stretched toward them. I smiled and acknowledged their applause while I stayed in place until the curtain touched the stage and the band played thirty two bars of a fast paced *There's No Business Like Show Business.*

The faint light the dancers needed to enter and exit the stage came on. I picked up the rhinestoned pants and ran off the stage while Tiara came on and stood in place, listened to her announcement and composed herself as she waited for her music to begin.

I had become caught up with the new band, the way they played, the spotlight and the great stage. I had forgotten about the girls upstairs. Now I would have to face them and see their decisions. I felt hot and sweaty and confident as I grabbed my wardrobe from the hook where Tiara had hung it and climbed the stairs.

The first to greet me was a smiling Miss Beverly Hills. I noticed her deep yet very feminine voice and then her hair. It was thick and full, with lots of body and the lightest brown with several shades of blonde highlights, the kind of hair that is God-given or that costs thousands of dollars a year to maintain.

"You looked wonderful on stage Brandy. I'm Beverly. Welcome to the Largo, I hope you like it here," she called from one of the two private dressing rooms out near the television room.

"Thank you, Beverly. I'm happy to be here with you," I replied and smiled back at her.

Carrying my costume I entered the main dressing room and saw relaxed faces and women going about their nightly work.

Althea, who had the biggest chest in the dressing room, looked up from her toenail painting, smiled, and knocked me out with her two big dimples.

"Did you get that corselet here in town? I love it. Who did it for you?" she asked, as I hung my wardrobe in the closet and slipped on a short green silk robe.

Sandra Lee who had long, straight, blonde hair and legs as delicate and muscular as a thoroughbred racehorse stood in four inch silver "Sky Highs," dressing for her first show.

"That color gold looks great on you," Sandra said.

I was accepted. It was subtle but I felt it. Now I wanted to see all the other girls' acts.

Chapter Twelve

Gorgeous Friends

Some dancers stayed at the Largo for years, becoming the core of the nightly program. I was one of those dancers, who wanted to live in Hollywood. I loved the Largo and the friends I made there. Diane, Beverly, Althea and Joni became the kind of friends I also saw during the daytime for lunch or movies on Sunday.

Diane Lewis started at the Largo a few days after me and we formed a close and lasting friendship. She was a natural blonde who dyed her waist-length hair black to look more dramatic. With her pronounced cheekbones, sharp nose and large, deeply set dark eyes she had an intense presence. Diane was a terrific dancer and after a few months of watching everyone's act and copying all their best moves, she turned herself into an excellent stripper.

Diane began performing as a Go-Go dancer on the Sunset Strip with her boarding school roommate, Cheryl Crane, who was Lana Turner's daughter. Diane had more classical dance training than any stripper I ever worked with. Growing up, she had taken a dozen years of ballet, tap and jazz lessons.

Her mother lived in Washington DC where she was a high level legal secretary. Diane and her mother had an aura of mystery in our dressing room where the girls were always on the lookout for news and gossip.

At eighteen, in a fit of rebellion, Diane married right after high school and became pregnant on her wedding night. Her daughter, Beverly, was a beautiful pink and blonde joy. By the time Diane arrived at the Largo, at age twenty-one, she was the single parent of a three-year old. Her only complaint about having a child was the change it caused in her breasts. No longer the smooth and round virginal breasts of an eighteen-year old girl.

The Twist, which Chubby Checker made popular in 1960, was still trendy in 1963. Diane did a blast out, rough and tumble Twist act. Her strapless red and yellow, knee-length, chiffon dress fit tightly at the waist and bodice while the skirt flared. The costume had a riotous pattern of stripes, squiggles and polka dots. The tiny red pants and bra underneath had layers of four inch fringe that enhanced every movement when the dress was removed.

The basic Twist was easy enough for most people to learn quickly, but the extra jumps, double turns, high kicks, splits, punches in the air and driving rhythm of her act were so wild men and women in the audience often danced around their tables and many tried to join her on stage. A few were successful but they didn't stay up there long. Over the years a succession of muscled, well-dressed, and persuasive bouncers took care of them.

No one could figure out why Diane took such good care of our star, Miss Beverly Hills. She caught Beverly's wardrobe during each show, took it to the dressing room and hung it up. She was always in Beverly's dressing room. It was noticeably unusual so everyone wanted to know what was going on.

Some said it was to steal Beverly's style and her new steps but I didn't think so. Diane had Beverly's steps memorized and did them better than Beverly after watching one show. Diane had her own special crisp and hard-edged style. So why did she continue year after year to coddle Beverly? It was generally acknowledged that both women were completely heterosexual at the time.

I felt that Diane was star struck and needed a woman to admire. She chose Beverly who was beautiful, happily married, had a little boy that she adored, had been in movies and several television shows and was a devoutly religious Christian woman.

New dancers came in and some of the friends I had made when I first arrived at the Largo left. Those of us who remained never heard from them or saw them again. Where do beautiful girls go when they leave their friends behind and take off for parts unseen?

I found out that some dancers become romantically linked with men who are jealous and controlling. These men will not allow their dancer to continue dancing. Many want "their woman" to stop wearing makeup and force them to wear drab, baggy clothing, keep their head down and not make eye contact with women or men.

Paula Price, a wide-eyed young beauty queen from Ohio, married a police officer who exercised complete control over her. He sold her car and threw away most of her clothes while she was grocery shopping for dinner. He then moved her to Rancho Cucamonga, a small town about fifty miles away from Los Angeles. She submitted to his wishes and disappeared from our view.

Dancers moved away for about the same reasons other people left Hollywood. They wanted to be closer to families and free childcare or followed husbands and boyfriends to what they hoped would be greener pastures. Others decided their big dream of "discovery" and silver screen stardom was not going to come true and moved back home to go to school or become cocktail waitresses and bartenders. Some stayed because they felt most welcome in Hollywood or had nowhere else to go.

Althea was at the Largo when I arrived and had her place in the pecking order carved out. She was the Mae West of our troupe and had been for a couple of years. She talked to the audience and teased them with witty, flirtatious Mae West type lines.

When the curtain opened Althea stood in the center of a stage prop, about eight feet tall and six feet wide, and painted to look like a magazine cover. She was inside a section cutout to match her body and the big red hat she wore. The word VOGUE was painted at the top. Althea's first song was *You Stepped Out of a Dream* and in her bright cherry colored satin suit, red stockings and satin shoes, large red picture hat with a two foot long feather and a matching umbrella, she was the curvy fashion model of men's dreams.

She never did a bump or a grind, mainly strutting back and forth across the stage, using her umbrella as a stylish cane, posing, talking and kidding with the men. Althea was a favorite of the audience and the club owner Chuck Landis for her wit and magnificent bosom. She had a sweet round face with killer dimples, a rosebud mouth, and a cap of short, wispy, dark hair.

Althea had been raised in a little town not far from Portland Maine, where she was thought of as "a fast and loose girl" by her parents, teachers and peers. She had the small waist and hourglass figure of Mae West but was bigger on top. Althea said she had driven the small town boys and men crazy while the girls and women shunned her.

"Not one woman in Maine ever said a kind word to me, including my mother," she said.

No one could see there was still a sweet little girl in the body that had matured so early. It had made her cynical and a little bit bitter but she was still hopeful.

Althea said she arrived in Los Angeles a virgin and remained so for quite a while. She lived at the Hollywood Studio Club on Lodi Place, just a few blocks from Hollywood Blvd. and Vine St. It was a chaperoned, dormitory style building run by the YWCA, exclusively for actresses and other young women in the movie business, such as film-cutters, screenwriters, dancers and singers, who wanted to stay in safe, regulated quarters. Built in 1925, it was funded by actors and studios concerned about the exploitation of hundreds of young women who were streaming into Hollywood hoping for a career in the movies.

Sharon Tate had lived at the Studio Club in 1963, while Althea was there. Other famous former residents included: Marilyn Monroe, Ayn Rand, Rita Moreno, Linda Darnell, and Kim Novak to name just a few. After I had been at the Largo a few months, Dreamy and I started driving Althea to work each evening.

These women became my friends. I felt I would keep Beverly, Diane and Althea as friends forever. They had not had easy lives, were not always sweet, but I could trust them not to want to hurt me in any way. We played Scrabble, read, knitted, and watched television together. We talked about ourselves, our sex lives and our families for six hours a night, six days a week in between dressing up to take our clothes off.

I didn't have to hide the fact that I was a lesbian from strippers as I did from most of the world. I was safe in the dressing room when it was illegal to be gay in California. Dreamy and I were afraid we would be arrested if we went out dancing together or gathered to have a drink with male friends who might look effeminate or lesbians who looked butch. We could be thrown out of a restaurant or club if the police were called because an establishment didn't want to serve "our type."

The Largo girls became close while we were there. We all wanted the same thing: to be the best dancer on the stage that evening, to do the best show we could even if there was just one person in the audience.

Dreamy's mother, Berylynn, called about ten o'clock in the morning. It was Friday, November 22, 1963.

"Wake up. Turn on the television!" Berylynn said as she gulped, groaned and hung up.

I obeyed and turned on the set, which was on the dresser facing the bed. President John Kennedy had been shot in Dallas and was being rushed to the hospital. I got back in bed. Dreamy and I watched television all day and into the night. We cried as we heard of the president's death and watched the crowds of reporters, police and onlookers outside the hospital mill around as everyone waited for further news.

How could this thin, ordinary looking man named Lee Harvey Oswald be the one to kill our powerful, handsome hero of a president?

Bernie called to tell me Chuck was going to keep the Largo closed that night. We watched history unfold. Needing to know more than what the television was telling us, Dreamy went for newspapers. The front page had a picture of Vice-president Lyndon Johnson being sworn in as president on Air Force One. His wife Lady Bird was on his right and a stunned Jackie Kennedy stood as witness on his left side.

Saturday, the 23rd, the Largo opened. We danced to an audience of eight men that night. I was glad to be there to talk to my friends at work about the death of our handsome president who could have done so much good if only he had lived. It was comforting.

On Sunday, while watching television for anything regarding the assassination, Dreamy and I saw Lee Harvey Oswald on live feed being lead through the halls of the Dallas Court House. He was handcuffed and surrounded by law enforcement officers. A man stepped into the television picture with a gun in his right hand and shot Oswald in the chest near his heart.

"I know that guy! I'm sure I know that guy! What did he do? Oh, my God, what did he do?" Dreamy wailed.

Oswald died two hours later in the same hospital President Kennedy had died in two days earlier. The most important question of the day had been "Why? Why did you kill President Kennedy?" Now that could never be answered.

The man who killed Oswald, Jack Ruby, was a Dallas striptease club owner, from Chicago.

*Club Largo Bowling League presentation of bowling bags.
January, 1963.*

Sandra, Tiara and Brandy cuddle around Dave while bowling at Largo.

Chapter Thirteen

The Pasadena Playhouse, 1964

Once Dreamy and I were settled in Los Angeles we started looking around for something other than work to amuse ourselves. We didn't want to go on the road, and though the Largo was a steady gig, I wanted more. The two classes at Los Angeles City College broke up the sameness of every week. I still was not satisfied.

I started thinking about attending the Pasadena Playhouse and with Dreamy's encouragement I signed up for a six-week daytime summer session. It was a famous acting school in the 1940's and 50's and many stars had attended the Playhouse. Phyllis Jacobson, my tiny Jordan High School drama teacher, had gone to the Playhouse and I wanted to go too.

I was excited. I wanted to learn more about professional acting and this was the perfect place for me. New York didn't appeal to me, while Los Angeles held everything I wanted including the movie industry.

In 1964 when I was able to apply, the application asked about present employment and I answered truthfully, writing that I was an exotic dancer and gave the name and address of the Largo. I was able to join the summer session and work. It was hard but it was only six weeks and I had a great time. At twenty-three I was the oldest in a class of forty-two students.

At the end of the summer session each person who wanted to continue attending the Playhouse but needed a scholarship had to perform a three to four minute solo piece that would be judged by the teachers. Those chosen would be considered for one of the five scholarships offered. I did a monologue from a 1958 Kim

Stanley movie called *The Goddess*, which was loosely based on the life of Marilyn Monroe.

The scene was going along well. My poor character was having a dramatic fit on stage in the small black box theatre used for student projects, when my jaw locked. It felt like an electrical explosion in my head. I was stunned. It had happened before in moments of stress, but not often. It knocked me against the proscenium wall, my knees buckled. I fell to the floor moaning and raised my head while looking out toward the audience. My jaw relaxed and unlocked. Without missing a beat I continued the last few moments of the monologue from the floor, rose shakily and left the stage in character.

The judges had seen true fear and pain and wrongly recognized it as acting. I am sure I would not have won the one-year scholarship otherwise, but I did win. Now I had a real decision to make. I couldn't work at night and go to school during the day for two semesters. Six weeks had been so hard I knew nine months would be impossible.

During the day from eight a.m. to three p.m. five days a week we had classes in fencing, ballet, body movement, scene work, history of Theater, elocution, accents and dialects, stage makeup, costuming, singing and acting. Rehearsals and performances were scheduled in the evening during the regular school year.

Some of the summer students had been told by their teachers they should try some other line of work. Some had been encouraged to go home and have babies. Want-to-be actors were hysterical, pulling out their hair, hitting their heads against the wall or quietly sobbing in hiding places around the Playhouse. Everyone was exhausted.

I had to talk to Dreamy. She had been supportive and very patient, driving me back and forth to Pasadena from Hollywood every day, and had done everything she could to help me succeed in summer school. If I went to the Playhouse for a year Dreamy would have to go to work to support us.

"I want you to go to the playhouse. Don't worry, we'll get along fine. Someday you're going to win an Oscar and it will all be worth it. I'll get a job waitressing and maybe you can substitute at the Largo when someone is sick. Let's see if we can make it for both semesters," said Dreamy.

It had been two and a half years since she had held down a job and what could she do? How much could she take? We didn't know yet.

Dreamy found a job as a waitress in a Hollywood barbeque restaurant. She liked working there and although she had never been a waitress she proved to be good at it.

The Star News, Pasadena's conservative newspaper, front page headline bawled **"STRIPPER WANTS TO ACT."** The story told of my scholarship win. There was also a huge topless picture of me hiding my breasts with crossed forearms, above the fold. Unfortunately the picture made my elbows look like elongated nipples and I seemed completely bare.

I was called into the Dean's office and asked to sign a pledge that I would not use the Playhouse as a publicity stunt to further my burlesque career. The pledge also made me promise not to allow photographers to follow me around the school and that I would wear clothing in class. That was real easy.

Dreamy said they were maligning my character, that it was insulting, but I had already signed the pledge when asked. I had always intended to wear something.

In 1965 a new Volkswagen Beetle cost two thousand dollars. I bought a clover green bug with stick shift, and a tan interior. We named her Perky and I learned to drive from N. Kenmore in Hollywood to S. El Molino in Pasadena. Terrified of the curved bridge into Atwater, I slowed down to ten miles an hour each morning while driving on it for the entire school year. The rest of the drive was easy after a while. It felt so good to be independent. It was worth every scary minute.

Dreamy and I fought over the long hours I had to spend in Pasadena. We had never been away from each other so long. I loved being at the Playhouse but it sure didn't help my love life with Dreamy. I didn't think it was helping me learn how to act any better either.

After stripping around the country and in Hollywood for three years, I wasn't a completely inexperienced girl any longer, even though I still thought of myself that way. My classmates and teachers looked at me and treated me like a "mysterious, lesbian of the world who has worked in dark, dirty, sex driven joints". I felt like I was putting over a delicious joke on everyone.

I was having a wonderful time even though Dreamy was not there advising me and protecting me. I didn't need as much protection as I once had and was more in control of my own life. Dreamy and I spent all of our free time together and I tried to include her in my school life, but it wasn't quite the same.

I hoped it was worth the sacrifice. Dreamy and I both hoped this training would help me get acting jobs and perhaps be able to make a living as an actress. It was a million to one chance but we took it.

Lysergic acid, LSD, was still legal in 1964 and easily obtainable. Half of the students at the Playhouse were experimenting with it and not attending class. Some were taking LSD every day and the school could do nothing about it. I could see actors around campus on their knees staring down ant holes for hours, watching tree leaves grow or conversing with their potato chips.

Dr. Cohen from UCLA, who was involved with the LSD studies there, was asked by the Playhouse administration to talk to us at a school-wide assembly in the large theater. We were excited, laughing with the speaker as he described the effects of the drug on people he had seen.

"We want you to be safe, in an atmosphere of trust if you take LSD. Don't do it alone or with a group of people who are all turning on. Respect the drug. Don't be greedy, and if you get in trouble with it give me a call," the doctor advised us.

We wanted to know more about the drug, how much of it we could take at a time, the best way to have a good trip and what to do about a bad trip.

I wanted to take LSD but Dreamy insisted I was not a good candidate. She was protecting me and I rebelled but I was afraid she could be right. She knew from my one experience with marijuana that I got paranoid when even slightly drugged.

When I looked around the school, I worried that I might have a bad trip and fall into another world and not come back, like the seventeen year-old high school football player one of the other actors took me to visit. He was staying near the Playhouse in his brother's apartment. The good looking muscular boy with brown eyes sat on the couch all day, looking at the refrigerator. He needed help to eat and move to the bathroom. His brother and sister, who had given him the LSD, didn't know if he would ever come back. They hadn't told their parents yet.

Dreamy and I survived the year. I had been in a few plays, which she had come to the Playhouse to see. I'd learned how to fence a little, knew a few yoga positions and some theater history. Dreamy was proud of me. I hoped she was, because she had worked so hard for me to be able to attend the Pasadena Playhouse.

I knew how much I didn't know. It was almost overwhelming. My hopes of learning how to act at the Playhouse didn't work out. I had wanted to start at the beginning, find a solid foundation and build on it but since I was so much older than most students and already a performer in show business they put me into advanced acting. I still had no foundation, only a second story experience, with nothing to stand on and nothing below to boost me up. My acting class was taught by a former student who wanted to be a playwright and knew very little about acting.

Sally Struthers, the tiny blonde curly-head, was the only one of our class that I know of to make acting her career. She was charming, made you laugh and was everyone's friend. You couldn't be sad around Sally. Soon after her playhouse experience she landed the part of Gloria in *All in the Family*, the television series that went on to become legendary.

By June of 1965 I was ready to go back to dancing, the spotlight, the girls and the money. Most of the students at the playhouse were five or six years younger than I, with little experience on stage or in life. I was the older, experienced lesbian stripper at twenty-four. It made a big difference. I didn't make any friends and felt out of place.

The Pasadena Playhouse was able to hang on for one more year, and then went bankrupt.

Chapter Fourteen

Top of the Sunset Strip, 1964-1967

It felt wonderful to be back at the Largo after studying at the Pasadena Playhouse for the last year. Diane had my "best seat in the dressing room" which was next to the water cooler so she sat next to only one other dancer, but I didn't care. The girls gave me a welcome home wine and cheese party. Chuck Landis, owner of the Club Largo at the top of Sunset Strip, had finally let us have alcohol in the dressing room as long as we bought it from the club and stopped sneaking it in as the dancers had done for years. The girls were probably his best customers. Most everyone had at least a couple of drinks during the evening, including me. I was careful though because now I was driving myself to work and back home.

There was a new dancer in the show. Baby Darling was a wiry-thin, muscular blonde who did her act in a short pink see-through nightgown with a matching dainty short robe. She either had her thumb in her mouth or was playing with her tongue and lips during her first two songs. Starting slow and sleepy, using *Baby, Baby, Baby* as her first song, by her third trailer she was running barefooted across the stage, up the wall, and bouncing off with a backward flip to an extended drum solo. People said she reminded them of the famous Candy Barr who had once worked at the Largo.

The first night back I followed Bett Casey on stage, a pretty girl with a dark cap of straight hair, big round breasts. She did a nurse act which included crawling to the edge of the stage while staring at "the patient," one randomly chosen man in the audience.

I watched while she chose a man about forty years-old who was wearing thick glasses and sitting at a front table with friends. She danced to that man only.

"Hey Ronnie, boy does she like you!" his skinny, dark-eyed friend said.

"Get 'er number. Here's a pen. Call 'er later, yea." He was panting now. "Give 'er y'er mouth. She wants y'er mouth Ronnie! Shit, that looks pretty good. Look wats she doin' ta Ronnie," the friend whispered as he leaned across the table toward Ronnie and Bett, his mouth hanging open, his long thin fingers inching forward.

She wasn't touching the man named Ronnie and she wasn't doing anything against the law, but it looked like she might, soon. No matter what he or his friends said she would not smile, blink or break eye contact. Bett stared and stalked her patient. It was fascinating to watch the smiling expressions turn to confusion, worry, and fear. That was the best part. That was the part Bett liked.

Chuck Landis was a shy, heavy-set man who always wore a black suit with a gray tie. He had a wife and two children that he kept away from his popular Sunset Strip club. Chuck left the work of dealing with the dancers' needs, daily dramas and complaints to a series of ever-changing club managers now that Bernie had died. Chuck usually arrived at work just before midnight to take a peek at any papers or messages the secretary had left on his desk.

July 20th, the night of Chuck's birthday, the dancers were excited to share the occasion with him. Most of us liked him, even though he was so distant. The girls bought him a huge square cake with his name on it and garland after garland of flowers made of blue and green whipped sugar-cream icing on top. We were looking forward to twelve o' clock when we would feast on cake and champagne with our elusive boss.

He didn't show up at twelve or at one. Baby Darling and Diane Lewis paced the hall in front of Chuck's office, each wrapped up in their own anger with him, and not paying much attention to each other. Occasionally they bumped shoulders in the narrow hallway. Rage made them gradually more irritable as the night was almost over and no cake.

Diane was dressed to go on stage in her pristine white bridal gown with yards and yards of taffeta in the full skirt with the long train and billowing tulle in her longer bridal veil. It was her actual wedding gown which she had converted to a stage costume and was very proud of it. She marched up and down the hall.

Diane became so frustrated she used the "emergency" telephone in the dressing room to call downstairs to see if Chuck was in the lobby. As usual she had been the one to organize the party, pick up the cake and order the champagne.

"Harry, where the hell is Chuck," Diane demanded when the lobby phone was picked up. "Has he called?"

"Yeah, sure honey. Chuck slipped up the stairs and into his office about half an hour ago, when he was sure there was no one in the hall," the club manager told Diane, with a bit of sly fun in his voice.

Ten dancers screamed when we heard that. We were wrapped up in the insult we felt Chuck had laid on us. We were reminded once again that he had no respect for us or our delicate generous feelings.

Diane ran to his office door, cake in both hands, with the rest of us behind her and began to shout "Chuck, let us in. Let us in you motherfucker. Here is your fuckin' cake. Put it up your ass."

She threw the cake down in front of the office door. It landed hard. Frosting flew half way up the door and all over the floor. Some frosting plopped onto Baby Darling's sweaty hair as she was coming up the stairs after her act. As she reached the hall someone bumped against Baby from the side and forced her into Diane who put out her arms to shield her wedding gown from the dripping body.

"What were you doing up here when you weren't catching my wardrobe, ya fuckin' cunt?" Baby Darling yelled as she reached toward Diane.

The bridal number was being announced on the loud speaker by Joe Crisa, the current master of ceremonies. Baby's bellow could be heard all over the club, including Chuck's office. Diane should have been downstairs ready to go on stage and making sure Baby's little night gowns didn't lay on the floor and get dirty.

Baby Darling blocked Diane's way down the stairs, grabbed the full taffeta skirt and ripped it off the main body of the dress. Most of the slippery taffeta fell to the floor as Baby reached for the strapless top of the gown.

Diane stepped forward, slipped on the tulle, tearing it as she fell in a heap. Baby held on to the bodice holding up Diane's breasts and yanked hard. The zipper didn't hold the dress together. Baby held the top of the dress in her hand as the bottom tangled between them. Diane sat up a little and was able to bite Baby's inner thigh.

Baby tried to raise her knee and hit the side of Diane's jaw but her teeth held on tightly. Baby raised the other knee and hit Diane under the chin. Black hair flying back, Diane fell on her back which made her breasts more accessible. Baby slipped on the taffeta and fell on top of Diane which put her in a good position to get hold of a recently inserted , triangular breast implant. The skin was thin around the edges of the saline implant and you could see exactly where to pry it loose. Baby tried to get her fingernails under the implant and tear it off Diane's body. It was lucky for Diane that Baby bit her nails; otherwise that strategy could have caused real damage.

They grappled on the floor in the middle of the bridal veil, rolling from one side to the other, knees knocking against hip bones, elbows punching groins and fists hitting faces. I had seen a few girl fights but never a stripper fight. These over-wrought women had found a way to release the night's tension.

The rest of us were mesmerized by the sight of these two feminine bodies, white taffeta and tulle smeared with blue and green milky frosting swirling around them, hitting each other with intent to maim. A few of us screamed as we huddled in the hall, held our breath, or gasped when an especially hard blow landed on a tender spot. But mostly we stared at Diane and Baby, sweaty, breathing hard, groaning and grunting with the effort of hurting each other while protecting themselves.

Harry, the current club manager who had been living with Diane for a few months, finally came running up the steps and tried to take Baby off of Diane, who had her muscular thighs around Baby's waist, and was just getting ready to smash the back of a spike heel into the exposed spine.

Harry, a tall burly guy, with smooth skin and neat black hair who looked great in a tuxedo, could hardly get them apart. He threw one into the dressing room, one into the television room and stood in the doorway between them.

"Brandy, you're almost dressed and ready to go on. You go on stage next. I'll tell Joe to announce you and let the musicians know. Get going," he said, reaching for the telephone.

I was so mad I didn't get to see all the throwing of costumes and makeup going on upstairs in the dressing room while I was on stage, but the audience and I could hear every word Baby and Diane were yelling at each other over the music.

There were about fifty men in the audience, all wanting to see the "fighting strippers" more than my act. Heads were twisting and turning trying to find out where the real action was.

When I got off stage, Baby Darling was already running down the stairs toward me. Harry followed. Baby had dressed and packed in the ten minutes it took to do my "Pussy Galore" act and had her costume bag slung over her shoulder, her makeup bag swinging. 'God help anyone who gets in her way,' I thought, as I put my back against the wall to let her pass. She threw the door open, entered the showroom, headed toward the front door with Harry right behind her.

Diane came back the next night ready to dance but Baby Darling never came back to work at the Largo. We started calling Diane "Slugger" and she was kind of proud of that. Going to a private girl's school for twelve years had prepared her for the outside world.

A rumor went around that Baby had had a nervous breakdown. We heard that her husband, an up and coming TV actor, had put her in the hospital but we never knew for sure.

As months passed pretty girls came and went from the Largo stage. The Whisky a Go-Go, a club just one block down the Strip, became popular and featured some big acts. Occasionally Jim Morrison, or some of the Mama's and the Papa's and other musicians working the Strip would wander up to watch our show.

The top part of the Strip, where Holloway Drive joins Sunset Blvd., changed radically in 1966 and 1967. Hundreds of teens, dressed fashionably in rags, sprawled on the north side of the street, their backs against buildings or lounged on corners. They waited.

They waited to see who would come along with some weed to share, who would walk up that might be in the mood to screw, who could give them a few coins or want them to join a band. Go-Go dancers, musicians, singers and side men, music producers, all walked past them going from Gazzarri's, past the Largo and down to Sneaky Pete's jazz club and to the Whiskey a Go-Go on the corner. No one wanted to move their cars as parking places were rare.

More and more young people flocked to the Strip. They moved onto the south side of Sunset, then further east toward Schwab's drug store. Long hair for men and women was mandatory if you wanted to look hip. Miniskirts, which had been an inch or two above the knee in 1963, became more mini which I loved. But it was work to keep your crotch out of sight.

Police and shop owners along the Strip hated the changes. Their reactions were in the newspaper for weeks. The Strip was no longer a place for sophisticated adults to play. Youngsters, who had little or no money to spend in the shops but were sly shoplifters, wanted to be near the clubs where their heroes were working. They had entered the playground and made it a slum. Broken green and brown beer bottles littered the Strip, graffiti covered shop fronts, cigarette butts, papers with food and cups full of vomit began to appear next to semi-conscious teens.

Some people called what happened next riots and some said they were civil protests but when the police came onto the Strip and started enforcing a ten p.m. curfew for those under eighteen, all hell broke loose. Buses were set on fire by enraged teenaged protesters and the police descended. Anyone who looked young and had long hair was knocked around, beaten and eventually arrested. The first riot was in November but there was tension between police and teens for months.

The Strip quieted down as the music scene gained momentum in San Francisco and the Bay Area. The "hippies," as they were now being called, moved up there too. Skirts were shorter and hair grew longer on the Strip. Drugs and cults became more popular.

I didn't know that cult culture had entered the Largo cast of dancers until a night in January when Marina, a belly dancer from a little island off the coast of Spain, who had been at the Largo for about six months made the announcement. We knew she lived with a younger hippie heroin addict, but now she said her lover was the "newly risen Son of God, Jesus Christ and all who see him must bow down and worship him."

One evening after crawling across the dressing room on her knees, dressed in only a belt of gold coins, Marina kissed Joni Carson's feet and tried to spread her legs. Marina turned her face away from Joni's momentarily exposed labia and declared, "We meet in my living room each evening after the clubs close to worship our Jesus. I am called Little Mary now. Would you like to join us for prayer?"

No one answered her invitation aloud. Some heads shook "no." Other dancers lowered their eyes, leaning back trying to hide behind someone else, pretending Marina was not looking at them imploringly over Joni's knee.

I was nervous. All conversation had stopped. Joni stood up, shook Marina loose and left the room. The next person who spoke had to go.

"Maybe," I said.

Marina crawled over to kiss my feet, which I pushed further under my chair. She hugged my legs and tried to draw my feet toward her.

"You won't be sorry. I'll let you hold my little girl while we worship."

Every eye in the dressing room widened. My hesitant half smile vanished. Dancers sat up straight and looked at one another with only one possible question in their mind.

"Who else has she made that promise to?"

All those eyes landed on me and I realized I did have to go and see how Marina's daughter was being treated at those worship sessions. I didn't know what I would do if I saw anything wrong. I talked it over with Joni, our current star and dance captain. Joni decided my "instincts" would let me know if I had to take the little girl with me or leave her there. But she didn't tell me how to get her out if I needed to.

I didn't mention that I was going to go to Marina's the next evening to Dreamy. She would have been worried and we would have fought about me wanting to go to a drug addict's nouveau-Christian cult at three in the morning with who knows how many other addict cult members, to possibly kidnap a child. We who had heard Marina understood I had to go, but it wouldn't make a bit of sense to Dreamy.

I followed Marina's car to her house the next evening after work. I felt wrapped in dread. It was only a few blocks, within walking distance from the Strip. No one was there yet. Marina put American cheese slices and some soda crackers on the table. She lit candles and incense, keeping the lights low. The sparse furniture in the living room was against the walls which left space in the middle for the "circle of worshipers" Marina was expecting.

"Where is your little girl, Marina?"

"She's next door, with the sitter. She'll sleep there tonight. Jesus is probably on the Strip with his disciples, trying to save souls and find junk. That's what he does every night," she said in an accepting manner.

I was so relieved. I didn't want to stay and now I didn't have to. The little girl wouldn't be in danger tonight. What about tomorrow?

"Does she stay with the sitter when you're at work?"

"Oh, yes," she answered. "My lord is always busy."

"I'm going to go home then, Marina. I'll see you at work."

"No, no, no, don't go! He'll be here in a while and when you feel his touch, his energy, you'll be able to see how special he is," she cried.

Leaving wasn't that easy but I kept moving forward as she turned from her nightly chores and pleaded with me to stay and wait for "The Living Jesus."

"Another time, honey," I said forcefully.

Marina left the Largo soon after that but I saw her at the Renaissance Faire in Agoura a few months later with her daughter. The little girl looked happy and healthy. I wondered what was really happening and if we "dressing room bitches" were as jaded and evil minded as Marina had screamed at us when she found out by accident why I had gone to her house. Who had blurted it out anyway?

Wally Green came into my life at the perfect moment. Life had been quiet for a while when I was introduced to a fabulous gay South African choreographer by ZuZuLa, another dancer at the Largo, who was having him create a new act for her. I loved him immediately and the feeling was mutual. Wally had tried to make it as a lead dancer on Broadway but that hadn't worked out. He sometimes called himself "The World's Oldest Chorus Boy."

Wally started taking me to fancy restaurants so he could be seen by directors and movie producers with a woman and I wanted to go with him. He took me to lunch meetings with famous actors but he never wanted to take Dreamy. That caused tension between us but Dreamy tried to be understanding. He was trying his best to become a choreographer for movies and television in Hollywood.

"I would love to create a new act for you Brandy. Have you ever thought of working with a choreographer? You could lift the quality of your act and your dancing if you wanted to do this with me," Wally offered. "I've got this great idea for a Hungarian Gypsy act, very classy and you've never seen anything like it. Now that everyone dances to tapes instead of live musicians, we can expand on the types of songs we use. "

I wanted it. I wanted it so much.

It took nine months to learn that act and I had to write down every step of the choreography because it was so complicated I kept forgetting it if I didn't perform it for a week or two, but it was spectacular for me. I did real gypsy steps while beating myself with a tambourine to classical music probably never heard in a strip club before. My mom had always told me her father was a gypsy so I thought this was just right, although I had never really believed her.

Dreamy picked me up after work on a cloudy September night in 1967. When we got home she turned toward me, took a deep breath, and looked at me like she knew this moment would be the last quiet time in her life for a long while. One hand held onto the dining room table. Her eyes were wide open with tension and not the relaxed green sleepy eyes I loved.

"We need to settle up our bills."

"Why? Are you leaving me?" I asked her only half seriously.

I was surprised that had come out of me. It was the furthest thing from my mind.

I could see she was relieved that I had said the words for her. Her shoulders dropped to their normal position and her grip on the table relaxed some.

"Yes, I am."

Now she just had to tell me why and when.

In the seven years Dreamy and I had been together I had never seen her even slightly interested in a woman who was not a stripper, so I wasn't prepared. I probably should have been aware of signs that her interest had changed, but I hadn't noticed any signs. I wasn't looking for them either.

Where was I? I was at work six nights a week. I left our apartment at 7:30 and returned about 2:30 in the morning after spending the night, semi-nude, talking and laughing with ten or eleven of the most beautiful women in Los Angeles and making myself look sexy and appealing for paying customers to watch, dancing and having a wonderful time with my friends.

Dreamy was alone at home and sometimes on Saturday night she would go out to a gay bar. I could see how she might be lonely, but I didn't expect her to be in another woman's arms before I could do anything about it.

I didn't know Dreamy had been seeing Mitzi, the curvy blonde bombshell that she had met in a gay bar. Mitzi had been with another woman for a year or so and immediately dumped her for Dreamy. They had been having sex for weeks.

There had never been a moment when I had not trusted Dreamy to do the right thing. What had I been thinking? Hadn't I heard this same story from other girls?

I cried and screamed. I wouldn't listen to her trying to make excuses.

"I'm holding you back," she said. "You've outgrown me and you don't see it yet."

I had been reading lines like that for years in books and plays. I had been to movies about breakups between men and women and seen all those lines played out on the screen. I knew I was hearing the classic break up lies used when one partner has fallen in love with another person and wants to be rid of the current "problem." Now I was the problem. I didn't want to hear it. I wanted to stay in our apartment and never leave her side, which she would not let me do.

Two nights later Dreamy picked me up from work and I saw a red mark on the inside of her arm at the elbow. She seemed relaxed. The tension of the last few days was gone, yet she was a million miles away from me.

"What happened to your arm?"

"The funniest thing happened," Dreamy said slowly. "On the way here I saw my old dealer from Chicago. I pulled over and talked to him for a while. He gave me a free shot. Isn't that funny?"

She was able to drive us home and get up the stairs. I was shaking and couldn't stop crying. I couldn't think of anything but Dreamy becoming a drug addict again. It would be my fault because I was the "problem" she wanted to be rid of.

"If you want to stay with me, this is the way it's going to be," Dreamy said.

I quickly packed a small suitcase and called the only person I could think of who would answer at three in the morning and wouldn't ask any questions before she said yes.

"Althea, I need to stay with you tonight. Can I come over now?"

"Yes," she said and hung up.

I moved out the next morning to protect Dreamy from herself. I didn't want to leave. I hadn't begun to realize I was making a permanent move but I couldn't let Dreamy hurt herself because I was selfishly holding on to her.

I was mad. I was hurt and mad, but I couldn't say anything bad to her on the way out. I loved her too much to be mean to her. I had never been mean to her.

I took the car keys and left my Dreamy days behind.

Chapter Fifteen

New Possibilities, 1968

The silver beaded fringe shook as beautiful black and brainy Billie Britain leaned forward to arrange her full breasts into the little bra for best stage presentation. While checking the fringe panel around her hips in the floor to ceiling mirrors on the closet door, the Largo's newest dancer sighed.

"They sure loved this outfit in Rome. The whole club was done in gold and silver. I looked like a pearl in a jeweled setting. Working in Italy was fine."

The playfulness of Billie's voice made me smile but the smile sagged. I was so jealous I couldn't stand myself. My eyes flew open and I had to hold myself down in the chair. There was only one kind of work Billie would do.

"What do you mean you "worked" in Italy? They have strippers in Italy?"

"Oh, yeaaah baby, and they pay gooood, too," Billie cooed as she wiggled her rear, making the silver fringe sway. She winked to let me know there was much more she could say if she wanted to.

I waited, not moving from the sight of her lips but she didn't say anything else. She just looked at me and smiled that smile thing she did on stage when she looked down and played so innocent. She could see I wanted it but she was going to make me beg for it.

"Billllieeeee, you tease. How did you make that happen? What's it like in Italy?" I squealed.

"I was living in New York and met a girl who had worked in Rome," Billie said as she put on heavy rhinestone earrings that covered her entire ear and reached her shoulders. "She told me to take a few days off and go meet her agent in Italy. I went over and didn't come back for two years. My mother sent my costumes and everything. You'll find strip clubs everywhere there are men, honey. I never felt so appreciated, and that's saying a lot."

Billie laughed and looked at her reflection in the full length mirror. She examined her small waist and round hips. She turned a foot to check the spike heel and smiled as if the whole picture looked delicious to her.

"Sometimes I'm sorry I came back but I wanted to get the duplex for my mom while I had the cash."

With one last check in the mirror, Billie floated down the hall and stairs to wait for her turn on stage leaving me in a brand new world. I was excited and had so many plans to make.

My head was spinning with possibilities. I had always wanted to go to Europe. When I was twelve my mother and I had started a bank account for just that reason. We were going to travel to London together to see if we could find the music halls my grandmother had sung in before she came to Hollywood. We had planned to go to Paris and maybe even Rome.

It was 1968. I felt like a thousand girls had come and gone and here I was, still at the Largo doing three shows a night. There had been some progress though. We now danced topless, which meant we didn't have to wear pasties any longer. No more spirit gum on the tender skin of our nipples or pulling and prying pasties off at the end of each night. No more cleaning the gluey residue off pale pink skin with harsh acetone. I had seen nipples the size of dimes and some the size of tea cup saucers on that same stage. I was ready to try something new and maybe even dangerous.

By St. Patrick's Day, I was down to ninety-seven pounds again. I was wearing a size three pumpkin-colored suit, with a mini-mini skirt and needed to buy some pantyhose at the drug store on Hollywood Blvd.

"You're in show business aren't you," the man before me in line said with no question in his voice.

This time I knew I looked like a showgirl. By now it was a practiced look and one I was good at. Perfectly applied makeup and long false-lashed eyes, bright red hair, expensive clothes from designer boutiques and platform shoes that showed off my legs and size six feet told the story.

"I'm Alexander Dobritch, owner of the second largest international circus in the world. You've probably seen my son on the Ed Sullivan Show. He is the youngest ring-master in history."

He said all of this proudly, with a confident toss of the head and an accent I would soon find out was Bulgarian.

"I'm getting this perfume for my wife. We just had fight and I'm trying to make up with her. She looks so much like you. Look at this picture," he said while opening his wallet to the photo section.

I looked at a small picture of a woman who was dressed flashier than I, lying on her back on top of a live tiger. Both were smiling toward the camera.

I smiled too and said, "Pretty impressive."

This man was bigger than real life. I found him fascinating. In his mid-fifties, he was not truly handsome with his thinning brown hair, but the dark Picasso-like eyes held so much energy, almost electricity, that I didn't want to resist him. There was a European suaveness about him I hadn't encountered before. I found myself thinking if he was single I would go out with him. I was shocked at myself.

"Take this perfume. I'll buy my wife something else. Come have dinner with me now. I have fallen in love with you. What can I say?"

We hadn't reached the front of the line yet and we were already half engaged. He bought the hundred-dollar bottle of Madame Rochas perfume, handing it to me like he wanted to give me the world.

I went up on the Strip with him and ate at a European type restaurant where they knew him well and called him Sasha. He ordered things that were not on the menu, in French. They hurried off to make them for him.

We talked about Bulgaria, the circus life and how wonderful he thought I was. Both Scorpios, with birthdays two days apart, I thought he might be my soul mate. I was swept off my feet.

Sasha could not believe I had never been to Las Vegas. I told him about my superstition that came from my first agent sending out pictures of a girl who had committed suicide while working there, saying they were pictures of me.

"I know all about superstition. A circus lives with superstition. Don't worry. That is not for us. Tell me what you think of me darling. Will you marry me? I'm a resident of Las Vegas. I can divorce in one day. Come to Vegas with me tomorrow."

I did go to Las Vegas with him a few days later. I had to talk it over with Dreamy first. She said I should make him a home-cooked Southern meal to seal the deal. She even offered to do the cooking. He loved it but I didn't think he was any more sealed than he had been.

Sasha didn't want me to work at the Largo anymore so I spoke to Chuck Landis by phone and took a few weeks off. Sasha gave me two thousand dollars to take care of my expenses. I put the envelope with the money into my refrigerator freezer under the ice cube trays. I had no idea what to do with so much money.

He was preparing for his circus to open at the Sports Arena in the heart of Los Angeles but insisted we go up to Vegas, get our wedding license, and look at the site of the new hotel and casino his business partners were building based on the circus.

I met him at his temporary office on Ivar Street just off Hollywood Boulevard late in the afternoon and we flew to Las Vegas five days after we met. I didn't know where Rusty the wife was, but we were going to divorce her while we were up there.

It was a short one-hour flight. He had a room booked for me at Caesar's Palace. I went up to the room, changed into a long black strapless evening gown of silk jersey and met Sasha in the large casino. After dinner we saw a show. Sasha left while the magician was on stage. He came back about fifteen minutes later, sat down and asked me to put something he was holding under the tablecloth into my purse. I reached for it and quietly put ten packets, each marked $5000 on the wrapper, into my purse so no one would notice. My bag wouldn't close but I held onto it tightly.

"I won. Do you gamble?" Sasha asked politely.

"Never have," I answered, well aware of the promise I had made myself in Texas never to gamble with my own money.

"Let's walk around and see who's here then I'll stake you at the Baccarat table. We'll see if you like it," he said.

We left the show. It was obvious to me that he couldn't wait to get back to the gambling tables.

There was a place for us at the Baccarat table, probably because of the hour. The tuxedoed guard held a velvet rope aside so we could pass through. It was only eleven p.m. and Vegas doesn't start getting hot until after midnight, Sasha had told me earlier.

He stood behind me so he could tell me what to do when the cards came my way. The shoe that contained eight decks of cards was eventually passed to me.

I slid the first card out and it went my way. I won money and Sasha was pleased. The next card I drew won money. The shoe stayed with me for three more draws. The last draw I only bet a thousand as Sasha had advised. I didn't mind losing that so much, since I had already won more than twenty five thousand dollars.

It was fun. Everyone in the room looked at the Baccarat table with reverence like it was something special, only for the high-rollers. The players were dressed in eveningwear. The women's jewels kept the elite mood of the table as they sparkled quietly, in the dignified manner of important pieces.

"I haven't taken a woman to that table, who actually won, for years. You deserve something special," Sasha said.

Sasha pulled me along into the furrier's shop that was still open at midnight. He stood a few feet inside, scanning the shop for no more than ten seconds.

"If that black mink fits we'll take it. Try it on darling," he said as he turned to me and the saleslady ran to take it from the display cabinet.

Her attitude said, "This happens once in a blue moon and when it does you better act fast before these new winners change their minds."

"This black swing coat is beautiful isn't it? Look how it fits her. See how full it is in back and the wide collar is very luxurious," she said, as her eyes and bobbing head tried to prompt me into making a verbal expression of joy.

"I've never even tried on one of these. We don't need them very much in Los Angeles," I commented.

Her frown was deep and immediate.

I had thought the coat would be hot and heavy but the satin lining was smooth and cool as I slipped it on. It was light on my shoulders, comforting and deliciously soft.

"I'll take it. Don't bother with a box. She'll wear it," Sasha said as he leaned over and kissed me on the cheek. "I'm very proud of my girl."

He paid with one of the $5000 packets he'd slipped me in the showroom. We left to see the site where Circus Circus would break ground in two days and start building the hotel and casino within the week.

We were to return to Las Vegas on the 17th of April for our wedding, our one-month anniversary, but by then Dobritch wasn't thinking of anything other than saving his circus.

Dr. Martin Luther King Jr. had been shot and killed on Thursday April 4, 1968. The audience size had diminished by fifty percent. Hardly anyone wanted to go to the circus.

Sasha called and wanted me to go down to the Sports Arena immediately. It was only ninety minutes before the show had to begin. His son was trying to get to Los Angeles but the plane had been delayed and wouldn't arrive in time for him to open the circus.

"Come in here" Sasha called from the animal tent. I could hear the tension and worry in his voice.

"Go put on this costume in the dressing room and come right back out here. This is our baby, our smallest elephant, Princess," he said indicating a huge gray form that was stuffing hay into her pink mouth. "You're going to get on her back, a trainer will help you, and ride her around the ring. Make one full circle. She knows the routine. Let her take you to the center ring, flip your left leg over her head and slide off her back. Use this whistle here. Hold the microphone in your right hand. Memorize this" he handed me a card, "and say it with lots of energy. Then blow the whistle loud - real loud and long!" he emphasized.

He looked exhausted. He was pasty gray and his hair was oily. In the short time I had known him he had never looked like that.

"Now the *Grand March* will start" Sasha said, like a conductor, leading me through what he wanted me to do. A spark of energy came into his voice as he explained the grandeur he loved.

"The musicians will begin playing and all the animals and performers will come out for their first introduction to the audience. All but one spotlight will leave you." Sasha put his hand on my arm to reassure me. "Go to the artist tunnel with the red curtain and stride through. Do you understand? Don't think your job is done when the lights are not on you and walk off casually. I want you to stride with purpose and joy, as though the best day in your life is about to begin."

I eagerly nodded and raced off to the dressing room I had seen earlier. He had convinced me I could do it. I put on the pink fishnet hose, the skimpy pink sequin costume, and the little jacket with gold epaulettes on the shoulders. I was living a life dream. My only regret was no one I knew was in the audience to see me and take a picture or two for my mother.

There might not be much of an audience, but there still had to be a ringmaster. People were afraid to go downtown now and they were sad. We all felt helpless and terribly sad that a national leader with King's integrity had been murdered. The Watts Riots had only been three years ago and no one in Los Angeles had forgotten them. Dobritch's greatest fear was that some people might think this was a good time to riot again and his animals might be hurt or let loose to roam the streets of Los Angeles.

I had no idea that even a baby elephant's back was so wide and covered with such tough hairy bristles. They were puncturing my legs as I rode the six year-old Princess around the ring. She wasn't all that tall compared to the adult elephants, and that thrilled me. There is nothing to hang onto when you're on top of an elephant, except the two round bumps on its head. No saddle, no stirrups, no reins to help you stay on, or tell the elephant which way you want to go. I had to trust that the elephant I had just met, knew what to do. The band played as I rode and Princess walked, swaying side to side, around the arena.

I was terrified at the thought of speaking to all those people. There were at least eight thousand people there but the stadium was only half full. Standing in the middle of the center ring, more than twenty spotlights on me, while the sparse audience was silent in semi-darkness, I announced in a loud and clear voice:

LADIES AND GENTLEMEN, CHILDREN OF ALL AGES, WELCOME TO THE DOBRIDGE INTERNATIONAL CIRCUS!!!!! LET THE SHOW BEEEGGGGIIIINNNNN!!!!!!

I blew the whistle hard, directly into the microphone. The band started again, the lights went up revealing colorfully costumed clowns, trapeze artists and riders on horseback, lions, tigers and huge elephants with their trainers walking beside them and beautiful girls in sparkly costumes standing on their backs, all entering the arena in single file for the Grand March. It was the mandatory introduction of all the performers, before individual acts would begin in each of the three rings.

I strode to my exit tunnel, with one spotlight still on me, turned, saluted the audience and disappeared behind the curtain. Being a part of the circus was a spectacular event for me. It was a childhood dream come true.

Two days later Dobritch called me and asked me to meet him at Scandia, an elegant restaurant across the street from the Largo. I left my mother and thirteen year-old sister, who had flown from Boston to Los Angeles for the wedding, and met him there. Sasha was at the far end of the bar waiting. He looked tired and sad, like he really needed the double shot of slivovitz he held in his hand.

We kissed in the European style, on both cheeks. It took him only a minute to say, "I can't marry you now. You don't really care, darling. You wanted to marry me for the money and the glamour. I don't blame you, but now there is nothing. It was wonderful though. We both had a good time. I am sorry, but you did get to visit with your mother and sister and I am sure they will understand."

I don't think I said a word. Just shook my head no and yes at the places he expected and listened to him. Sasha kissed my hand, kissed my cheek, looked into my eyes for a short moment and left me sitting there.

I felt relieved I would get my own life back but I was sick to my heart too. It had all happened so fast. Lesbian, engaged to a man, dumped, lesbian again. We had never had sex or even kissed passionately. I had known Sasha for three weeks and had been consumed into his world for that little while. Then I was bounced out and on my own again. I would never meet another man like Sasha. I was sure there weren't any more.

By May, Dreamy was still happy with Mitzi. She was not taking drugs, as she had threatened, but Mitzi drank heavily and Dreamy joined her. I would get up each Saturday to have breakfast with Dreamy while Mitzi was working as a hair-dresser.

They had been living together since September, cuddled up in my old Hollywood apartment.

I was still recuperating from the sudden breakups with Dreamy and Dobritch. At least it was sudden to me. I moped, buried myself in books and didn't go out for days at a time, except to work back at the Largo.

Dreamy and I tried to preserve our friendship as I was learning how to deal with the women who started making advances toward me now that I was single. She gave me advice on how to handle them at our breakfast meeting. Girls I had known and worked with for months and years suddenly decided they wanted to find out what lesbians did in bed and they wanted to find out with me.

My friend Althea hadn't been at the club for about a year. Johnny had decided she could make more money as a topless waitress than dancing at the Largo. She didn't seem too happy with the job. Her personality was more suited to being a performer than a server as she could tease on stage and still keep her bottom out of pinching range.

Althea was six months pregnant when I moved away from Dreamy. We leased a luxurious two bedroom apartment at the top of the hill on Primrose Avenue in Hollywood. I had always called Althea "the straightest girl I ever met" and she was exactly who I wanted for a roommate now. I knew she would never touch me.

Johnny, her boyfriend and the baby's father, was with his parents in Iran. I didn't know when or if he would be back.

Althea was an extremely private person and had just listened as other dancers explained in great detail how they had been hurt in love or by some family member. She never said much about herself. I had known her long enough that I knew more than most people. She did tell me before we moved in together that she had broken up with Johnny. He had insulted her in a way that she could never forgive.

"Yes, Johnny finally called from Iran and I told him I was pregnant. After all we have been through together in the last two years, he asked me whose child it was. That was the end for me. I'm finished with him."

Johnny was from Teheran and extremely handsome, with lots of dark hair and large brown eyes. He said he was from a wealthy family that owned emerald mines. He worked as a car valet at an exclusive restaurant on the Sunset Strip and made most of his money in tips. Althea had met him and fallen madly in love.

I decided to give Althea a baby shower. It was a first for me. Most of my lesbian friends had not had babies yet as they were still working as strippers.

All the Largo girls came to the shower and showed up with fancy gifts. Two cribs, three strollers, a high chair and enough clothes and soft tiny shoes for five babies came in the door that day.

The phone was in Althea's bedroom and it rang every twenty minutes all afternoon. It was always for Denise, the glamorous, five foot eight inch, blue-eyed platinum blonde, who had been called Miss Hollywood while she was at the Largo. She couldn't dance but she sure could walk great. Denise was there when I started but just stopped coming to work one day. She was so secretive I never got to know her but Althea had kept in contact.

I felt sorry for tall, blonde, delicious Denise who should have been on top of the world with her spectacular good looks. Most of the girls thought there was something weird about her. I guessed this caller might be the reason she seemed so strange and almost afraid.

It was late spring when Diane and I were in the television room at the club, nude under our short silk robes, watching Robert Kennedy speak at the Ambassador Hotel. He was our guy. We were excited and toasting each other with vodka martinis. It was almost midnight and we only had a couple of hours before the night was over.

"What was that? What happened?" Diane squinted at the television set trying to see between the people swarming around Kennedy. "Well, he fell down. No! No!"

Dancers who had been playing Scrabble or reading ran into see what was wrong with Diane. What had made Diane scream so loudly? She could only point toward the black and white television screen.

"Robert Kennedy has been shot. He is lying on the floor of the Ambassador Hotel here in Los Angeles," we heard the news commentator say.

It couldn't be happening again. It was just two months after Martin Luther King Jr. I didn't want to believe it, couldn't believe it.

A girl who looked very much like me was our house guest for several days in July. She had the same long strawberry blonde wavy hair, same freckles and blue eyes but was a few inches taller than me and rail thin. She called herself Worth and had worked with Althea as a topless waitress Althea had invited her to stay with us as Worth said she had given up her apartment and was on her way back home to New York City.

"Let's go to Rome and become movie stars," Worth said as I was driving down Wilshire Boulevard toward the apartment in my clover green Volkswagen bug.

I made a screeching right turn into the Robinson's department store parking lot, parked and looked at her.

"When?"

Worth blinked, shook her head, and laughed in surprise. "Do you have a passport? Can you just go? Are you kidding me?"

"I don't have a passport but I'll apply for one tomorrow morning. Why? Can you just go? What will we do?"

I liked Worth. She was fun to be with and I thought she would be a great traveling companion. What an outrageous duo we would make on the streets of Europe. The Italians would love us.

The layer of sadness that had settled over the United States after the assassinations of our leaders was dark and heavy. I wanted to go somewhere else. I wanted to go anywhere it wouldn't feel like another disaster could catch us off guard and kill someone wonderful at any moment, if there was someplace like that.

"We'll go to Rome and get someone to take us to the people who make movies. Lots of American actors go there and become big stars. Let's go in September. I should be able to save enough by then. You have the money already?" she asked.

"A few thousand dollars saved," I admitted. "I played around with the idea of being straight for a few weeks, met a guy and won money with him in Las Vegas. Diane Lewis told me to pay off my credit cards with it and I did. Now I just have the rest of the money and nothing to tie me down. How about you?"

"I can get it," she said.

We chose September 1st to take the flight from New York to Rome. I would have been single exactly one year to the day. I got a one-way ticket to Rome with a three-day layover in New York City on the advice of my theatrical agent, Miles Ingalls.

Miles was more than helpful. He had once been a big time agent but now had a small one-man office on South Beverly Drive in Beverly Hills. He loved to take pretty girls to lunch, across the street at Ma Maison, and show them off like it was the "good old days."

Miles arranged for me to stay at a hotel in New York, courtesy of a friend who owned part of Hialeah Racetrack in Florida. He gave me a Zeiss Icon camera and said, "Have people take pictures of you every day. They'll be useful when you get back to Los Angeles and we want publicity shots." He was 'old school' and still had some Hollywood tricks up his sleeve.

A client of his was returning home for a few months and Miles arranged for me to stay in his apartment while I was in Rome. It was just four doors off the stylish Via Veneto. Miles arranged everything for me and that meant I must really be going to Europe.

I couldn't think of anything but my trip and wouldn't listen seriously to anyone who tried to get me to think "reasonably." Dreamy said she was terrified. My mother was all for me going to Rome, and perhaps Paris. That was good enough for me. She cautioned me to bring lots of money. That was not a problem.

Althea went into labor in early August. I took the place of the daddy in almost every way. I raced her to the hospital down Wilshire Boulevard as she lay in the back seat of my Volkswagen bug. I held her hand in the labor room as we waited for her to dilate. I waited with the fathers-to-be while she was in the delivery room. We had a beautiful healthy baby boy she named Craig to take home.

Althea thought I was crazy to take off with a woman I hardly knew.

"I don't even know Worth very well, Brandy. I only worked with her a couple of weeks and I don't know anything about her. What if she leaves you in the middle of Europe all by yourself or gets involved with some weird people there? What will you do?"

"I am going to take two of my costumes and the music to go with them so if I get into trouble I can work there and at least buy a plane ticket home. Miles has already set it up for me to meet an agent in Paris, so I have contacts. Don't worry so much," I answered.

Three days before I was to meet Worth in New York, she called.

"Brandy, I feel so terrible. The New York police are looking for me and I am hiding in another state. I can't leave the country now. I am sure they would take my passport at the airport and hand me over to the cops if I tried. I'm sorry. I can't talk anymore, goodbye."

I never saw or heard from her again.

Hysterical was the word for the next three days. Dreamy said this was a sign that I needed to stay home.

"Go to Las Vegas for six weeks, Boobie. When you come back tell everyone you went to Europe and had a great time. Who's gonna know the difference?" Mitzi asked.

My beautiful mother said, "Why do you have to travel with someone else? Mind your own business and you'll do fine on your own, that way you can do whatever you want, whenever you want. Have a wonderful time and don't forget to take a box of See's Candy for the flight."

I still wanted to go to Europe. I needed something new to think about. Maybe the Italians weren't killing their best men.

Chapter Sixteen

New York City, 1968

Entering the plane for the flight from Los Angeles to New York my mind was on keeping my eyes open and my mouth shut. I immediately spilled champagne all over my seatmate's beautiful navy blue suit while trying to sit down and my mouth popped open to apologize. I was carrying the black mink coat Dobridge had given me in Las Vegas. It just nudged his wine glass which flew into the poor guy's lap. How do you carry a bulky coat like that in an airplane without getting into trouble?

I had never been to New York City – never traveled anywhere alone. An upgrade to first class for the flight through some highly connected friend of Miles employed by the airline was a lovely surprise. When all the cleaning up was done, I settled down and drank a champagne toast to "success" with my seatmate, Mr. Plough.

As the trip progressed, we talked, ate and drank our way across the west and Midwest. Plough was about sixty, grey and paunchy, with a comforting air of fatherly knowledge and authority. He lived in the United States six months of the year and in Israel the other six months due to his large international corporation's needs.

After our T-bone steak dinner and red wine, he taught me how to dip cigars in brandy before smoking them. As we smoked leisurely and drank from the deep snifters of brandy, Plough had a warning for me.

"Since you're going to be wandering around Europe and don't know where you are going to wind up, I have to tell you this. Don't let anyone talk you into going to the Middle East. I go for business and to visit friends a couple of times a year and I know two men, very wealthy men, who I could sell you to, right now, for fifty thousand dollars on the hoof."

I leaned up in my seat and turned to get a better look at his face.

"What do you mean, on the hoof? What does that mean? How could you sell me to anyone?"

The pretty stewardess refilled snifters in the first class cabin and emptied crystal ashtrays. I could see she was fascinated by our conversation.

"If you're in Saudi Arabia or someplace like that, I could walk down the street with you and a man might come over and casually ask how much money I would take to sell you to him. You could be looking in a shop window minding your own business. If I wanted I could name a price and after receiving it just walk away and leave you with this stranger. Yes, some people do walk around with that much money on them in the Middle East. You wouldn't know the language or exactly where you were and the guy would be a native of the area with ties to people there. You could scream and yell all you wanted to and no one would help as he pulled you away calling you his stupid wife."

Plough took a slow drag from his cigar. His words and his sad expression alarmed me.

"That's just how it works. Be sure you can trust any man you walk down the street with or have coffee in a café. It could even happen in Europe if you're in the wrong place, so be careful."

For the first time since my decision to leave Los Angeles, I was afraid. He was serious. I realized I might not be able to control everything on this trip. Someone could force himself into my life without my permission or even my knowledge until it was too late.

By the time we reached New York and our seven hour flight was over, Plough and I were good friends. He gave me his business card and looked at me with a worried frown.

"If you get into trouble, let me know. If you need anything, let me know. Just call."

I felt good having that bit of paper in my wallet like a little life preserver.

Mr. Musi, my host, had thoughtfully sent a car to the airport for me. I met him when I arrived at the Hampshire House, a thirty-seven story residential hotel in Manhattan, directly across from the Park. My room on the nineteenth floor had a green and yellow September view of Central Park and the city that was breathtaking.

Miles had said his friend's name was Antony Musi but when he called my room and I met him at the bar, he asked me in a flat almost expressionless voice to call him Tony.

"You're the redhead. I'm Tony. It's late and you're tired. Go do the tourist thing tomorrow and have dinner with me after. Dress."

He sounded rough and curt but the charcoal suit he wore was a tailor's masterpiece. The material was light, the cut clean and crisp. Tony had a swarthy complexion and unexpressive black eyes set in a thin sharp face. There were no smile lines around his eyes although he must have been in his fifties. I thought he looked like what he probably was, a slender, well-dressed thug.

"Make a day of it," he said as he pressed two folded one hundred dollar bills into my hand and left me sitting at the bar alone.

I was a tourist on my own in New York City and did all the tourist things the next day. I climbed the tight and narrow spiral staircase into the crown of Lady Liberty, Mother of Exiles, in New York Harbor. Even though the guard tried to herd us toward the downward spiral, after the hot crowded climb, I stood at one of the immense windows in her crown looking toward the Atlantic Ocean savoring my moment. I thought about my grandmothers and grandfathers who had died before I was born and how they had first seen this monument from far out in the Atlantic Ocean. I was sure most of the other climbers were reflecting about their families as well.

I rode one of the many elevators to the top of the Empire State Building. The morning before, I had been in the smoggy grey and beige of a warm Los Angeles day. Now at the tip top of New York City were cool clear strong breezes and pure white clouds in a pale blue sky. It was almost fall in a city that had four seasons. I loved it. But even this would have been better if I had someone special to share it with. I took a deep breath and tried to push thoughts of Dreamy out of my head.

Later that afternoon I was walking down Fifth Avenue, ambling along, looking at the tall buildings and beautiful shop windows. I loved New York.

A raggedy man with long grey hair, a big belly and a greasy face walked toward me. He was no more than three feet away from me when he tugged a huge, live, grey and black rat from his jacket pocket and flung it by the tail in front of my face.

"See my rat?" he sang out, and belched loudly as he leaned toward me.

I choked down the scream that rose to my throat. I didn't want to open that pathway to germs and parasites and kept my lips crushed together. I turned to look at him with the poison stare I had perfected to use on men who did not understand the meaning of "NO." How many gawking women and children had he terrorized with that trick, I wondered.

He was gleeful as his cloth wrapped hand put his pet back in the jacket pocket where it sheltered. Half a long New York block away he kept turning to see if I would have any more reaction. I was frozen to the sidewalk with fear. I was dizzy. I heard "See my rat," over and over. People on the sidewalk with me now looked like the rat. They were all dressed in black and grey.

I was wearing black fur, too. I had been afraid to leave my coat in an unguarded hotel room.

That evening my host, Tony, who owned an apartment at The Hampshire House, met me in the lobby bar wearing a tuxedo with black bow tie. He took me to a dinner club in New Jersey, saying he was a "sort of partner" in the business. We were in the back seat as his driver took us over the George Washington Bridge from Manhattan to Jersey City and I realized Tony's face had no life in it. His whole demeanor was stiff, including his walk and his voice.

The club looked like a Las Vegas show room with a dark red curtain at the front of the stage, rich black leather booths near the front, and tables in the rear. Tony was welcomed like a conquering hero. He was escorted to the center booth with the highest back protection that I thought was probably bulletproof. A chilled bottle of champagne rested in an ice bucket next to the table.

Tony introduced me, but did not mention the names of several men who came to say how happy they were to see him. They looked like they were cut from his same mold; dark, forbidding and dangerous.

I was only there because I trusted Miles Ingalls and I began to wonder how much I trusted him. Miles was generous with his help and his contacts. But how did he know tough guys like this? And how did he think I would fit into this picture? As escort or as Tony's bed partner? I couldn't imagine gentle, sweet Miles with these gangsters.

I could tell it was my job to play the part of "glamorous bimbo who is crazy for Tony." I had on a floor length peacock blue silk with deep cleavage and my mink coat. At least that made me look like an expensive bimbo.

He also introduced me to the clear Greek cordial called ouzo. We drank most of a bottle while we watched the crooner sing Italian songs. *That's Amore* and *O Solo Mio* were big hits as the audience sang along with the handsome young singer.

Tony's lips curved upward a very small twitch as he started to relax. That's when I started to worry about what was going to happen when the evening ended back at the hotel. I wondered if I was playing my part of adoring female too believably and that I would be asked to perform my thanks at the hotel.

The singer came to the table after his show and respectfully thanked Tony for being in the audience that evening. He sat down when asked and accepted a drink from the bottle of ouzo when it was offered. He did not look at me or speak to me except when we were introduced and when he said goodbye.

Tony opened my door and walked into the beautiful lavender and creamy-white room after me. He sat on the lavender velvet sofa.

"Come and stroke my forehead," he said.

I didn't say a word. When I was seated, Tony leaned over and put his head and a shoulder in my lap. He closed his eyes. I was nervous as I gently passed my hand over his forehead and then up to the thick dark hair. I could see my hand shake and he must have felt it too.

Tony tired of this hoax when he saw I was not going to make any amorous advances. He sat up and rose to leave.

Tony put five one-hundred dollar bills next to the television set on the desk. Walking toward the door, he said, "Be a good girl. I'll see you for dinner tomorrow at seven. Dress." He closed the door softly. I spent the next day shopping for another evening dress that would not add much weight to my suitcase. I had not expected anything from Tony. He was already paying for my hotel room as a favor to Miles. The least I could do was use his money to look special that evening.

The more expensive the gown the lighter was the material. I decided on a black silk jersey cocktail length with a deep cowl neckline and three-quarter sleeves.

Dinner was at a small, refined Italian restaurant in Manhattan. I was again expected to play the role of bimbo in front of friends or associates who came to the table to greet Tony and express their wishes for his continued good health and happiness. It seemed very formal to my Southern California ears. The only time I had heard people talk like this was at Mickey's Showbar in Cleveland Ohio and I knew what that meant. Tony must be a made man, a man with power, a "big gun" in the Mafia.

I smiled, nodded in agreement with his every remark and looked at him as if he were the finest man on earth. I did not ask questions about his business interests or his personal life but I was awfully curious about him.

Tony left me at my door when we returned to the Hampshire House. It was a relief to be myself and alone. I had worked hard at being the perfect bimbo that night. I had not wanted to be alone the last few days, but now my solitude was a treat. I felt like my face was going to crack from hours of over-smiling, over-yessing and over-fondly looking at Tony. I was ready for the late afternoon flight to Italy the next day. I wanted to learn something, to see something new and breathe different air.

Chapter Seventeen

Zucchini and Pizza: Rome, 1968

The American sailor, who sat next to me on the flight from New York and during the train ride into Rome from the outlying airport, helped me into the taxi and told the driver where to take me. I had no idea we had American naval bases in Italy but he said we did and that's where he was going.

Confused and tired from so many hours in the airplane without sleep, and the time change, I leaned back for the short ride. It was afternoon. The three and four-story buildings around the train station were golden, faded yellow, and ochre in the sunlight. I could feel my shoulders relax in the warmth of the late summer Roman day.

Suddenly, at the first stoplight, the back doors were yanked open. Two middle-aged Italian men jumped in on either side of me. I couldn't understand a word but from the ecstatic facial expressions, quick fluid hand gestures and bodies wiggling on both sides, I could tell they wanted to say something. They screamed at me in the most friendly way, like they had always known me, and wasn't it great that I was home?

"Tell you friends leave," the taxi driver yelled to be heard over the ruckus. "The light, she change."

I looked behind. A taxi with three wide-open doors was in back of mine. Its driver was yelling as he hurried toward us, fists tight and swinging.

"These are not my friends. Make them get out of the car," I shouted while trying to protect myself from grasping hands and the lips exploring my neck.

"Bella, Bella, Madonna, Carissima, Roma, Roma, Via Veneto, Bella, Divina, Sola? Amore Mio, Te Amo, Te Amo, Stella Mio."

What were these men saying? Some of the words I thought I recognized but why was this guy's hand on my thigh? I felt a hand trying to get under my bra strap.

"Get these men out of here! No, no, go away!" I pleaded with the taxi driver, yelling and pushing the men out at the same time.

Horns blew and other drivers slowed down to see what was happening. With both hands, I lashed out against the invasion of my mini-skirt and fought to keep hold of my purse and my bra at the same time.

My taxi driver jumped out of the car and with the burly driver of the other taxi, dumped the Italian would-be lovers onto the street. Looking at me like all this bother had been my fault, the driver returned to his seat and drove toward my borrowed *pensione* near the Via Veneto. The two happy intruders were still in the street blowing kisses and singing loudly as we left.

Soon the driver made a rough stop in front of the grey flat façade of the building I was to stay in. It was on a narrow side street, four doors down from the often star-studded sidewalk cafes and nightclubs of the famous Via Veneto.

My first look at the white iron double bed made me take an involuntary step backward. The mattress had a wide, deep, body length dip in the center that made it look like a canoe. I knew a mattress had to be very old to look like that but the sheets and blanket seemed clean.

I decided to sleep on top of the thin green blanket, completely dressed in a long sleeved tee shirt and a soft pair of blue pajamas and socks. I spread a full skirt on top of the blanket, wrapped a folded skirt in a tee shirt to make a little pillow and put Kleenex in my ears to keep out unseen but possible cockroaches. I covered myself with the fur coat and, finally, slept.

Baby Ruth chocolate candy bars and two bags of Planters peanuts, purchased at Kennedy Airport in New York and meant to last for weeks had to stand in for breakfast, lunch and dinner. I stayed in my room for two days, only leaving to go to the shower and bathroom about fifty feet down the hall.

The room was a large square and had probably been the main living room at some time. The walls were vaguely white. I was sure they had not been painted since the building went up. Two magnificently tall and wide windows opened onto the little street below.

One wall had a few shelves covered with cereals and macaroni in open boxes, a few wine glasses, cups and plates. There was also a little sink and a hot plate. A small wooden table covered by a bright blue and yellow cloth with two mismatched chairs, were in the middle of the room. I could live there if I had to but I didn't want to.

I was paying forty dollars a week for this room which included maid service and was in such a prime location, that it seemed worth trying to work around the bed problem.

Hanging out the window and peering down two floors toward the Via Veneto was enough excitement for a while. I was afraid of the Romans.

I had seen the fruit stands on the corners full of red and orange cut melons, and the fancy stores along the Via Veneto when I arrived in the taxi. Rome was so different from what I imagined. It seemed rough and soft at the same time.

Two days after arriving in Rome the smell of frying garlic and onions drove me out to look at the city. I was famished, and ready to try my luck in Rome once again. Following my nose, I ran down the two flights of wide grey marble stairs and walked timidly out to the street.

The September weather in Rome was about eighty degrees, sunny and heavy with humidity. Wearing a baby blue micro-mini skirt, bare legs in strappy silver high heels and a light silk blouse, I was still sweating. My hair started to frizz which made it stand up higher on my scalp and grow wilder at the sides.

I looked like a typical tourist in 1968 Los Angeles. But this was 1968 in Rome, a city that carried more than two thousand years of setting morality restrictions on one shoulder and fashion standards for the world on the other.

I turned right, my nose telling me where to go. Reaching the tree-lined Via Veneto I turned left and passed the famous Excelsior Hotel. Two blocks down, just inside a small restaurant, I saw a steam table with green and golden brown zucchini that looked and smelled just like my mother's, fried in butter with garlic and onions, sprinkled with paprika. It was familiar in every way and a woman holding a huge serving spoon beckoned me to enter.

"*Mangiare! Mangiare!*" rang out to the street as she smiled and waved her spoon at me.

The zucchini had called to me from three blocks away and I had answered. The steam table also held meats in luscious thick red sauce, plump clams in rich creamy white sauce, shiny spaghetti in olive oil and parmesan cheese, and broiled tomatoes with golden brown cheese on top. I smiled at the stout server and pointed to the zucchini, salad, meat and some roasted potato and received the plate piled high after paying at the register.

Standing at the bar and eating with the noisy smiling people who were already there, I felt successful. I had found a way to eat in a foreign country. The lettuce and tomato were so fresh and crisp they tasted like they had been picked that morning.

Chewing enthusiastically and looking at the other patrons I saw that I was one of very few women in the room and the only one who showed the slightest bit of thigh. Not one bare knee could I see, and no uncovered elbows. The men had on dark jackets over white shirts even though it was boiling in the crowded restaurant.

I found out that it takes nerve to do well in a new place. I hadn't had much of that before I left Los Angeles but I was learning quickly.

I felt like I hadn't spoken to a woman in years. If that continued it would be painful. There were so many men but I was feeling lonesome for the sound and company of women.

Not everyone was happy with the way I ate. The next evening, after walking in the Borghese Villa and gardens and wandering in Roman plazas all day, I looked into a small restaurant and saw they served pizza. I knew pizza. My aunt in Boston had introduced me to pizza in 1955. It had not been popular on the West Coast then and I loved it.

It was about six o'clock, early for a Roman dinner, so the restaurant had only one other customer. He was a distinguished looking gentleman with silver hair and eyebrows and a matching full and wide silver mustache.

My small cheese and olive pizza arrived steaming hot and juicy and I was starving again. I started to pick up the first piece with my hand as Aunt Mary had taught me at Rocky's in Boston when I heard three chimes from across the room. I tore my eyes from the pizza to see the silver haired man across the restaurant tapping his water glass gently with a knife to attract my attention.

Once sure he had my eye, he very precisely showed me his knife and then the fork and proceeded to cut a small bite from his imaginary pizza. He opened his mouth slightly, mimed inserting the pizza and chewed slowly. At the end of his performance he looked at me with a slight smile and one eyebrow raised as if to ask, "Did you understand?"

How kind that was of him. He had noticed an obvious tourist and had gone out of his way to make sure she did not make a fool of herself in public. I was glad I had traded the short skirt of yesterday for a pair of light slacks. What signs would he have made about the micro mini? This was Italy and there would be other pizzas and situations along the way when I would need to think carefully and assess the situation before I acted.

The sparkling water of the Trevi Fountain in central Rome had drawn visitors for over two hundred years but the hordes of Americans and other Europeans that admired the fountain during the summer were gone. I felt lucky that afternoon. I was one of the few to be cooled by the water flowing into the basin in front of Neptune and his sea horses.

The rush of blonde and redheaded Scandinavians would not arrive until October and November, so my red hair, in the throng of brunettes, brought attention toward me as I stood trying to capture the scene with my little camera.

"Let me take your photo, *Signorina*," said a man's soft voice close to my ear.

I turned and was only inches from blue-green eyes that looked directly into mine. He smiled and I could feel my shoulders relax.

"You are here alone, Cara? This is a terrible mistake. Have a coffee with me and we can look at the fountain together. But first let me take a beautiful picture for your memory book."

His voice was melodious and he spoke slowly so I could understand his English through the lovely Italian accent. I didn't know people still spoke so flowery in Europe.

His smile was gentle and sweet. The light brown hair with streaky blond highlights gave him a boyish, innocent façade. I handed him the camera and let him pick me up. He was right. I am sure I did look lonesome and vulnerable. I had been in Rome for over a week and had not had a conversation with anyone since arriving.

"My name is Marco but yours can only be Venus."

He dribbled on like that for a short time as we drank little cups of espresso and then I wanted to move on without him. I reached for my purse and started to stand up when he pressed my wrist down with two fingers that felt like steel bars.

"I can never let you go, Cara mia. But let us walk along now."

His voice didn't have quite the same soft melody now and I was sure I wanted to be rid of him. He sounded too sure of himself, too confident he had some claim on me that would make me do as he wanted.

I started to walk and Marco walked beside me. I stopped responding to his comments, thinking he might see he was being ignored and I wouldn't have to say anything unkind to him. As I was thinking that, Marco grabbed my wrist and pulled me into a building with open double doors and up a grand staircase into what looked like a ballroom, full of gilt and mirrors.

A man who was speaking on the telephone was in the far corner and Marco, still holding on to me, walked us toward him. He stopped about fifty feet away from the caller.

"Stay here. I'll just be a moment," Marco said firmly. As he turned away from me to be closer to the phone caller, I could see his smile fade and turn into a harsh expression. He made quick hand motions to the man on the phone and then he jutted his chin toward me.

I spun and ran down the stairs, out the open doors and down the street. He ran out after me and I ran for several blocks without looking back. I ran turning and twisting in different directions in case he was still following me. I pulled a pink and white flowered silk scarf from my purse, covered my head with it and went into a small church that was far from the fountain where I had started.

There were several women, all dressed in black, sitting and praying. Judging from their tight squints and pursed mouths they didn't like the way I looked but I was not going to be pushed out of my temporary refuge by the stares of a few viciously pious women.

Sitting there for about an hour, looking at my surroundings, I kept an eye on the main doors, the side doors and the altar. I thought about the situation I had put myself into. Dreamy had told stories of dancers she knew who had taken up with people they wouldn't have normally looked at while they were on the road. They were lonesome and they had been hurt or killed.

I felt so stupid to be caught off guard like that. I knew better. I had listened to Dreamy's stories over and over as she had new audiences to tell them to.

I thought of Brava Tutti, the young Italian stripper in Houston, Texas who had given me the stage name Brandy Wilde. She had been kidnapped and held for many days before she could escape. I remembered thinking at the time that could never happen to me, then gangster Tony Boots in Cleveland tried to kidnap me and take me to Brazil to make me marry him.

I wondered where Worth was at this moment. I hoped she wasn't in jail or trouble somewhere. If she had joined me on this trip as we had planned, I sure wouldn't be sitting here waiting for danger to pass. Maybe we would have been protection for each other.

I thought about Lorna Love in Cleveland and how she had disappeared into thin air. No one had heard from her after she left Mickey's Showbar in the middle of the evening dressed in just a low-cut pink evening gown and her high heels. I had sent her costumes to the agent but there was no missing person's report filed anywhere unless Lillian had done it. I hoped so. I felt bad for never having thought to ask the police about her. I prayed for God to protect me, and make me smarter. I made sure the scarf was on good and tight when I left the church.

"Miles, Miles, I can't stand it here anymore," I shouted over transatlantic phone cables a few days later. "These men are too much for me. That director you asked me to call, took me to dinner, but then in the middle of my salad he reached over the table and bit my bottom lip and blood dripped all over my sweater. Then he had the nerve to insult my poor sweater by saying it looked awful on me.

"Then a guy I met at the Fountain of Trevi a few days ago was weird and possessive with me too. To top it off, today I saw his face in the International Herald Tribune in an article about white slavery in Italy. He had just been caught along with some other men. I can't stay here anymore. There are just too many men. I am alone and these guys are too aggressive for me. Do you have any ideas? I don't have anyone else to ask. Tell me what you would do."

"Take it easy baby. Have a nice glass of wine, maybe two. Try to relax," Miles crooned from more than 6,000 miles away. "Pack your things and go to the train station. Get a private sleeping room for the overnight trip to Paris. I'll call Bernard Hilda, my former partner, and you go to see him when you get there. He'll have some ideas for you. I'm going to call a little hotel, near the Sorbonne, for you. I'll let Bernard know you're going to be there.

"This hotel is in the middle of everything and the staff speaks English. When you arrive in Paris tell the taxi driver to go to Hotel Central on Rue Champollion. A nice room will be waiting for you. It's midnight here. I'm going back to sleep now but it will all be ready by the time you reach Paris."

I did exactly what he said. I packed immediately, left a note of thanks to my absent host and went to the train station to book a couchette and wait for my trip to Paris to begin. I was excited again and hoped that all the wonderful things people had told me about Paris were true.

The train left Rome at seven in the evening. It took fifteen hours to reach Paris but it was an easy trip. My private compartment was a tiny brown and olive green cell. The seat attached to the wall pulled out to become a bed and there was a small basin in the corner for washing. I slept well despite my excitement, the noise, and constant rocking of the train.

I awoke early and watched the French countryside pass by from my own velvet curtained window. Huge rolls of yellow hay dotted field after field. Horses stood in the cool morning sunlight, swishing their tails and resting their heads on the fences.

I ate buttered croissants and half a loaf of French bread with apricot jam and drank the creamy hot chocolate the porter served. It was heaven. I was warm, well fed and traveling in luxury to what I knew would be the most beautiful city in the world.

Chapter Eighteen

The Pretty and the Pigalle

"*Oui mademoiselle,*" "*Bien sur mademoiselle,*" and "Whatever you like, *Mademoiselle,*" were phrases like honey to my ears. These were sweet French words and phrases that were a little formal and reserved but most of all safe. The French language did not feel hot, staccato and insistent like Italian. It was cool, liquid and crisply melodic.

Just one block off Boulevard Saint-Michel and a block from the Sorbonne University, the small and inexpensive Hotel Central was in the middle of student and bohemian life in the Latin Quarter. Miles had arranged for a room with private bath and continental breakfast for twenty-five francs, five dollars a day. When I saw the hotel's bright little lobby and breakfast area I was grateful and my trust in Miles restored.

I registered and received a large brass key from Madame Simon, the hotel owner, who had obviously been a beauty in her youth. She was now gray- haired and her skin was softly wrinkled about the eyes and neck but her bone structure was classic and aquiline. Her blue eyes were sharp yet kind, and when she smiled at me, I liked her immediately. This was much better than Rome.

I gave her my passport as she requested and it disappeared under the counter. As I stood there waiting and worrying about her keeping my passport and when I would get it back, a short, squarely built man with a little beard approached the desk and put his small hairy hand on my shoulder.

"You are Brandy something, yes?"

I had been enjoying the feminine loveliness of Madame Simon's eyes and figure. I frowned, as I turned to look into the small, masculine, black eyes that glinted beside me.

"Yes, you are! I saw your show at the Largo last week in Los Angeles. How happy for me that you are here. Let me take you to a coffee. Have you seen the Avenue des Champs-Élysées? We could go there?" he asked with an accent I couldn't place.

He had said just the right thing to seduce me to go outside. Somebody here knew me and wanted to show me the Avenue des Champs-Élysées.

Tired, yet excited to be in Paris after a lifetime of waiting, I put my suitcase in my room and flew downstairs to catch a taxi and run off with this stranger who didn't feel like a stranger because he had seen me nearly naked and had recognized me in a foreign country with my clothes on.

It was the middle of the afternoon and the sun was shining on Paris. We drank strong black coffee from tiny cups and ate French pastry with raspberries and whipped cream as we sat outdoors on the Avenue des Champs-Élysées. I felt like I was sitting inside a postcard, staring at the people who walked along with their shoulders back and heads held so proudly. It was style. It looked like they were almost aware of being on display on what I thought must be the most beautiful street in the world.

I hardly heard a word my companion, Tufic, was saying. I know he said he was from Beirut, Lebanon and that he had loved my show. "Oh, yes. I remember that orange scarf. And what you did with it. Marvelous." He slowly closed his eyes as he raised thick eyebrows and looked as if he were trying to see me pass the silk over my breasts one more time.

Who was this guy anyway? Hadn't I learned anything from my Roman experience? I was exasperated with myself and torn between leaving him here to go back to the hotel by myself and lingering a while longer on the Champs.

We walked toward the Arc de Triumph, looking in shop windows and lingering at many, especially the Guerlain perfume shop which involved all of my senses. I could smell, taste, see, feel and even hear the green, gold and amber floral and citrus scents. I couldn't get enough of this street, the lights, the magnificent 19th century buildings and the atmosphere. It was twilight by the time we reached the Arc and went into Le Drug Store.

Tufic told me the French were having a fit because the tall neon sign with the name of the large shop that sold everything, from pharmaceuticals to diamonds, was in English.

"Oh, la, la, la, the French have a government department just to protect their French language from pollution by foreign words," he said with a head waggle as if making fun of them.

You see, I told myself, he can be interesting. It'll be just fine.

"Let me buy you something beautiful," Tufic pleaded. "Do you like those nice gold earrings? What about that watch?"

My smile drooped. Oh, no. I knew what that could mean. He was going to think he deserved something for his "kindness" and I didn't want any more trouble. He was from a culture that thought women should be at home taking care of their husbands and children; only whores danced on stage in Hollywood. Buying coffee was one thing, but a gift of jewelry or perfume was different.

"I don't see anything I want, Tufic. I'm fine. Really," I said with a smile which I hoped would get him off the "let's barter for sex" track.

It was dark when we took a taxi back to the hotel. I was exhausted, full of pastry and just wanted to sleep.

Tufic tried to take my room key from me while we were in the lobby. I made sure Madame Simon, who all these hours later was still behind the reception desk, saw me holding on to it. I wanted her to know I was not allowing him to come into my room.

"No, Tufic, you were charming, and it was a wonderful afternoon, a beautiful day. But now it's over and I'm tired."

I wanted to be nice but I hadn't had a moment to myself since I'd arrived after a sixteen hour train trip. As I turned and climbed a few stairs I heard the most awful yowling behind me.

"Noooooooooowaaaaaaaaayiiiiiiiiiiiinoooooooooooo uuuugggggghhh," Tufic wailed.

I fled up the remaining stairs, quickly went into my room and pushed the one small sliding metal lock on the thin wooden door. Looking at that little lock I thought about the stout chains and dead bolts on my New York hotel door. Well, one can't have New York and Paris at the same time, I decided.

Tufic screamed and cried outside my door. He mumbled and then he yelled. I could hear Tufic clearly for several minutes as I stood tensely just behind the door and wished for him to leave. I couldn't sit on the bed because I would be too easy to jump on if the lock failed to hold him out in the hall.

Silence.

I was sure Madame Simon had asked him to be quiet or leave or something. She didn't seem to be the type who would stand for him bothering her other patrons for too long.

He must have gone to a bar and had a few drinks because about one o' clock in the morning, he started pounding on my door and yelling louder than before. He was in a threatening mood now.

"Let me in there you whore, you. I know what to do with you. I'll fuck every hole in your body. Twice. Let me in. Let me in there. Who's in there with you? Let me in."

It seemed to go on for hours. The telephone in my room rang and rang. The night guard kept calling from the reception desk, begging me to let my boyfriend into the room or at least open the door and talk to him. After the first few calls, I refused to answer. I sat on the little wooden desk chair with my feet pressed against the door waiting for Tufic to go away.

By two in the morning I was too tired to care. Tufic had started groaning in what was probably Lebanese and the guard had drained his supply of English long ago. As long as the lock held I was satisfied. The door rattled when Tufic pounded on it and I didn't know how long it would hold together.

I heard a man in the hall yelling at Tufic in some language that was not French. Someone stomped along the hall and threw

Tufic down the stairs. The sound of him hitting the walls and screaming as he landed hard on the tile in front of the reception desk competed with the shattering slam of a room door. It was quiet. I slept on clean, crisp, white sheets.

The next morning, trying to make myself look as small and dignified as possible, dressed all in black, I cautiously went downstairs for the promised breakfast. Was there anyone with a heavy beard lurking around the three little tables? Madame Simon ignored me, which I thought was probably the sophisticated way French hoteliers handled such things. I was sure it was not the first time something like that had happened in her hotel.

Two young and very skinny men drinking coffee looked up and nodded hello. I was both embarrassed and starving.

I had never heard of a continental breakfast. At this hotel, like the train, it was two croissants, a long lovely piece of freshly baked baguette, unsalted butter, and apricot jam, with a huge cup of coffee or hot chocolate. It was served in the tiny lobby by Alma, the chambermaid, before the rooms were vacated and she had to change the beds and clean.

Alma had one long black braid and carried a key ring displaying the Communist hammer and sickle that she hung prominently from her apron pocket. I was shocked to see anyone so comfortable wearing that symbol. In the United States we were at war with the Communists in North Viet Nam and in a cold, tactical war with the Soviet Union. I soon learned that France had a legitimate Communist political party that represented thousands of French citizens.

Sustained by French bread, fat, sugar and caffeine, I joined the swollen river of strolling students on the Boulevard Saint-Michel. Strolling was a favorite Parisian pastime and I could see why.

No matter where I was in Paris or what time of day it was, as I looked around, I could see something magnificent, something extraordinary that I would never see in America: a businessman standing on the bus in a well-cut black suit, black face covered with a dot and dash pattern of tribal scars, wearing an English bowler hat and leaning on a large umbrella; the crepe stand on the corner with the woman who never spoke but filled the thinnest of warm crepes with delicious sugar and butter and sold them for two francs apiece; the architecture of buildings that were older than the United States.

I was struck by the sweet toasty smell of roasting chestnuts that filled the boulevard as I turned into the Muse de Cluny, which was a block from my hotel. I had only heard about that smell in Christmas songs and here it was.

My mother had urged me to see the huge, red, five hundred year-old *Lady and the Unicorn* tapestries. She said they were considered some of the finest art works of the Middle Ages and they were right here. When I saw them I felt like I was fulfilling one of my mom's long held dreams.

After three or four days of taking city tours and seeing so many beautiful sites I was very blue. Seeing all these wonderful things alone depressed me. What was I going to do with myself? I couldn't be a stripper much longer. I was twenty- seven and in my prime but I would soon be too old to make a living from revealing my body to the public. What else could I do? What was I doing here wasting my time? I had never had so much time alone to think about myself. I didn't like all of this introspection. I liked to have a job, do it the very best I could and move along to the next task with no doubts or second thoughts.

I met a pretty blonde woman named Erika at my hotel who was from Vienna and in Paris on business. She worked for Rover automobiles and was amused and amazed that I had never heard of the Rover. She said it was very famous in Europe. We had dinner together at a Basque restaurant on the Boulevard St. Michele. The food was good, she was good company and I felt much better. Erika left the hotel the next day but talking to her helped me get over my dark blue funk.

Before I left Los Angeles I had promised Miles that while in Paris I would call and try to visit his old friend. Bernard Hilda was also an agent, now working to supply the clubs of Europe and the Near, Middle and Far East with musicians, singers, variety acts like the well- known ventriloquist Senor Wences I had seen many times on the Ed Sullivan Show as a child. The address alone would have drawn me to his office. Thirty Three Avenue des Champs-Élysées was written in gold and black above the massive entrance doors.

Bernard was short and pear shaped. I didn't know when he had moved from New York to Paris but his pleased expression let me know he was settled in and enjoying himself.

"You're crazy, Brandy. Why do you want to travel around Europe as a tourist, paying your own way, and not getting to know anyone but other tourists?" Bernard asked with a New York accent from his extra wide chair behind the desk. "You should meet Lily de Saigon, our new agent just for exotics. She's working at Le Sexy right now but she used to work all over Europe, Viet Nam and Thailand. Name it and she's been there. Lily could fix you up with something nice."

Bernard's office matched the elegance of the building. The walls were covered with silver and gold printed silk and the immense desk was polished dark wood and held three telephones. The two matching silver velvet straight chairs in front of it were uncomfortable and not meant for lingering chats. This was a business office and judging from the number of acts in the waiting room, business was pretty good.

We talked for a few minutes as he tried to convincw me to stay and let his office represent me. I finally agreed to work with them, but only if they found someplace interesting for me to go. He stood and ushered me into another office, not quite so richly decorated, where I looked around for Lily de Saigon.

I was looking for a beautiful, dainty Vietnamese woman but no such person was there. The woman sitting at the desk was not Asian and must have been at least forty- two, maybe forty-five years old. She was Caucasian, definitely French, with sharp features, grey eyes and unremarkable dark hair in a bun at the nape of her neck, which was held in place by a chopstick. This was a stripper?

Lily turned slightly to look at me and my first impression of her changed. From her penetrating expression I saw she was a woman who had confidence in her own opinion. She was much prettier when her attention was focused on you. After being convinced by Bernard Hilda to stay for a few more weeks, I hoped Lily liked what she saw and would take a professional interest in me.

"Lily," Bernard said to her "this is Brandy Wilde from Los Angeles. She is thinking of working around Europe or somewhere for a while. See what you can do for her. Show her some of the clubs, if you can. Take her to Le Sexy." Bernard bowed from the waist in a gesture of respect to Lily and left us together.

Bernard was amazing. He had said, "Europe or somewhere" in such an off-hand way. It was like he had melted the whole world and put it in his own little pot to spoon out as he wished. Maybe it did feel that small and manageable to him, but to me it was still huge and scary. I seemed to attract all the weirdoes here. It had never been that way before I left home. Had it?

Looking quite glamorous, Lily pulled up to the Hotel Central in her shiny, black, English, Morgan convertible. I had seen a few of those in Los Angeles and thought they looked like movie star cars. Sitting behind the sporty wooden wheel with the top down, a red silk scarf fluttering at her throat, Lily looked more than good. She looked happy.

It was ten p.m. and we were off to Le Sexy, the second best strip club in Paris. I wondered why we started so late. I had always been at the Largo and other clubs around the States at eight or nine o'clock at the latest. I felt like the provincial, small town girl I was.

I looked like a big city girl though. My hair had grown out a little since I had arrived in Europe and was full, curling and strawberry blonde. In complete stage makeup and dressed in deep cobalt blue form-fitting pants and belted jacket of silk jersey without a blouse or bra, plenty of gold around my neck to cover some of the cleavage, and navy blue spike heels, I felt I could match any stripper in Paris for looks that night.

We arrived at Le Sexy and Lily had a waiter show me to a seat in the back so I could see everything: the stage, the bar and the audience. The stage was small but the whole club was small and crowded. It had an intimate feeling, everyone all close together, smoking, drinking, talking and laughing loudly to be heard above the music. Most paid some attention to the dancers but not much.

I saw four acts and was shocked at how strong they were. The girls went down to a tiny black or jeweled patch which covered whatever pubic hair they had not shaved off, the lips of the labia and the anus. The patch took the place of a G-string so there were no strings at the hip-line which gave the impression of real nudity.

The first girl, Angelique, was a tall blonde with blue eyes but her features were coarse and her costume was cheap, wrinkled and looked like she had never hung it up. I didn't recognize her music but it did have a good raunchy beat and her grinds were smooth. She did a lot of floor work, her legs waving in the air, the black patch looking squarely at the audience between the large buttocks. She rubbed herself all over but did not inspire much interest from the audience or from me. As an opening act, I thought she was a disaster.

After working in clubs for almost seven years, I had some pretty clear ideas on how a show should be set up. If I owned a club, the first act would be very pretty, not too strong, but a good dancer who used up-tempo music, with beautiful costumes. The audience has been waiting for the show to begin, and it's good to give them a warm and welcoming first impression.

The blondes and redheads would be mixed up with the brunettes and no two blondes, or two redheads, would be next to each other on the program. The girls would have to be sexy, but not all in the same way. Some men like to see the angel they could never have undress for them, while others want someone who looks easy to get so maybe even they might have a chance with her.

Most of all, in my club, the dancers would know how to tease and enjoy it. The tease is most important. If you have that, you don't need spectacular looks, a fancy costume or even know how to dance very well. Make the audience feel good and think you want desperately to make love with them, but just not right now. Make them think they could make you change your mind, and you will have them in the palm of your hand. If you can do that with a smile, every club owner would want to kill their competition so you would work at their place.

At Le Sexy, the second act was a young blond man who wore a baby blue military costume with gold braid and looked gay. He was a baton twirler and good at it, but he seemed out of place. I started looking at the patrons, comparing them to audiences in Los Angeles. They were more stylish, smoked much more, and most were drinking hard liquor – no beer. They spoke mainly French, so I figured Le Sexy was not a club frequented by tourists.

Lily de Saigon went on stage next and she looked pretty, all in black lace, but her act was not special. I had been hoping she would be wonderful and gorgeous so I was disappointed. She was in her mid-forties and her age showed on stage – cellulite in the back of her thighs and sagging breasts. She did play with the audience, shooting one guy a bump, or glancing over her shoulder at someone once in a while letting them know she was interested in them. I liked that. She didn't smile but she winked a couple of times which was almost as good.

The little pubic patch Lily wore to cover her mons was of rhinestones on flesh colored lace and looked almost pretty. Her music was French blues, which I thought sounded more like jazz and uninspiring, but her act was much better than Angelique's. The audience started getting in the mood to see a good show. They looked at Lily and they applauded for her. I don't know who that Angelique was or how she got in there.

Babette de Bon Bon was the fourth act. She was a ravishing, dark-haired beauty. Solemn, and without much personality on display, but what she did show was terrific. She had large, high, round breasts, small waist and hips, a muscular rear end, long legs that moved with grace. Babette looked like she could tear you apart. She didn't move much like a stripper, but she didn't have to move at all to be delicious.

Babette smiled once. At the end of her number when there was nothing left to divulge except her teeth, she smiled and the audience sighed in a chorus. So sweet, so adorable these teeth, the audience seemed to moan. They loved her and they showed it with applause and their undivided attention. They were riveted by her sensual body and beautiful face.

A magician came on stage and Lily was suddenly next to me at the bar. It was time for us to check out the clubs in Pigalle.

Lily said, "The Crazy Horse Saloon is the best club in Paris, of course, and probably the whole world. Le Sexy is the second best club, but the clubs in Pigalle are something special to see, especially for the dancer. I think you will find them interesting."

Serious and business-like, Lily had her agent hat on now. We were off to collect the commissions. The little Morgan rumbled through the streets of Paris just as the night life was about to reach its peak.

Half nude and showing it off in the cold midnight air, girls and women stood in little packs on corners and leaned together against shop doorways on the Rue de Pigalle. They smoked leisurely as they stretched and arched their backs to push their breasts forward or showed off a bare leg, moving it slowly under the high slit skirt to reveal a hairy crotch. An older blonde played with her exposed brown nipple, trying to make it look inviting.

I looked at Lily. I was surprised. Hollywood Boulevard, with its young runaways willing to do anything for a ten dollar bill, had seemed wild to me that summer of 1968. I guess it was, in an amateur type of way. The Rue de Pigalle was strictly professional and loaded with lingering, loitering men who looked ready to pay for action if they could make up their minds which, among all the bodies being thrust in front of them, would get to suck their penis.

"La Rue de Pigalle," she said with a small shrug and a "that's show business" attitude.

We drove another block to the first club we would visit.

"The girls here do one show a night for twenty francs and then they can move on to another club to do the same show. If they can find a few clubs to work, they can make a living," Lily said. Something in her tone suggested that dancing here was not a good living.

The mountain of a man taking money at the door knew Lily and let us in right away. The inside was painted flat black but the weak white light from the stage helped me find a maroon velvet seat at the back of the small theatre. There were seven rows with eight seats in each and no drinks were served. All the money was paid at the door for the entrance fee. A man could see thirty or more dancers if he sat long enough. Each act lasted about eight minutes.

There was nothing fancy here. It was just the starkness of women taking off a few bits of clothing and walking back and forth across the stage. No flattering lights, no pretty costumes, no smiles and no personality. These women looked like they would rather be mopping floors. They might have been zombies for all I could see. I felt terrible for them. The music was taped so there was no fresh or immediate feeling from live musicians either. It made me sad for the dancers and for the audience who sat there like grey and brown lumps. I saw two acts and I never wanted to go through that again. It was torture.

"Lily, I can't sit in the audience again and watch those shows. Let me get out of your way. I'll take a taxi back to the hotel and talk to you tomorrow," I suggested.

"Oh, you wouldn't get half a block in a taxi from here," she said. "I'll drive you back and do this tomorrow. I'm tired anyway. I want to see you dance at Le Sexy about four in the afternoon. Bring your costume and tape so we can see what you're used to."

That sounded like an invitation to compete. I was sure Lily was wondering what I was like on stage and who was I to judge the women I had just seen. That sounded fair to me. I am sure she knew I had judged her act as well. Now it was my turn to be judged.

Half an hour later, as I was trying to get to sleep I thought about all that had happened to get me here. The Texas ranch and the girls dancing on a flat-bed truck in the middle of the pasture, Mickey's Showbar, the Mafia club in Cleveland, the Crystal Palace in Duluth where the musicians were wearing overcoats and ear muffs on stage and I almost froze in the twenty seven degrees below zero weather, wearing only pasties, panties and high heels. Then in Hollywood, I danced at the Largo for five years. I had overcome many obstacles, and realized I was prepared for Paris. If not now, when?

The next afternoon Lily was waiting for me in front of Le Sexy. She took me back to the dressing rooms. They were not too bad. There were mirrors and seats and closets. After Pigalle, I hadn't known what to expect. I was already in full makeup, false eyelashes in place and fine black lines carefully painted under my eyes to look like lashes and make my eyes look huge on stage.

I had brought my gypsy costume, the eight pages of handwritten choreography to make sure I remembered the complex steps, and the taped music to Europe with me in case I might want or need to work to get back to California.

Everything was ironed and brushed. My black knee high boots with the three inch heels were polished. The green, orange and lavender ribbons on the tambourine were bright. I felt ready.

Before she went to the sound booth to put on my tape, Lily told me there would be no stage lights, only the lights used during the day time to clean up the bar. No flattering colored lights or shadows for me that day. Fair enough. There had been none in Pigalle either.

It was good to hear the music start and know that it was loud enough and I could hear it clearly. I could see by her raised eyebrows that *The Theme from Zorba the Greek* was not what Lily expected to blast out into the dingy club. That was fun for me. I wanted her to be surprised.

The rich purple velvet skirt was cut in a double circle and stopped a few inches above the knee. The underside was lined in lavender silk and the leaf-green low cut blouse was neatly tucked in. A long orange scarf around my waist, I held the tambourine lightly as Wally Green, my choreographer in Los Angeles, had taught me.

I kicked and twirled, teased to the empty chairs and bar stools, smiled to the music, finally taking off the skirt at the end of the first song. The tape segued into *Golden Earrings*. I shed my blouse and was left with just a lavender corselet, that zipped up the front, pink, purple and aurora borealis rhinestones covering the front panels and sprinkled around the back, a pair of tiny pale lavender satin pants cut so the sides reached my waist and did not cut the curve of the hip line.

The last song, *Ochi Chornye* by Rachmaninoff, was very fast. I made the tambourine hit my bottom with loud smacks, hit my arms, hit my thighs as I whirled from one side of the small stage to the other. I threw the tambourine off stage with the rest of the wardrobe, unzipped the corselet and threw it on top of the growing pile.

The orange scarf slid across my breasts and gently caressed my body. It too was eventually tossed aside as I stood stage center with arms above my head and the music ended with a triumphant surge of horns and drums.

I went directly to the dressing room, hung up my wardrobe, and began to towel myself dry. I had not performed in a few weeks and was wet, like I had just stepped out of a shower.

Lily came back stage already excitedly talking to me before she came into the dressing room.

"Brandy, I'm calling Monsieur Bernardin, owner of the Crazy Horse Saloon to see if he can give you the audition tomorrow. He has never had an American dancer there but you are not so very American. This is good. Your act is not very sexy, but if he likes you he will provide your costume, probably change your name to something he prefers, choose your choreography and music, everything," she trilled.

As Lily paced down the hall and back to the dressing room, she was making plans.

Chapter Nineteen

The Crazy Horse Saloon in Paris

"*I* don't think you understand what an important club the Crazy Horse is for you. If you work there a year, you can go to any of the best clubs in the world for top money. Your reputation in Europe and the Orient will be made."

Lily was excited and rambling on as we walked up the Avenue George V, but she grew quiet as we approached the tall man, dressed in a red and black Canadian Mountie uniform, who guarded the doorways of the Crazy Horse Saloon.

I realized then she was seeing me as a long-term investment and intended to make a great deal of money from my career. She thought I could strip years into the future -- just as I was wondering if my dancing days were almost over. Her words made me feel better when I needed more confidence. I was still on my way up instead of on my last lap around the track.

"We have an appointment with Monsieur Bernardin at three," Lily said, as the red-coated Mountie opened the door with a flourish after his large assessing brown eyes had lingered on us for a moment. We did look exceptionally good. Lily had her hair in a flattering chignon, without the chopstick, and I had dressed in a black silk jersey jumpsuit that emphasized my small waist.

The wide entrance lobby and hall that led to the showroom were luxuriously carpeted in thick midnight blue plush. The walls were painted cerulean blue and accented with deep pink boarders. It looked clean and bright even as the afternoon sun poured through the glass entrance doors.

There was no smell. I couldn't help but compare this club to the dingy Le Sexy and the dark boxes of Pigalle with their smell of sweat, semen and tobacco that stuck to the hair in your nostrils. Even the Largo, the best strip club in Los Angeles, smelled like a bar in the morning.

"*Bon jour*, Lily. This is Brandy? I am Agate, M. Bernardin's secretary. Let me take you to the dressing rooms," said the graceful, tall young woman who offered a slender hand to shake mine. "We have just finished a special photo shoot for an Italian magazine so all the girls are here and also the usual newspaper reporters and photographers that follow them everywhere. We will all be able to see you dance," she said joyfully.

I was glad Lily was with me for support. All of a sudden I was terrified. I felt woozy and stumbled against the wall. Lily grabbed me, but Agate saw it and laughed.

"You are so funny, Brandy."

I did the same gypsy act that I had done for Lily at the Sexy but this time the house lights were dimmed and I had an audience of about twenty five people. Pink and blue lights on both sides of the stage and a bright pink spot light from the lighting booth behind the audience were focused on me. It felt very familiar, and although the stage was narrow and tiny, I found room to fit in all the steps.

The sound system at the Crazy was wonderful. The music was full and clear. I could hear each violin in *Ochi Chornye*, my last number. I smiled a thousand watt smile, and lifted my chin while taking a victorious bow. I was wearing only tiny violet silk break away panties and knee-high black boots at the end of my act.

As I was dressing Lily came back to hurry me into the main room to meet M. Bernardin.

"He is very excited about you," Lily gasped with one hand on her chest. "He told all the girls how much he loved your act. Of course it is not suitable for his stage but he never hires anyone unless he sees them on his stage first. He flies girls in from all over Europe if he likes the look of them but he hires very few. How lucky you are, to be in Paris already. Incredible! *Marveilleuse* !"

Relieved to have the audition over and exhilarated that I had not made any mistakes that would be obvious to them, I entered the showroom and Lily ushered me toward Bernardin. The other dancers backed away a few steps as if giving the king room to reign. He was of medium height, about fifty, wiry and slender with closely set eyes, but his self-confidence gave him an immense presence. I smiled while being introduced and his voice exploded into the silent club.

"Why don't you smile like that?" he demanded of his dancers. "That's the one marvelous thing about American dancers. They smile. And look at that hair! So funny!"

The nine, extraordinarily glamorous women who were the crème de la crème of European striptease shifted their beautifully made-up eyes toward me. The room chilled. Only Agate, who had taken her cue from Bernardin, told me how much she liked my act and how different it was from any show she had seen in France.

I knew my hair was wild in color and curl but it was natural. There wasn't much I could do to change it even if I had wanted to, which I did not. I loved my hair even though it was short now and thought it was my best feature. Did he have to insult me in front of my agent and all the girls?

"This is good," he said as if I were a fine wine and he was tasting me on his tongue. He was deciding what to do with me. "I have all the dancers I need now but if she can stay in the area I can use her about January fifteenth ," he said to Lily. "I can see her as a heroine of the nineteenth century. Our choreographer is from Los Angeles. Victor Upshaw. Maybe you know him? Come back tonight at ten forty-five," Bernardin ordered us. "Television crews from the U. S. and Mexico are coming to interview me about the Crazy Horse."

I didn't say a word. It seemed like Bernardin was trying to be charming in front of the reporters but he did not ask, he demanded. His voice held just enough disdain to make me feel unsure about working for him. The photographers were taking pictures of us talking as if all Europe would find a new addition to the Crazy Horse show fascinating. Lily nodded that she would have me back at 10:45. She seemed amazed that she had pulled it off.

This was late September and I had to "stay in the area" until January fifteenth? How could I do that? What would I do? I had the money if I wanted to live on a budget but not for traveling and enjoying myself for four months. I had been in Europe for almost four weeks and was lonesome for feminine company. There were too many men and not enough women here.

"But for now, you will do the television interview," Lily insisted when I told her I didn't want to work with Bernardin. "What an opportunity you have," Lily scolded me after we left the Crazy. "Photographers are always there. He has important people in to see the show all the time. Many of the girls get movie parts and become famous or marry millionaires." She was frowning at me now. "You must do this. The Crazy Horse is like no other club. I can find something for you until January. Don't worry."

I did film the television show in Bernardin's comfortable salon that night. Newspaper reporters and more photographers crowded together along the rich black leather bench to ogle little Rosa Fumeto, from Italy, and me. Television cameras and lights and eighteen people took up most of the air in the salon.

Bernardin described the allure of his club to the American and Mexican interviewers.

"We have the best of everything here. We have the best dancers, the best liquor, the most beautiful costumes, the most handsome waiters in Paris. The most beautiful girls from all over the world come to Paris to work at the Crazy Horse. Here is one who is an American, our first American, the hair so funny, and she is so talented. Look at that talent."

He started talking about what kind of show he wanted me to do. I didn't understand much as the interviews were in French, Spanish and a little English. But, I did finally understand the reason I was there. To show the viewing public what Bernardin said was true. Rosa and I were examples of all the women who were climbing over each other, clawing to get a chance to work for him. I didn't like that at all.

I saw my first show at the Crazy Horse that evening, and I had to admit it was the most beautifully costumed and choreographed show I had ever seen. There were gorgeous lighting effects of geometric patterns and cityscapes on bare flesh. The girls were all pretty, though most were too small busted for American taste. The silvery astronaut, the spider woman who climbed a rope web and other characters created for the five to seven minute acts were interesting. I especially liked the idea that every act was a story, every dancer a special character. Some were exciting while others showed off the feminine body to its best advantage.

One very busty blonde, Bonita Super, who had only a blue marabou piece on her head and a silver G-string on her body, stretched long legs, kneeled or sprawled on her back in graceful and sensual positions on a large, blue velvet pouf that slowly turned round and round. The lights dimmed to black, Bonita changed position, and when the lights came up there she was. Her facial expression was serious as she looked at the audience looking at her. That was the act. Bright colors and patterns of the New York skyline and other cities reflected on her body and the screen behind her. It was a beautiful lighting effect that I had not seen before and was enough to make the act memorable without much action.

I kept thinking what a great act this could have been for Jackie DeWitt, our Miss Ohio, at the Largo. Jackie could hardly walk across a stage in high heels. She kept her knees bent as she walked and looked awkward no matter what she did. This act would have been a perfect way to hide that from the public.

The Crazy Horse audience appreciated the girls and applauded wildly. They happily enjoyed the comedians and vaudeville acts which no American group would have tolerated. Here, they paid one hundred francs per person, about four times the cost of my hotel room with breakfast, to see this show which included one drink or half a bottle of champagne. I had the chilled brut champagne and it was perfection.

The audience, mostly dressed up tourists, hunched together on small, blue-carpeted platforms of differing heights. The short stools and tiny tables were almost impossible for the extremely handsome waiters to pass through. They seemed to crawl over us while balancing small trays full of drinks and ice buckets holding bottles of champagne. It created an intimate atmosphere though there must have been more than two hundred of us sitting there.

The mirrored bar at the back of the showroom exhibited bottles of the finest spirits available in the world. It was filled with men, some looking at the four gorgeous blond men mixing the drinks, but about sixty were standing with drinks in hand watching the girls on stage.

Tired and happy to go back to the hotel when the show was over about 1:30 in the morning, I compared this show to the Largo in Los Angeles. It made me proud. I had not realized what a good club the Largo was or how well our show measured up with what was considered "the best striptease club in the world."

Later that morning the telephone woke me. Lily was in a panic. Her voice sounded shrill and tight.

"Come to the office right away. The girl who was going to start in Tel Aviv on Friday has broken her leg and we have to send you there on Wednesday. You need pictures and another act. Hurry! Hurry! Get down here now. We only have four days for a new act, costumes, pictures, music, choreography, travel and your haaiirrrrr!" Lily yelled.

I had to admit it: my hair was different than most of the French women I had seen on the street or in the clubs. Theirs had no height, no curl, no spring, while mine stood straight up and could not be tamed to lie flat. The very simple, hair hanging straight down look was in now. With my naturally curly hair, I probably seemed old-fashioned to these style-conscious trendmakers.

Lily decided an LSD hippy act would be the best we could manage in such a short time and I went along with her. The costume and psychedelic techno-pop music could be simple but wild and she did not think anyone in Israel had done an act like that.

It was rush, rush, rush for four days, nights, and into the early mornings. We rehearsed seven to eight hours a day then did all the other things like fittings and shopping. I had to learn a nine minute act in two days and it was a much stronger presentation than I had ever imagined I would work. Legs spread open and no pants. I was going to wear a gold and silver rhinestone patch like the French girls and show it in the last moments of my act.

"*Elle et Lui,*" I said as I hopped into a taxi after leaving Lillian's apartment.

"The club *Elle et Lui, mademoiselle*? Are you sure?" the driver with the greying walrus mustache said, while turning slowly, arm across the top of the front seat, to look at me again.

I nodded yes, pulling my black mink coat closer to my chest. Dressed in tight black pants and a cashmere sweater, with only a red Hermes scarf for relief, I felt warm enough to venture out after midnight. It was late September and already cold in Paris. A friend in Hollywood had told me I had to see this club and the show while in Paris. I might not have another chance.

"Pay good attention for your safety," the driver cautioned as I was paying him. He was leaving me there alone and he looked worried.

As I turned away from the taxi I saw the bouncer and knew why the driver was concerned. A large tuxedoed blonde, with a face as sharp as a cleaver, stood by the maroon velvet door-rope. She was allowing women patrons to pass through and turning away men, if she decided by one look at them they were not gay or not sophisticated enough to enjoy the show without causing trouble.

I walked in and was met by a woman who looked about twenty years old in a black tuxedo and crisp white dress shirt. Her dark hair was cut in an Elvis Presley style with the same high pompadour. I couldn't see one feminine thing about her, not her walk or her square figure, as she ushered me to a seat at the bar. She was not my kind of girl, but I am sure she was attractive to many women who liked their women to look like men.

"My name is Leigh. Would you like to buy me a champagne?" she asked, in a surprisingly delightful, girlish voice.

I looked around the bar and saw women sitting together holding hands over the little tables or with their arms around each other. The lights were dim but I could see six or seven women with masculine hair styles, in tuxedos, dancing with women, some in dresses some in fancy pant suits, on the small dance floor.

"No, thank you," I said with a polite smile.

I had done that kind of work for eleven weeks at Mickey's Showbar in Cleveland, Ohio. I knew it was not easy to offer your company and have it turned down. The idea of having older femmes, perhaps even married women, looking for and paying for handsome butch gigolos' was a new concept to me.

On the outside, I thought I looked very sophisticated, sitting there in my mink coat, martini in hand, part of the scene. On the inside, I felt like a provincial girl, trying not to stare. I was so surprised, looking at women in their forties and fifties flirting and trying to entice young butches to kiss and fondle them.

The club lights dimmed further as the show started. A tall woman dressed in a long gown of deep blue, dark and sultry, danced to pursue a young, frightened blonde in a thin white gown around the dance floor. The chase music was slow and menacing with a heavy tom-tom drum backbeat. The blonde turned toward the brunette, moved her hips seductively, lowered her eyes, then turned to run across the stage as if she was ashamed and afraid.

The woman in blue grabbed the girl's light dress. She ripped it off and pushed the little blonde onto a small bench in the middle of the dance floor.

The dark woman knelt and forcefully spread the blonde's legs. She slowly removed the girl's G-string, turned her to show us the fair pubic hair, forced her to lie down on the bench and pulled back the labia to reveal the clitoris. She lowered her head as if to drink from the vagina while pinching the tender nipples as the blonde screamed.

Their show consisted of oral sex, nipple pinching and sucking, quite a bit of writhing hip, moaning, screaming "no" while panting for more, nipples dragging against clitoris, tongue dripping with saliva and other fluids.

Just when I thought the act was over the blonde was able to convince the brunette to lay back and be sucked and entered by the blonde's little hand as well. The audience drank champagne and toasted the turn-around.

Their act was about twenty minutes long but no one was counting. Even sitting at the bar with an unobstructed view, I couldn't tell what was real sex and what was not.

The couple stood and bowed to applause as the music ended and left the dance-floor, each with an arm around the other.

A few minutes later the following act, Adamo and Eva, was announced. The music had just begun but I could see from the first steps they were world-class Apache dancers. Their dance movements were strong, crisp and completely finished. They could, and probably had, worked in finest clubs around the world.

Adamo looked like Michelangelo's powerful statue of David in a white draped loincloth. He had the same sensual type of muscular beauty, softly curled hair and full lips.

Eva was a tiny blonde, in a red tunic that split up the side. Adamo threw her up in the air, turned, twisted and tortured her by withholding his love all around the dance floor, taking off her clothes as they danced. When Adamo would not pay attention to her, Eva stalked him, threw herself at his feet, bit him and clung to his legs so Adamo could not move away.

Their spectacular act was over when the only shred of cloth they had between them was the skimpy white G-string worn by the glistening Adamo.

I was amazed. What a strange and unusual experience. No one at home would believe I had seen such a show all by myself while surrounded by dressed up butches.

The next morning I took a taxi to Pigale to meet with Lily's photographer. We still had to take the black and white glossy 8x10 publicity pictures. I fought and wiggled to move between three posing prostitutes in front of the stairs to go up to the photographer's second floor studio. He wasn't there, but a note attached to the door said he would be back soon.

I was afraid to be trapped on the landing between the gruby-looking pass-by tricks, a guy who looked like a pampered pimp dressed in black velvet and silver boots, and the three working girls trying to do business at ten a.m., so I made my way down again.

With my arms full of costumes, a deflated blue plastic blow-up chair, the air pump, and my make-up case, I waited on the street in front of the stairs just like the other girls. During the half hour I waited one girl, a skinny blonde with few teeth, went around the corner twice and came back, but she was the only one who got work.

I was offered work I think, but I couldn't be sure as I wouldn't leave the safety of our stairs and walk to the car that had pulled up to the curb. I shook my head no while the other girls nodded their approval of my decision and motioned their willingness to go.

The little photographer, who looked like an old terrier, arrived with apologies to the girls and a bottle of Pernod for us. He fixed us both a drink and we spent two hours taking photos in front of a white paper backdrop.

The next day Lily and I chose four pictures that had turned out especially great. I was very proud of them. Even though I was completely nude in two pictures you couldn't see more than what was necessary to show off my figure.

Lily managed, arranged, choreographed, taught and figured things out so well, that on Wednesday I was in the air heading toward Israel with everything needed for two acts, plus a four week contract in Tel Aviv at seventy five dollars a night to be paid each evening before I left the club. I had never earned so much money in my life.

Chapter Twenty

Israel, September 1968

I'd always wanted to see Israel but didn't think I could ever afford to make a trip like that, so far away and exotic compared to Los Angeles. The Six Day War had ended several months earlier but Lily assured me that Israel was safe now and it was lots of fun. I had told Bernard Hilda if he could find someplace interesting for me to work I would do it. Little did I know I probably would have found almost any place in the world "interesting" as I was curious about everywhere and had hardly been anywhere.

The long, cramped flight from Paris left me irritable but as soon as I left the plane, I felt better. I stepped onto the airfield in Tel Aviv and was covered by a sky full of blazing stars. I could actually feel them shining on me. I felt warm breezes off the Mediterranean Sea embrace and comfort me as a short chubby man walked toward me.

"I'm Cuba, the owner of the Cabaret Sabra," he said taking my arm. "You don't need to go through customs."

I'm being kidnapped, was my first thought. No one will be able to find me because there won't be a record of me entering the country. I opened my mouth to wail and quickly shut it as Cuba steered me over to a little counter connected to the outside wall of the main building. Several uniformed men stood watching from there as the passengers disembarked.

"Just walk over here and let this guy look at you. I'll have someone wait for your luggage. Right now, I'm taking you to dinner. We're hungry."

One of the men in uniform nodded at us and Cuba put pressure on my arm to turn me toward a long white Cadillac convertible with the top down. A driver waited while holding the back door open. The smiling middle-aged woman in the back seat moved over a few inches. A convertible. I would still be able to see the stars.

Cuba sat in front with the driver while introducing me to his wife, Jordana. Her name was the same as my favorite character in Leon Uris's book *Exodus* and I was thrilled. I had wanted to be Jewish ever since I had read that book when I was eighteen.

"You have stars here. I have never seen stars like this." I couldn't take my eyes from the sky. I felt amazingly well, alive and happy.

Cuba looked at me seriously, like he had never seen a woman who had just been on a plane for ten hours look so joyous, and asked, "What is your mother's maiden name?"

"Tauber," I said. "It's French."

"No, it isn't," Cuba said. "You're one of us. You just don't know it yet."

"Oh no, I'm Lutheran," I told him wide-eyed with surprise.

"Ask your mother," he suggested with the only genuinely kind smile I saw on his face for the next month.

"That's General Moshe Dayan," Cuba said of the solitary man sitting one table away from us with his back to the wall, in the Middle East restaurant. "He is one of our country's greatest heroes."

General Dayan's eye shifted slightly toward Cuba and showed no expression. The other eye was covered with the famous black patch.

Cuba's chest swelled with pride to be noticed. I had recognized the slender man as someone special from his attitude and his erect posture. Dayan looked like he was the only person in the restaurant who was totally alert to the sounds in the street, to the topics of conversations around him, what the others were eating, and what each patron looked like in case he needed to identify them after a bomb blast.

To sit in the same restaurant with the man who had led the armies of Israel in the recent Six Day War was an honor. Unstoppable tears flowed slowly down my cheeks throughout the meal even after Dayan had gone.

I had never been overtly political but I felt that Israel needed to protect its people and their way of life. Constant attacks from the larger surrounding countries had made me furious. When the war broke out, everyone expected Israel to lose. I had no idea my emotions would over-take my usually stolid composure. Jordana and Cuba looked at one another and their expressions shouted, "Oh, no. Not another dramatic *artiste*."

The Hotel Ami, on Am Israel Hai Street, where Cuba had booked me for the four week engagement, was across the street from the Mediterranean Sea. The hotel was about a mile from the Cabaret Sabra. My room was tiny but modern with a single bed against the wall, one large window and a private bath. I didn't mind the size because I didn't plan to be there much and the price was right. Ten dollars a night included my breakfast, a telephone in my room and a 24-hour a day guard at the reception desk.

I happily walked to work each evening on the narrow sidewalk beside the water. It was light and warm at eight in the evening and I was next to the Mediterranean. The sea was calm and smooth compared to the Pacific Ocean in California. There was no sound of crashing surf and no waves. Burbles of warm, bathlike water softly approached the sand, giving it passionless kisses, retreated then repeated.

Cabaret Sabra was a homey, dim little neighborhood strip club. It was the second best club in Tel Aviv with the Caliph, up on the hill, being the best. The audience arrived in shirtsleeves to spend the evening, drink their fill with friends and family, and see a good show.

The first thing I saw on entering was a highly waxed, ebony black bar where six attractive women, aged between twenty and thirty, sat on black leather stools looking toward the doorway. They did not sit together but had space for men to sit between them and I realized they were B-girls. They knew who I was, as my 8x10 glossy French photos had been in front of the club for two days, advertising me as the coming attraction.

The women looked me over, judged me quickly, and most turned their eyes away in unison. Only the tall blonde with the large brown eyes and long graceful neck kept looking at me while the other brown, blue and light green eyes moved back to the door to see if "anything good" was coming in. I found out that Cuba let them talk quietly and smoke but they could not sit together or drink anything unless a customer bought it for them.

The pretty B-girls were not allowed to leave the club during working hours to turn tricks behind the building or somewhere else of their choosing, but after work they could do whatever they wanted. They were at Cabaret Sabra to look thirsty, seem hungry for companionship and to make money for Cuba six hours a night.

When I arrived the first evening it was early. I was able to give my music tapes to the sound man and put my costumes in the dressing room I would share with the curvaceous, olive-skinned belly-dancer, who was already there applying fragrant oil to her body.

"Hi, I'm Natasha from Brooklyn. Just put your things anywhere you can find some space."

"Hi, I'm using the name Clarice Gillis now. Not very sexy, is it? I don't know why but my agent felt it was better if I used the name on my passport."

I was surprised and relieved to run into another American dancer. My first thought was, maybe we could be friends. Maybe we could run around together and make little trips around the city.

"I was a tourist and got caught here during the war. Never thought I would live anywhere but New York. I love the feeling of fellowship, the closeness and spirit of the people. I don't want to live anywhere else now. Couldn't go back," she explained while shaking her head. She spoke in a hurry – barely stopping to breathe.

After her speech, she added that she was married to an Israeli and they had bought a house. She was "settled down," which was my cue to know that any running around Natasha did would be with her husband. She was friendly though, and cheerful and she shared information generously.

Brushing her heavy, waist length hair she said, "You know we have a nine-piece band this month. I think they have the same agent you do, out of Paris. They're all from Nicaragua."

That night we each did two shows. Natasha's costume was of magenta satin and gold silk chiffon with gold chains, and countless large and small gold coins hanging on her bra and chiffon skirt belt. She danced barefooted to the sensual Middle Eastern rhythms. She was on first and as sexy as any dancer I had ever seen. The audience loved her.

I did my gypsy act to create the best first impression possible. It was colorful, the audience would be familiar with the music and it was very different than Natasha's act. I was supposed to be the star of the show but I didn't feel like I could match her sensuality or the extravagance of her costume. The royal purple velvet, orange silk and bright green satin materials of my costume were rich but nothing could match the thousands of dollars in real gold that Natasha had riding on her breasts and hips.

Cuba sat with two older men at a large table with the best view of the dance floor. There was no stage and I felt awkward and exposed starting my show in the middle of the dance floor instead of behind a curtain as it had been choreographed. The band and all their instruments were set up on a ten-inch platform.

There were several wives and girlfriends with their men in the club for the first show. The women were tan and muscular, no matter what their age. Their hair, mostly in waves and curls of brown and black, flowed loosely onto strong bare shoulders. I loved that.

The tall blonde at the bar turned from the door and sat facing the stage for my entire act. Cuba didn't seem to notice. He was too interested in the opinions of the old men at his table to pay attention to a B-girl for those few minutes.

The audience yelled and clapped, stomped their feet and beat the tables with their fists before, during and after my act. I had never had such a wonderful reception.

Then the audience got up and danced to the music of the Managua Knights and the small club shook.

The Managua Knights were a band of nine handsome boys with dark slicked-back hair, wearing white dinner jackets, black trousers and white shirts with bow ties. Their leader, the most handsome, the most slick of all, was Sergio Velez, the saxophone player. He looked like the Elvis Presley of horn men, sexy and shy in that same little boy way that Elvis had that made women want to take him to their breast.

They improvised to the tune *I Left My Heart in San Francisco* during my introduction. That became my theme for the entire month. Each time I entered the showroom, after my act, even in the middle of a song they were playing between shows, they played a few bars of *San Francisco*. It became a contest between the musicians to get it right each time. I knew that first night I would always be reminded of Tel Aviv when I heard that song and never of San Francisco.

"Is the audience always like that?" I asked Natasha. "I thought that older guy with the white hair in front was going to have a heart attack while he was putting the money in your belt."

"I know, they were loud, weren't they? But for Tel Aviv they were a little quiet because it's Shabbat and they don't want to draw too much attention to the club. The Orthodox don't want anything to be open on Friday nights and they control the laws here. Yeah, these guys are good audiences. They're nothing like the bastards in New York or Los Angeles are they? We know how to enjoy ourselves," she said as she nodded, "Yes, yes, yes."

I had been in Israel for three days when I discovered that the entire Munich Philharmonic Orchestra had arrived and was going to stay at the Ami Hotel with me. It was an historical occasion. About ninety people, mostly men, were in the first orchestra from Germany ever to be invited to Israel. It was always the same: so few women. I exchanged glances with a few of the musicians, but did not venture further to become acquainted with them.

While I was having breakfast in the lobby, a middle-aged, balding man dressed all in gray approached me. He introduced himself as Moshe and asked to speak to me. Coffee cup in hand, I nodded, but did not ask him to join me.

"I have a dear friend who saw you dance at the Sabra and would like to offer you a shopping tour to express his appreciation and enjoyment of your show. I have a car and will take you to the shops. You can buy whatever you like."

Moshe looked sober, docile and respectable at ten in the morning, but I was unsure of his motives and I am sure it showed on my face. I had been down this road before.

"Mr. Stacher is an American gentleman and would like to do nothing more than make you happy," Moshe said with a soft but persuasive voice and a gentle smile.

What else did I have to do all day? Who else had appreciated me and wanted to buy me presents? I quickly considered Moshe's kind face, his polite posture of deference, his open manner and the way he was dressed all in soft nonthreatening pale grey. I felt safe in the middle of the city with people around. Mr. Plough's warning on the airplane came to mind but I reminded myself, this was Israel. I was bored and friendless which is a bad combination for a stripper on the road.

"Where shall we go?" he said with a winning grin, as though he knew the exact moment I had made up my mind.

"Everywhere."

I had never shopped in the presence of guards, loosely holding rifles on their shoulders with pistols at the waist. They searched my purse when I entered the mall and several of the stores had their own security men and women. Every man and woman of age and living in Israel had to serve two years in the army to protect their country. They were always on call to serve if they were needed to fight in a sudden outbreak of war.

Part of that protection was to search bags and parcels carried into public places like malls, markets, theaters, bus stations and all kinds of public and government buildings, for bombs and guns. The Six-Day War had been fought in June of 1967 and fifteen months later things were still tense. The United States had existed almost two hundred years and was considered young by most governments. Israel was twenty years old and under attack every day somewhere in the country.

Moshe took me to a small English-type boutique for young women and I liked everything there. I didn't have room in my suitcases and I didn't need anything but it was still fun to shop.

I came out of the dressing room wearing a black wool knit dress with orange piping, a matching orange coat lined in the same color satin, and a black felt picture hat. I thought I looked like a glamorous French schoolgirl.

"This is Joseph Stacher, Clarice. The American gentleman I was telling you about. He is your host today," Moshe told me as he gestured to the man who had joined him.

Joe was near seventy if not there already. He had thinning silver hair and was dressed for the warm Tel Aviv September weather in slacks and a light cotton shirt. Joe looked as if he had been transplanted from a Florida resort and like many of the retirees of that state he was trim and tanned. He was not tall or regal or handsome but when he smiled at me his face was understanding and kind. That smile told me he knew how it was to be away from home, that he had known showgirls before and he wanted American company too. I wondered how I got so much information from a smile, but my lightning opinion did not change during the weeks I knew him.

"That looks great on you. Good color with your hair. We'll take that outfit. What else have you tried on?" Joe asked as he took over the scene.

Paris 1968
Candy Capitol

He acted like we had known each other for years and were picking up our conversation where we had left off at our last meeting. He made it seem so natural and comfortable. From the way he handled fabric and his quick dismissal of some styles, it looked like Joe knew quite a bit about women's clothing and I didn't feel awkward or shy with him. I was having fun.

I recognized Joe as the man Cuba sat with at the best table in his cabaret. He wasn't very tall but he gave off a feeling of physical and mental strength. His dark-eyed gaze seemed like it pierced the skin of men but when he looked at me his eyes were gentle. He was used to being the boss where ever he stood but he was not mean or cruel.

"You know I used to own the Moulin Rouge on Sunset Boulevard in L. A. Nice showroom, good parking."

Joe sounded like he was reminding me of something but I was learning this for the first time. He wanted to let me know who he was while maintaining the little play of being long time friends that we were acting out.

Two coats, orange and navy blue, with matching dresses, the black hat, a gold bracelet and a new suitcase later, we left the shopping center and Moshe took Joe back to the big Sheraton Hotel on Hayarkon St. where he said he had lived for years. Moshe dropped me and all my bags at the Ami. I knew I would see them later at their usual table.

The four weeks turned out to be a good run in Tel Aviv. I was paid every night before I left the club and saved every bit I could. The Israeli pound was worthless in the rest of the world and not even listed on the monetary exchange market so I had to change my pounds into dollars before I left Tel Aviv. About two weeks before I was to leave Israel, Lili surprised me with a contract for six weeks in Singapore for a thousand a week plus my hotel room. I started worrying that I would not find a place to exchange my Israeli savings.

When I had been in Tel Aviv for ten days, Joe, Moshe, and his motherly dark-haired wife Janice drove us south to see the large church built over the spot where they think Jesus was born in Bethlehem. From there we went to Jerusalem and the Wailing Wall. I couldn't speak through my tears and trembling sighs.

The souk in East Jerusalem was crowded with stalls displaying everything from fruit ready for the table to wooden bracelets made of many tiny hand-painted pictures of Jesus, rosaries for the tourists, women's shoes and children's clothes for the locals. The smells of warm people eating falafels from the stalls, red, orange and green vegetables ripening and spoiling together, the ochre, orange and brown spice mountains in large round baskets, combined to make me stop to take in huge deep breaths. I wanted to take all of this back to Tel Aviv with me.

I cried all day. I didn't sob, but tears ran down my cheeks and my face was wet the entire afternoon in spite of the warm wind off the Negev-Sinai desert. Janice held my hand and comforted me.

Joe made sure we walked the Via Dolorosa where they say Jesus carried the cross to Calvary. My heart was deeply touched to stand in these religious places. I had never known anyone who had actually been here, hadn't been prepared for the emotional surge.

Joe gave me money to give every priest and rabbi we saw, and there were plenty. Roman Catholic priests, Orthodox Armenian Catholic priests, Protestant ministers and Moslem Imams who guarded the holy places of the three major religions in Israel were all recipients of Joe's generosity.

The next Saturday, our night off at the Sabra, the four of us drove to Haifa, the largest city in northern Israel. We went to the Dan Carmel Hotel that sat high on a hill, for lunch. I was ecstatic about the view that overlooked the city and miles of the blue Mediterranean Sea. The ships I had seen in the curved harbor earlier now looked like fancy toy boats in a grand bathtub.

Joe bought me a pair of velvety blue sapphire stud earrings from a small jewelry store near the Dan Carmel. Each two carat round central stone was surrounded by a circle of small diamonds. I was entranced.

Natasha, the belly dancer, was right. Living in Israel was wonderful. Haifa was the most beautiful city in the world. Why was I letting Lily pull me out of here to work in Singapore?

Evenings when I wasn't sitting with Joe at the club, I hung around the front bar and talked to the B-girls if they weren't busy. Aviva, the tall blonde I had noticed before, was more than interested to keep me company. She was a Jewish immigrant from Morocco but had chosen an Israeli name to go with her new country. The last Saturday night of my contract she asked me out.

"You know Mandy from London is here now. She has big disco and everybody goes there. You want to go tonight? With me?"

Aviva leaned toward me, bit her lip and grinned like a mischievous little girl. Her light brown eyes dared me to say yes.

"Yes."

I knew we would end the evening at her apartment and I looked forward to that.

Mandy Rice-Davies was famous in Israel, and around the world, for being part of the Profumo Affair. The English sex scandal had helped bring down Prime Minister Macmillan's Tory government, just a few years earlier, in 1963. Mandy was the beautiful friend and business partner of "party girl" Christine Keeler who was having affairs with John Profumo, the English Secretary of State for War and Eugene Ivanov, a Russian military attaché, at the same time.

Mandy was in Tel Aviv, having a great time and making a ton of money from the club she had named after herself. Every young cool Israeli wanted to go to her club, be Mandy's friend and dance to the beat of modern Israel.

The club was so big and dark I couldn't tell what shape the rooms were. I had to give all my attention to the two thousand or more pressing, sweating, aggressively hip-swaying and jumping side to side dancers. People at the bars on the edges of the rooms were screaming to be heard over the viciously loud music of the Doors *Hello, I Love You* and *Those Were the Days* by Mary

Hopkin. There was no air, just the dancers' hot wet exhales. They were winding up for a big night. It was 2:30 a.m.

Mary's words hit the mood in the club and the feeling inside the country. I listened, with Aviva's long slender arm resting on my shoulders and was amazed. I wanted to remember forever where I was, what I was hearing, seeing and feeling at that moment.

Those were the days my friend
We thought they'd never end
We'd sing and dance forever and a day
We'd live the life we choose
We'd fight and never lose
For we were young and sure to have our way.
La la la la...

Aviva had asked me a hundred questions about the United States, my life there and my travels in Europe and sexy girlfriends. That night, in her bed, Aviva had many questions about my body. She touched and probed, licked and sucked until all her questions were answered.

The B-girls told me more and more about Joe. They said he was a gangster, a member of the Jewish Mafia, who was not able to return to the United States because of crimes he had committed. I didn't care about any of that. He was as nice to me as any man had been. No matter what power he had, or used to have, he was probably a lonesome person who felt just as displaced as I did.

I found out he was good to all the strippers who worked for Cuba. The B-girls didn't want me to think I was special or something. Most of them were Jewish girls from Morocco and Algeria, where, with the help of other men, they had escaped lives of poverty to wind up at the Sabra Cabaret selling their time, and occasionally their bodies, to men from all over the world.

Joe bought me a bottle of pink champagne every night and kept it chilled, waiting for me, at his table.

"This is the only kind of champagne the Queen of England drinks. I hope you like it," he had said the first night I sat at his table between my shows. What could I say to that?

It proclaimed his status as friend and protector of the lead dancer and made it comfortable for me to drink in the club. I was beginning to like champagne very much.

I still hadn't found a bank or any place to exchange my money, without taking a huge loss because of transaction fees imposed by the banks, when Joe asked me about it.

yHow about your Israeli pounds? You want me to change them to dollars for you?"

"You could do that for me, Joe?"

"Yeah, easy. It comes in just like clockwork from the U.S. I still got some connections, ya know."

I only knew I wanted to return to Israel someday. There was so much more to see. I wanted to know whether or not I was in fact Jewish. Cuba had been so certain of it. I would ask my mother about many things the next time I had her all to myself. She was very secretive about her early years, her lack of a father, her mother's life and death. She did tell me she was raised in an orphanage and had run away from it when she was twelve, to work as a mother's helper and put herself through high school, but that was all I knew. I was her first-born and I deserved to know.

Chapter Twenty-One

Singapore:
The Police and Little Pinches

*F*our suitcases that held everything I owned were pulled away from me gently but with determination. The tall young Indian man, with huge brown eyes, who now had the bags smiled imploringly.

He gave me a card that read Freddie Yu Theatrical Agency. Lily de Saigon, in Paris, had written a note and sent it to Tel Aviv with the contract, telling me Freddie would be my contact agent here and that I would be escorted to the hotel they had arranged for me. After so many hours on the plane from Israel I was ready to surrender some control, relax, take a shower, have a drink, and sleep.

"My name is Edward and I have a car waiting outside for you, Miss Clarice," Edward said, with a precise English accent. He handed off my bags to the waiting porter.

I hit a wall of air so hot and humid I could walk no further than the open doorway of the little airport. Edward very politely held my elbow while trying to drag me through the door and steer me across the sidewalk into the sleek black Mercedes.

"It's air conditioned, Miss Clarice. Please enter." To the uniformed Chinese driver Edward said, "First to the Tropicana for rehearsal."

"Oh, no," I panted. "I need to go to the hotel first. I couldn't sleep on the plane. It's been more than twenty-four hours since I've slept. I need to rest and change before I meet anyone."

"The police tribunal is expected at the club at two p.m. to review your dances, Miss Clarice," said Edward. "You will just have time to give your music to the musicians and the sound man, and dress in your first costume before they arrive. We must not keep them waiting. I hope that is not inconvenient for you but you are the first striptease artist we have had here in Singapore. The police will decide if there are any parts of your dance that are too, uhmm, sophisticated, too French, for Singaporeans to view. If they judge some part is unsuitable for Singapore, it must be taken out before your first show this evening."

My eyes welled with tears of frustration as I dressed in my purple velvet and orange silk gypsy costume to perform for the police. I wanted to put my emotions to the side and do the best show I could for them but my knees were weak and trembly from exhaustion and nerves. This was my first tribunal and I hadn't even been warned about it. Freddie, the agent, and the Shaw brothers, owners of the Tropicana, would be there too. I had to convince them they were getting an act worth the huge amount they were paying me. According to Edward, I was making more per week than the Prime Minister of Singapore.

I was to be part of a French Review called L'Amour de Paris. I came from Hollywood, which many people felt was the capitol of glamour and wanton behavior.

The singer, Mario Bertolino, who according to his advance publicity sang like Mario Lanza, was to be the star of our show. He came from Italy.

Les Silhouettes were six musician/dancers, young men and women who drummed and played different kinds of flutes behind a screen, while colored psychedelic patterns of light played on the screen and lights behind them cast their shadows forward. They were from Peru and Chile. The stage was at least forty feet wide and quite deep so we would all have a challenge filling it and not looking small and insignificant.

Adamo and Eva were the only true Parisians in the show and they were wild. I remembered seeing their act in Paris at the famous lesbian club *Elle et Lui*. Apart, they would have been gorgeous to watch, together they were breathtaking. Adamo was over six feet tall, with dark loosely curled hair worn to his shoulders. He looked like his muscles came from hard physical labor and not standing in front of a mirror watching himself lift weights. To put clothes on that body was a crime.

Eva was a curvy blonde, slender and petite with the smallest waist I had ever seen on a grown person. It couldn't have been more than eighteen inches. She was a very talented gymnast as she had to be for Adamo to throw her around the stage and up in the air as their type of dancing demanded.

Back in Paris, in a show of sadomasochistic lesbian sex acts, their adagio dance was thrilling because of their skill and the beauty of their bodies. At the end of their show Adamo had torn off all of Eva's clothing. By the time he had bitten off Eva's G-string, they only had one very small piece of clothing between them.

The tribunal of three pudgy Chinese policemen, in dark wool gabardine uniforms, who looked like they took their work quite seriously, sat on the right side of the stage behind a long table. Straight chairs had been set up for them and tea was available on the table if they cared to refresh themselves.

At two o'clock exactly, the silvery curtain opened for the police inspection of L'Amour de Paris. They wanted to see my French act first. I performed it just as Lily had choreographed it for me, except for a few little things. I left out all the caressing of my waist, buttocks, breasts and thighs that she had insisted upon. I took out all the floor work on my knees she had demanded we include in this act. I did strip down to my silver and gold beaded G-string though. I had been booked to undress all the way to the G-string. The agent and the Shaw brothers, owners of the Tropicana, were in the large showroom watching to see what their money had brought them from the sexiest places in the world. This might be their only chance to see it in Singapore, and they knew it.

The police took an entire song out of my act that sounded like the blood in your brain was traveling in psychedelic waves and over the beach of your body. The song was three minutes long, and the basic theme of my act. In Singapore it is against the law to sell, buy and take drugs. My French act was all about taking LSD and how sexy and yummy it made me feel, the colors I could hear and smell, and how I could draw you in to see it and long for it with me.

The officers of the tribunal wrinkled their brows and wiped the sweat away with tea napkins when it fell from their jowls onto their white shirt collars. They seemed horrified at the effect the music and dancing had on them. They didn't want to create any precedents that others could follow, so my French act became six minutes long instead of nine.

The pudgy tribunal found no fault with the gypsy act and passed it as performed, although I had to keep on my beaded pants and could not show the G-string at any point in either show. I had no problem with that but I knew the club owners had been hoping for leniency from the police.

Everything needed for my show was already in the immaculate pink and gold dressing room. I had to go to the hotel, put away my personal items, shower, rest, eat, and be back in four hours to start working until one in the morning. Since we only performed two shows each evening it would be an easy schedule but it was seven nights a week.

The main showroom, on the second floor, The Orchid Lounge was the size of a ballroom, filled with comfortable chairs and round tables. There were wooden circles in the middle of the tables to hold the platters of food. They turned like a Lazy Susan to make it easy to serve yourself with chopsticks. Most of the audience would have dinner there before the first show and almost all would use chopsticks to delicately eat the cashew chicken, white rice and other fragrant dishes. True to its name the Orchid Lounge was decorated in shades of lavender and flower petal white and was delightfully air conditioned.

The orchestra, set up on three tiers, stage left, was shielded by a lavender scrim so they didn't take away attention from the performers. Fifteen men would play introduction music between acts and popular English and American songs for couples who wanted to dance during the intermission between shows The music for my act and the other performers was all on tape, which made it easier for entertainers to travel and always have the same songs and quality of music.

The Tropicana building held three other clubs: a mirrored dark and noisy disco on the first floor, a fine dining restaurant, and a small quiet lounge behind soundproof glass doors for social and business meetings where alcohol was required. It was a popular place and the Singaporeans had lots of money to spend. As a free port, with no money charged to bring products into the harbor of Singapore and no money charged to export it again, everybody had a job. Everyone worked. Even young children could be seen chopping vegetables in food stalls and cutting fabric for clothes. There were no beggars on the street in Singapore.

Two young Chinese girls, Annie and Wei-Wei, were sent to help blow up the blue plastic chair, place it on stage each evening, take care of my wardrobe and me. They were tiny and almost looked like children. They must have weighed about ninety pounds and were four-foot-ten or shorter, with long black hair and no makeup, but they had to be at least eighteen to work in a nightclub.

Annie was the first to gently pinch my arm and pet me sweetly. She kept her eyes down while she felt my skin, as if I would not notice her touch if I could not look into her eyes. Three little pinches satisfied her for the moment and she looked at Wei-Wei. Her nod seemed to say, "It's real."

Wei-Wei made her own chance to pinch my blonde-haired, pale arm within a few minutes and then stroked my face and tugged at my curly, red hair. Her body touched mine. It felt like she was trying to put her head on my shoulder.

That was too much. What was all this touching and pulling, nestling and shy smiling about? I didn't want to offend them but I was not going to let these little girls maul me either. I frowned. Both girls stepped back quickly, their heads bowed in embarrassment.

"You look like doll," said Wei-Wei, head still down, eyes up, and a mischievous grin on her thin little face.

They giggled nervously, held hands, leaned toward each other, and peered at me. As soon as I smiled they relaxed and started working smoothly together, moving the blue chair out of the dressing room toward the stage.

That was the beginning. The pinching and petting of my arms, the touching and pulling of my hair, the little hands feeling my cheeks, nose and eyes and occasionally my rear-end continued for the entire six weeks I was there. Female strangers on the street, school girls, shop keepers, and all of the waitresses, cooks assistants, and lady bartenders at the Tropicana pinched and fondled me whenever they could find me. They snuck up to me backstage, in the dark and started pinching and giggling.

I had to stop the hair pulling right away. I knew they were trying to find out if I had a wig on or if my hair was real. People have wondered that since I was a child and often asked my mother why she dyed my hair. I was used to that. But, I wanted my hair to look special on stage and the girls were getting aggressive about pulling off what they thought must be a wig.

They wanted to know what I felt like, as my arms had hair and freckles. Compared to their silken, smooth and unblemished skin I knew mine was a novelty. I would suddenly feel someone trying to pick off the freckles or wipe off the makeup that made my skin more pink and white than theirs. If they started giggling before they reached me, I could turn to protect myself by making a stern face, but if they came up quietly, I was pinched.

Mario, the Italian tenor, did not rehearse with the rest of the show and he did not perform at the Orchid Lounge that evening.

"My troat, my troat," he had moaned during the afternoon as he pawed at his neck and closed his eyes tightly. "Oh, I can not sing in this humidity. It is too much for me."

Freddie Yu, the agent who had put this "French troupe" together came up onto the stage while the police were there. He had tried to talk Mario into singing for them, but Mario would not sing. Mario groaned, he sighed in agony and twisted his heavy body into tortuous positions but he would not sing. He threw his arms and hands about him but he would not sing.

"No one works in Singapore without permission of the tribunal. If Mr. Bertolino decides he wants to work here he can come down to the police station to perform for us, if we have time to see him," the middle pudgy said as he stood up to leave, his chair loudly scraping the wooden stage.

The first night audience of more than 600 Chinese businessmen in conservative dark suits, married or courting couples, and American or English men filled the Orchid Lounge completely. Most of the women were dressed in gorgeous floor length sky blue, gold, red and black heavily embroidered or brocade silk and satin cheongsams with stiff Mandarin collars. Heavy gold necklaces and rings with immense sapphires and other precious stones enhanced their traditional gowns. The side slits of the skirts revealed their unstockinged, yet silky, calves up to the knee.

Men wore tailor-made suits of luscious light wools, silks and sharkskin. Gold watches and large rings seemed to be the necessary accessories to each suit.

The ladies and gentlemen were extremely polite as they applauded, as if they wanted to make the smallest amount of noise possible. I had no idea what they were thinking. Their expressions were bland but they nodded to each other, with tight smiles that showed no teeth, as if they had been given a slightly pleasurable experience. If there was ever an audience completely opposite, in every way, to the raucous partygoers in Tel Aviv, this was it.

It was a disappointing evening for the whole troupe. We had all worked hard to give the beautifully dressed and bejeweled audience a good show under difficult conditions. We were tired and sweaty as we looked at each other with sad eyes and drooping mouths that said, "Oh well, maybe tomorrow night we'll make them enjoy our company."

Les Silhouettes did their show that evening wearing black body stockings. The constantly changing colors and patterns on the screen were mesmerizing and the Peruvian music had a beat that would make anyone want to sway and move their hips while watching. The Singaporeans were stick still.

I thought Adamo and Eva were a wonder to behold as I waited in the wings to follow them on stage. Adamo threw Eva up in the air, threw her by one arm over the closest tables to the stage, through his legs and onto his shoulder. They took up every foot of space they were offered. At the end of their show Eva had on a bra and they both had on full pants. I was kind of glad about that because that made my act different. I was not as good a dancer as Eva or Adamo so I was pretty happy I was the only one who got to show a lot of skin.

As the temporary star of the show, the last act, I stripped to a very small pair of gold and silver beaded and fringed pants, set high on the hip, that brought more attention to the buttocks and pubis than a G-string would have as the beads glittered and the fringe twinkled with each shake under the spotlights. They were exactly like, but smaller than, the pants the tribunal had approved but I didn't think they would remember if they came back to see that their rules were being observed.

The troupe was getting ready to leave when Freddie Yu rushed in full of news followed by two waiters carrying four chilled bottles of champagne, a dozen fluted glasses and a tray of tiny pink and white cakes.

"Congratulations!! Congratulations!! What a great show. I stayed in the audience for a few minutes to hear what people were saying and they love all of you. They thought you were brilliant Adamo with your Eva, and Clarice was our beautiful doll. Even the women adored you." He was so excited his voice was high and squeaky, his eyes rolled to the ceiling. "We were successful beyond all hopes. We'll sell out the house for the whole six-week run. We don't need the Italian singer to draw them in after tonight. Oh, what a night! Let him work some place they don't have an exotic dancer and be happy there. I shake my hands of him, right?"

The wine was flowing, the waiters were turning in place trying to press glasses into our hands and the hall between the dressing rooms was so crowded that it took me a moment to realize what Freddie had said.

"Mario refused to work with a striptease act in the show, Freddie?" I questioned softly with no expression on my face or in my voice.

All the brown eyes in the hall turned to my face then to Freddie's for the answer. French, English, Spanish and Chinese conversations around me stopped as we waited. The poor man looked horrified that such an insult had just dropped from his mouth.

Edward, the assistant agent from the airport, looking cool and handsome in his summer weight tuxedo and ruffled white shirt, joined us at that moment, followed by the Master of Ceremonies for our show, Tommy Wong.

"Yes, Miss Clarice, and now you are our star and he is no longer needed. Congratulations to you all on a wonderful show. Will you have more champagne, Miss Clarice? You deserve it," Edward said smoothly with a smile and nodded for the waiters to pour.

I was happy with the new situation. Mario and his manager had both asked me up to their hotel rooms in the short time we had known each other, so now I wouldn't have to worry about that anymore. My smile was the cue for the conversations in French, English, Spanish and Chinese to resume.

Tommy Wong was a skinny kid of about twenty-three, dressed in jeans and a white tee shirt wearing a cigarette behind his ear. He had the rich, full, resonant and beautifully trained voice of a mature, upper crust Englishman. It made him a perfect Master of Ceremonies for the Orchid Lounge, as he was up in the sound booth, behind the second tier of tables where he could not be seen. He told us during rehearsal that he was a disc jockey on the radio during the day. It was obvious from his curled lip and cocky walk that Tommy thought he was the next James Dean. His face confirmed what Freddie had told us. Our show was a hit.

The apartment Freddie had arranged for us was large and clean but awful to look at. The only good thing about it was the short walking distance to the Tropicana. In that very expensive and almost exclusively commercial area, an affordable large apartment was hard to find. The two bedrooms and living space I shared with Adamo and Eva was full of grass-green, cushioned rattan furniture. There was a huge institutional type bathroom with four shower nozzles, side by side, jutting out of one wall.

The place was plain, used, and worn. Three hundred Singapore dollars per week, which was one hundred American dollars, gave me a home and a simple breakfast each morning around ten when I awoke to more heat and sun.

I hardly ever saw Eva or Adamo at the apartment. It was like having the place entirely to myself. Where they went and what they did during their time off was a big secret.

I was lonesome as usual, but I tried to be adventurous during the day. I walked up and down each side of Orchard Road until I knew all the jewelry shop owners and the tailor who was making me evening gowns and stylish dresses for afternocns. I had left Los Angeles September 1st and had brought mostly winter clothing with me. The pale leaf- green wool mini-skirt I had been wearing out in the sun was already leaving a tan line across my thighs. I had never had a tan line in my life.

The only department store was Robinsons. Its dark polished wooden walls and large ornate cabinets looked like antiques and I was sure they had been there for many decades. The merchandise was simple and years out of fashion.

All I had to do was give the tailor a Vogue magazine and show him photos of what I wanted him to make. He had a vast array of the finest fabrics from all over the world for me to select from. He measured and I picked up a dress that was an exact replica of the picture a day or two later, with perhaps a few changes I had asked for. It worked perfectly every time.

I received a contract from Lily de Saigon, in Paris, letting me know I would start working at the Crazy Horse Saloon on January 20, 1969, for one year, at thirty-five dollars a night for seven nights a week. When Lily started off on her quest of getting me into the Crazy she said I would have to be a super star to get twenty-five a night. I wondered what she would call me now.

I couldn't stop smiling to myself. I would live in Paris. I would fall in love with a beautiful French woman who would be madly in love with me. I would wear gorgeous clothes and fantastic costumes. I would dance at the best and most famous striptease club in the world. Maybe I would be famous. To top it off I would earn more than those catty dancers at the Crazy Horse, who had all agreed my hair was funny-looking.

I took a trickshaw to venture further into the city or when I felt too hot to walk. The trickshaw was great for sightseeing. A man riding a bicycle pulled a rickshaw behind him with a seat that was wide enough for two people, or one lady with all her shopping bags. It was slow enough to let me see everything while covered with a sunshade above and fast enough to create a welcome little breeze. The trickshaw was easier on the driver than the rickshaw, which was pulled by a man on foot, so I didn't feel guilty about using them. There were so many trickshaw drivers. They stood smoking in groups, or sat napping in their trickshaw next to the hot cement sidewalk, waiting for someone like me to walk by and hire them for a little ride or for the afternoon.

In the evening I walked the seven blocks of narrow sidewalk next to the drain, called a klong, down the hill on Orchard Road, to the Tropicana. I passed the tailor shop whose owner didn't have enough work and was always in the doorway smoking, and the little market with many kinds of fruit I had never seen before.

As I walked along, I could see how Singapore society was set up by looking at who had what type of job. The shopkeepers were all Chinese, except in "Little India." The guards, who also opened the doors of the jewelry stores and restaurants for customers, were all Indian. The men and women who swept the street, carried sand and rocks for the construction of new buildings, and did most of the menial work for the Singaporeans, were Malaysian.

I couldn't figure out why the cement trenches on the both sides of the road, called klongs, were there. I was told they led to the ocean and were to keep the streets and walk ways from being covered with rainwater and flooding the little shops. There was so much rain every day it washed the streets clear of almost all the spit. Singaporeans spat often and plentifully. It rained hard for about an hour and then the sun came out again leaving heavy, humid, hot air behind all day and into the evening and early morning.

Tommy Wong, our young M. C., asked me to go out for a drink after the show when I had been in Singapore for six days and I was ready to see something besides shops and restaurants. I worked with this guy so I wasn't worried.

He wanted to go to a disco and show off in front of his friends but when we arrived he didn't know anyone there.

"Have you seen the house of the dead?" Tommy asked as we walked back toward his new red roadster convertible.

"Is that another bar?" I asked, completely unaware that Tommy had suffered recent trauma and wanted company to revisit the horror.

"You'll see," he said as we sped through the narrow and dark back streets of residential Singapore.

The air was hot and the full moon cast shadows on the houses as we passed. It was after two in the morning and I had just decided to tell Tommy I did not want to go dancing at another bar when I saw lights up ahead.

We stopped near the entrance of a large building. Tommy got out and quietly greeted the few men and women sitting outside on rattan chairs. It looked like they were waiting for something. There were long tables that held hundreds of candles and platters of decorated food. The heavy smoke and smell of incense invaded my nostrils. A brightly painted silver and pink paper castle on one table had a tiny paper man dressed in gold at its doorway. He had a red paper car, packets of green paper money scattered around and three pretty little paper wives stood ready to serve his every wish.

Bells chimed from inside the building, wood hitting solidly on wood sounded loud and hollow while the chanting of men's voices filled what little air was not already full.

The men and women on the street greeted Tommy with smiles and shook his hand as they sat among the candles and food offerings for the spirits. A man tried to get Tommy to join them in a gambling game but he declined and bought a lottery ticket instead. These people were waiting for death.

Once inside the gate I saw pyramids of oranges and cakes, more paper cars and yachts and paper diamond rings. Professionally prepared platters holding the finest pastries and fresh tender fruit covered long tables in the middle of a rectangular courtyard that went on for several hundred feet. Black flies loudly buzzed around the platters and dived in to eat their fill.

Tommy and I walked between rows of three-sided rooms that faced the courtyard. We could see bunk beds stacked three high, almost to the ceiling. They held coughing or moaning and twisting men who looked a hundred years old. Some sunken eyes and mouths widened to see us there. Others had no idea they were still in the world of men and women.

Two rooms near the entrance were bright with candlelight, filled with chanting priests, and striking bells, among the incense. Orange robes, yellow fire and golden brass bells blurred together as the smoke of incense became heavier. The hollow thwock of wood on wood kept a steady pace as I shivered from the hot sweat dripping down my back and the weight of sadness around us.

Tommy took my wrist and pulled me further down the courtyard, past dark and dimly lit rooms. He finally stopped. I saw tears on his cheeks. Flies landed on his face. His eyes were fixed on one narrow bed that now held a slender figure, covered with a sheet.

"My father was there." Finally he said, "No family wants someone to die in their house. It's very bad luck," he explained.

I was freezing cold while dripping with sweat. I had never known anyone who had died and I was terrified. Turning away from Tommy and the sight of dozens and more dozens of dying men on each side of the courtyard that seemed like it went on for blocks, I walked quickly up to the front gate, with my eyes straight ahead.

The cheerful banter of the people waiting and watching stopped when I joined them on the street, shivering in the heat, to wait for Tommy. It was after three in the morning.

When Tommy came out of the death house he had been drinking. I had not seen a bottle on him or a drink for sale inside the walls. He was unsteady on his feet and looked glassy-eyed. I didn't want to get in the car with him. But I didn't know how to get out of there.

We had gone four or five blocks when the little convertible veered too far left and half the car toppled into the klong, and skidded until we banged into the walkway that crossed it to allow for pedestrian traffic. The car leaned in, with the front wheel caught in the narrow waterway. Tommy was sprawled backward, his head resting on the cement. There was blood on his forehead and a light rain had just started to fall.

I stood on the red leather seats in my high heels, grabbed onto his shoulder for balance, climbed across him and out of the car. Nothing happened when I shook him. He just grunted. I wanted to hit him and leave him there for dead. Angry at Tommy and feeling stupid for allowing myself to get into this dangerous predicament I left him there, passed out in his snappy little car with the rain pouring down on the perfectly smooth red leather seats.

I walked toward a street that had more light. A taxi passed and I grabbed it. There hadn't been anyone on the street a few minutes ago and who knew when another one might come by. I had no idea where I was but the driver didn't have to know that. I told him the name of my hotel at the top of Orchard Road. We started rolling up the street and I didn't look back.

Tommy Wong might have been a voice with no body for the next five weeks. Whenever I saw him, he was just leaving the room. I never spoke of it to anyone but he had suffered a tremendous loss of face. He introduced the acts very well, but he never let me see him again, and I didn't want to.

Chapter Twenty-Two

The Women of Desker Road

Breast of chicken curry at the InterContinental Hotel on Orchard Road was breakfast every morning as soon as I discovered it. The little coffee shop, with orange plastic chairs, was plain but the curry was spectacular in every way. Yellow, thick and spicy, juicy and hot, the whole chicken breast resting on a high bed of white rice made my mouth water, and was a great way to start the day.

A tall and slender boy came over to my table and introduced himself.

"I lived in London for a couple of years and I can tell when a girl is too good-looking for most people to approach her. May I sit down?" he said, pulling out an orange chair. "I'm Winston Tan and I own a club called the Fireplace. You may want to visit soon. What have you been doing? I'd say not much. You look depressed," he said, looking into my eyes.

This guy is lounging in my booth, looking about fifteen years-old and he tells me I'm depressed? He was right of course.

"Just trying to learn something about Singapore. Where do you shop around here?"

"We have nice jewelry shops in the hotels. Would you like my secretary to take you shopping? I can send her to you with a car and you can go anywhere you like. Good. She will be at your hotel in an hour. And by the way, if you want to change your Singapore dollars into American money, the Bank of America here is a branch of yours in California, so it will be very easy for you to put your salary into an account. It was lovely meeting you. Goodbye."

Winston strode out looking very confident, tall and willowy. He was a good looking guy and a foot taller than anyone in the shop. I tried to figure out what had happened. Did I let another guy pick me up in a new town but the same kind of place and the same old way? Well, yes. There weren't any women who wanted to talk to me. What else was I going to do today? My God! He really knew a lot about me. He already knew where I was staying and where I was from. I guessed the Tropicana always put their out of town acts in that ugly place.

True to his word, Winston's secretary arrived almost as soon as I got to the apartment. She looked young but I couldn't tell much about the age of the Singaporeans. She was neat and trim in her western style navy blue suit and white blouse.

"Good morning, Miss Clarice. I am Angela Wong. Mr. Tan has sent me to take you shopping and show you some of Singapore. Would you like to have your astrological chart drawn up today? Would you like to go to a famous fortune- teller? Do you like to buy jade or gold? What about temples, a tour of the harbor in a junk or the Tiger Balm Garden?"

At noon it was already ninety-nine degrees with ninety-five percent humidity. It was a chore to slog through the heavy, water-laden, air. Better to go someplace cool.

"Think of the coolest place and let's go there first," I said while walking out the door into the bright wetness.

A black Lincoln sedan and an Indian driver waited in the parking lot. Angela spoke to him in English and off we went to I didn't know where. I just knew the car was air conditioned and for the moment that was enough. I felt so relaxed talking to an enthusiastic, lovely woman who was there to help me enjoy her city. Winston had made this possible.

Angela was the first to warn me of a Malay Prince who came to Singapore regularly in search of women he could steal, with the help of his driver and bodyguards. It was said he took them back to his palace, far over the border in Malaysia.

"The prince loves Australian and English showgirls, Miss Clarice. You must be very careful. He has been at this for years and no one has been able to stop him, not even his father. We never hear of these stolen girls again, Miss Clarice, so do be careful. Don't go anywhere with strange men as one of them could be a bodyguard," she said with the innocent eyes of a young girl telling a ghost story.

When I burst out laughing, stopped and started up again over and over, she became frantic. Her slender hands fanned my face, her breathing became harsh as she leaned in toward my ear and yelled. "What's wrong Miss Clarice? Are you alright? May I help you? Stop laughing! "

I thought of how my trip had been going so far and I laughed until I my cheeks were covered with tears and I laughed some more. Shaking my head and getting my breath back I let her know I was alright. Later, I heard this story many times from bartenders and waiters. Even Freddie Yu told me about the criminal prince.

"In Singapore we have many groups that stay together and maintain their own culture on this little island," Angela told me as we drove along. "We no longer belong to England. We became our own country only four years ago. We are small, about the size of your Chicago, but have one of the largest ports in the world. Chinese always busy, always busy. Many are Indian. Indians want to work too. There is a joke that Malasians only work when they want to eat. So it goes. Chinese are on top part, with more businesses and more money. Indians in the middle, and most Malays on the money bottom."

I doubted it could be that simple. It looked more complicated but I had seen who had the job of shop owner, who had the job of shop guard and who had the job of shop cleaner in just that order.

Madam Aquila lived and worked in a cool, blue-gray atmosphere. Not only were her hair and eyes gray, but her long draped robe, massive jeweled necklaces and heavy bracelets, all of silvery cabochon moon stones , were gray as well. She sat in an ornately carved, wide, wooden armchair upholstered in grayish blue velvet, and placed on a dais. It was about eight feet from where my much smaller seat was placed.

Her head would be about two feet above mine when I sat down. That meant I would have to look up to see her and I felt sure my expression would become one of adoration because of the angle. It was just as she had planned. The showgirl in me admired how she made sure her audience of one could see the entire picture.

My next thought upon seeing her was, how did this plain, bulky western woman who seemed to be sixty-five or seventy years-old, become a famous fortune teller in Singapore, of all places. I wanted to laugh, just from the dramatic way she presented herself and the tension she inspired, but tried to control it.

"Be seated, my dear," she said softly. Her accent was not immediately recognizable but it could have been Russian or Hungarian. Clearly, she wanted this to be a theatrical experience. The low bowing male servant who had taken the envelope with forty American dollars enclosed and ushered me into the room from the adjoining hall, the furniture placement, the color, the costume, the voice and the hint of lavender in the air, all set the scene for a mystical moment in time. It was a moment never to be forgotten.

"You are obviously a Scorpio. In what year were you born?"

I wondered how she knew that very particular thing. When I told her the year her eyebrows raised to the top of her forehead. "Oh, yes. You are a dragon. What was the hour of your birth?"

The hour interested her and she sat up a little straighter and leaned toward me to get a better look.

Madam Aquila's voice was deep and serious as she warned, "A double dragon. You know by now you will never marry. No man would want to have a double dragon Scorpio for a wife. This combination is too strong for a man. Try women if you have not already. You must wear moonstones, as I do. There is danger everywhere, not only in the Far East, and they will protect you from harm. I can see that you will stop working in about two years but that is all for now."

I was dismissed.

My twenty-eighth birthday was coming soon and I would spend it in Singapore. I hoped I would not be at the beck and call of strangers when I was Madam Aquila's age. Poor thing had to put out at a moment's notice. What happened if she wasn't inspired to say something?

Most of what she had said was not a surprise, but her bluntness about trying women was a shocking thing for a woman of her time to say. Madam Aquila must have seen a great deal of the world before her gray chair days.

I was curious about her reading and now that I had started along this path I decided to collect fortune-teller readings and astrological readings while I was in Singapore. I had known I was a dragon. Children who live in San Francisco, as I had, learn at an early age what sign they are due to the large Chinese population. However, I did not know there was such a thing as a double dragon. That sounded exciting.

Angela had been waiting in the hall and rose to leave with me. We hurried to the gold shops in the center of town to buy moonstones. We bought cat's eye moonstone rings, faceted and cabochon silver-gray moonstone necklaces and gold bracelets for Dreamy and Mitzi. The reading took about ten minutes, but the shopping took hours.

Many of the little shops along Gold Street were open air, family run stalls. Some were upscale stores with air conditioning, large mirrors and handsomely dressed salespeople. A few shops were run out of suitcases, or boxes set up on the sidewalk. All sold only gold and jewels and each was full of dark yellow, pale green and pink gold. I was too busy to feel the heat. Many moonstones, large and small, went home with me and I smiled all day. I was a double dragon.

The shopping for jade, silk and gold went on for days. I had clothes made and sent Christmas presents to my parents, my little sister Michele and to Dreamy and Mitzi. Staying in one place was becoming boring. Nothing was happening. It was hot all day and night. I had my astrological chart drawn up five times and my fortune told by Chinese tellers, Indian tellers and Malasian tellers. I lounged as all strippers do on the road. I hadn't lounged as much since my first roadshow with Lillian and the girls in Houston.

Edward, the assistant agent, married a beautiful, tall and elegant Chinese woman while our show was there. He and his bride invited everyone in the cast to the wedding and we all went together to this most extravagant, exciting ceremony.

It was a spectacular event, traditional in every way. The bride started off with a western style white wedding gown and changed clothes five times during the many hours of the ceremony and dinner. Her last dress, a gorgeous, form fitting cheongsam was made of thick, bright red silk.

She also wore the long, heavy twenty-four carat yellow gold link necklace Edward had given her as a wedding present. She would wear that all of her life as a symbol of her family's status.

Giving the bride gold jewelry was both an Indian and Chinese tradition, we were told by Freddie's secretary Mary Soo, who sat at the cast table and told us what was happening. She was half way between our nanny and our matron at this event, and tried to be tactful about the obvious animosity between some tables. Black glares, muttering and some finger pointing drew Adamo's attention.

"Why do all the people at that table keep standing up and sitting down," Adamo, our apache dancer, asked Mary Soo.

"I'm very sorry for you to see this," Mary said. "I think they are trying to decide whether to stay or leave. Being Indian, and very proud, they feel insulted by some of the Chinese guests. When the father stands they all stand and when he decides he can stay at his nephew's wedding for a while longer they all follow his lead and sit down. Sometimes it is difficult to be an Indian person in Singapore. The bride is 'Strait-spawn Chinese,' meaning she was born in Singapore and not in China. Her parents were born in China. They, and their relatives, have different ideas about who it is proper to marry. I'm very sorry," she said with her eyes down as if she was studying the tablecloth.

A 'sit-down' dinner for four hundred, featuring shark fin soup and birds nest soup, were included in the ten course meal served on round tables. Toward the end of the meal the bride went from table to table pouring tea for her guests and saying a special word to each one. She received the traditional fat red envelopes of money from almost everyone. We in the cast had been advised by Freddie to contribute fifty dollars each and our envelopes went into the deep well of the bride's silk purse with all the rest. If every person there gave about the same amount, it might have paid for half of the wedding.

A few evenings after Edward and his bride went off to Sri Lanka for their honeymoon I found out that Winston was in terrible trouble. The police had raided his club. Ten customs officials had burst in, throwing tables and chairs against the walls, looking for narcotics one night after closing. They said they had received tips that drugs were being sold there. I knew that could not be true. Winston was a straight arrow kind of guy. He didn't smoke anything and drank moderately but never more than one or two drinks in an evening. He was called down to the police station and warned, although he was not told what he had done to receive the warning.

When I was invited to his parents' home for dinner, I found out his father was the head of the Salvation Army in Singapore and quite an important man. He said he had gone to the police station to see what he could do to help his son's business.

"Winston, a confidential source in the police department told me that gangsters planned to close the Fireplace. It's difficult to obtain a liquor license and get permission to open a new club so the criminals ruin the old established clubs, buy them for low prices then change the name and build them back up again.

"Someone will come to you with an offer to buy your government permits. The offer will be very low and they expect you to be grateful for anything they want to give you," said Mr. Tan.

About the same time two lean and bearded hippies from London, James and Malcolm, approached Winston and said they would redecorate his club for their room and board, a little spending money and tickets to go to their next destination. It didn't sound like too much money at first, but it could add up to a great deal. James and Malcolm were almost identical if you didn't look hard.

They wore silver stud earrings and their shoulder length braided hair was intertwined with blue and white beads and small silver bells. Well-worn pale jeans rested low on skinny hips. Among the very formal Chinese and Indian men of Singapore they could have been Martians and drawn less attention.

"We're traveling the world," said James, "remodeling clubs and some houses just to be able to travel and stay in places for a while."

From the pictures they showed us they were talented workmen and designers. Winston decided to close the Fireplace and update the club, hoping he could get past these bad few months and reopen with a fresh and modern look.

Parts of Singapore were beautiful and seemed very safe for the tourist. However, there was a tremendous amount of corruption, extortion, prostitution, and illegal gambling which a foreigner would not see if they didn't meet and talk to a great many local people. It took several weeks for me to see and I had to be led by the hand to very out of the way places. It was said by the locals that bribery was just part of doing business and you could get anything done for a price if you asked a Malaysian to do it.

Mr. Richard Lim, a partner of the Shaw brothers who owned the Tropicana complex, fell madly in love with me before the Christmas holidays and wanted to make me his second wife. I never found out exactly what a second wife meant in their culture but it seemed to mean mistress. Freddie told me it was a common practice and might be the best thing for me to do in Singapore.

I didn't want any part of it. Maybe if it had been Mrs. Lim who had fallen in love, but no. I found out in that way Freddie was a pimp as well as an agent.

Mr. Lim wanted me to stay in Singapore. He offered, through Freddie, to make me the manager of the Orchid Lounge showroom and buy me an apartment. He hardly knew me. What was he thinking? I couldn't figure it out.

I don't think Mr. Lim had ever been out of Singapore because when I mentioned I was reading *The Forsythe Saga*, he bought me the entire set of thirteen, orange hard bound books. They must have weighed five pounds each. How did he think I could ever travel with them?

Winston became my constant companion. He arranged for me to meet the only two lesbians he knew.

"To be homosexual is against the law here so it is unusual to find someone who will admit to it. I do know one couple who has been together for six years though. I think they would agree to meet you if you would like to meet them?"

The next night I felt like I was going on a secret mission as Winston and I walked from the Tropicana to the Goodwood Hotel after my second show. Margo worked with a trio who played piano, sax and drums at the Goodwood.

"She is amazing. The most beautiful and popular singer in Singapore and has been for five years. If anyone finds out she is a lesbian there will be a riot at the Goodwood," Winston cautioned me.

Standing five foot seven Margo was taller than most of the population in her country. With long brown hair and wide expressive eyes she was reminiscent of band singers in the 1950s, wearing strapless evening gowns that exposed most of her large breasts.

She was Chinese and English, an unwelcome combination in Singapore society. It often meant your mother had been involved with, or raped by, an Englishman, one of the invaders, a colonizer who deserted her when she became pregnant. That was Margo's story. She and her mother shared the bitterness of that truth.

It was a four block walk from the Tropicana to the Goodwood and at two in the morning I was a little worried about going there alone. But when Winston couldn't be there I did walk the warm, seemingly deserted, dark streets. If Margo wanted to see me I wouldn't resist.

Anita, her partner, was a painter of Chinese and Malaysian heritage. She was a slender woman with one thick braid of beautiful black hair that hung past her waist. Shy and quiet, Anita always directed attention toward Margo and away from herself.

I fell into instant infatuation with both Margo and Anita. I wanted to buy them presents, wanted to be with them every night, loved Margo's mother and I loved them as a couple. They were lovely together, gentle and funny, supportive of one another and they liked me. I was the only other lesbian they knew and they were fascinated with me. They wanted to know everything about me, how I found out I loved women, and what I did about it. They would call and make sure I was going to walk the few blocks to see them after my last show.

Anita and I sat in the audience, drinking vodka gimlets, and watching Margo sing and flirt with her audience. She sang American and English pop tunes, ballads and torch songs of the 1930s, 40s and 50s which were still popular in Singapore. Her strong contralto voice was divine. Beauty and warmth radiated from the stage to her audience. A week passed and I thought I was more in love with Margo.

The problems started when I wanted to take Margo to Paris. Feeling guilty about it, I nevertheless did everything I could to get her to go with me. I knew I would be as lonesome in Paris as I had been for the past few months and I was trying to guard against it. I felt awful about trying to get her to leave Anita yet I was so very attracted to Margo. I really did feel she could become popular in Europe if she worked at it. But she was more comfortable in Singapore being a big fish in a tiny pond.

Margo, Anita and I were in the disco at the Tropicana one evening when a young American guy passed our table and dropped two hand-rolled cigarettes.

"Have a good time girls," he said as he walked on and disappeared like an apparition. It was against the law to possess drugs in Singapore so he had risked a great deal to give us this gift. Margo didn't want to waste it but Anita and I were suspicious. Who knew what drugs were inside?

Margo wanted to smoke so the three of us smoked. That was the only night we were alone for a few minutes, drugged and loose enough to talk about her going to Paris with me.

"You won't like me once you know me better," Margo said when we were alone for a rare moment. "I'm really a bitch, hard to get along with and I always want my own way. What would I do there anyway? Here, I feel comfortable and I am taking care of my mother. You want me to see your agent in Paris and what could he do for me?"

She drank scotch, put her arm around me, fondled my breast and kissed me.

"He'd just send me on the road like you are now and how could we be together that way? You're right that professionally I have reached as high as I can here in Singapore. How do I know they would even like me in Europe? No, Anita takes good care of my mother and this is my home, but come here and let me kiss you again."

In her own determined Chinese way, Anita rode this out quietly and politely without saying a word to me. She knew from experience that everyone fell in love with Margo and I would be gone soon. Maybe not soon enough, but I would not be taking Margo with me. Anita was the constant in Margo's life, the known, the worshipper and the ultimate winner.

I was going to have a few weeks off during January before my contract started in Paris, and couldn't figure out where to spend them. It was so exciting to have the choice of traveling anywhere in Europe or even the Middle East before starting to work in Paris. I could not go to the Far East as China was still closed and America was bombing Cambodia, Laos and Vietnam. I couldn't fix on one place. What about Athens or London?

The hippies fixing The Fireplace advised me to go to Katmandu, Nepal or Bangkok Thailand. They talked about the handmade jewelry and crafts, the art and the friendly people. I was thinking about going to Kashmir in India. I didn't want to go anyplace hot. I was told I could get to Saigon for a few days to see the war if I wanted to entertain the troops. Singapore was only an hour away from the war by plane. Did I want to see the war?

Some of the Australian dancers I met in Singapore had entertained the soldiers in Vietnam with the USO and they said Saigon was special. The only real problem with that was my time off would coincide with their big New Year holiday season and the North Vietnamese army concentrated on bombing the city at that time of the year instead of the countryside. I didn't think about that destination for too long. It turned out that the 1968 TET offensive by the North Vietnamese was the largest to date and Saigon was captured by the north for a short while.

Winston introduced me to a young woman named Vicky Noon who had just returned to Singapore from London for what she called "a long vacation." Vicky had been a police-woman in Singapore before she left and was now on holiday from her work at Scotland Yard. She was taller than me, with a lovely figure, surprisingly large breasts and wore big glasses with heavy black frames. While not pretty, Vicky had some European style and sophistication about her after living in London for two years.

We had fun together. Vicky said she was straight and had just broken up with a long- time boyfriend but she acted possessive and very interested in me. I didn't mind even though I was not interested in her romantically. Winston got jealous I was spending so much time with Vicky and dropped out of my life for a few days.

A whole new Singapore opened up to me the last five days I was there. Vicky introduced me to Rose and Ann, friends of hers who were current members of the Singapore Women's Police Force. They obtained permission from their supervisor to take me in their police car to see the tent cities of prostitution, set up as semi-permanent venues away from the middle of the city. I had not heard about them and had no idea what I was going to experience.

Rose and Ann, both very plain girls, with square muscular bodies and hair chopped off just below the ears, had lived together for five years. Vicky told me in Singapore there was no thought that two Chinese girls would be gay together.

"They would be horrified to even think about it," Vicky said. "They just won't. The Eurasian girls are different, like Margo and Anita, but not the Asians."

I didn't care what Vicky thought. Rose and Ann looked and acted like lesbians, especially in their own home, where I was invited to have lunch before we made our way out to the tent city called Desker Road. We held a contest of who could eat the hottest and most chili. Would it be the Strait Spawn Chinese police women or the Southern California girl who ate Mexican food for breakfast lunch and dinner when she could? I won, I think. They were very good hosts so I am not positive I won, even though I ate the hottest of red, green and orange chilies but the food was delicious.

Ann and Rose lived in a government-owned building in Queenstown. A hundred or more apartments all with the same floor plan. They had two little bedrooms, a living room, and a small kitchen with a two burner hot plate and tiny refrigerator. The bathroom did have a flush toilet but only a drain in the floor and a thick black hose that hung from the wall for showering.

Ann and Rose had never had a Caucasian person in their apartment before and they kept looking at me to see how I was reacting. I was fine, but they seemed nervous.

Many buildings just like theirs formed Queenstown. Each apartment rented for twenty one dollars American. At street level there were restaurants, pharmacies, acupuncturists, little grocery stores for the tenants and sparse playgrounds for the children. It looked like private homes were on their way out and the trend was to have everyone, except the very wealthy, live in rabbit warrens.

We drove toward "Little India" a neighborhood with low cost housing and shopping of all kinds. Bright silk and cotton hung, fold after fold, from the roof of the stalls and small shops. The smell of sheep and pig blood, mixed with human excrement was over-whelming. You could smell "Little India" blocks before you could see it as the government didn't spend much time improving conditions there.

It was late afternoon when we reached Desker Road, a drab brown, beige and grey area of more than two hundred tents, separated by wide dirt paths with not a bit of green or softness. Only the women's colorful yellow, pink and purple sarongs and saris as they walked to get water from a constantly running pipe, gave relief to the eye. Indian guards with knives and guns at their waists took money from Chinese and Malaysian customers while standing by the tent door flaps to protect their master's human property from those without funds.

Women who were not busy having sex sat in front of the tents, sipping tea or cold drinks from the vendors' carts, waiting for the next customer to choose them. Their eyes, like dark stones set in dough, regarded us with flat stares.

We four women and one man rode in the police car. Ann, Rose and the driver wore their dark police uniforms. We cruised the dirt pathways between tightly packed rectangular tents. Ann said that each held four or five cots separated by curtains.

We looked at everyone going into or coming out of the tents. Each one looked back at us. The cruel and fierce faces of the tent guards looked as if they were wondering why the police had come back so soon. The passive, dull and dead looking faces of the women who carried water and grey rags beyond the door flaps, into the tents, seemed like they never wondered about anything. The defiant faces of the men, who came to penetrate the old and sagging flesh of these tired women, looked at us too.

"I don't see any Chinese women here, Rose," I said.

"If there are Chinese women doing this kind of work, it's in houses closer to the city and I don't know about them. There probably are a few. They would get much more money than these girls, as they would be rare -- too expensive for Desker Road. They probably have some Chinese girls in Malaysia. The men who own these women on Desker Road are paid three Singapore dollars by each customer. That's about one dollar in your American money," she replied.

"The women never get any of the money made here. They may have sex twenty or thirty times a day, or more, and can never better their position because they are given nothing but food, and a cloth roof," Ann added. "They sleep and work on the same cot."

We left Desker Road and drove a few minutes to the Johor Road section. It was smaller than Desker. There were fewer tents, but more misery. I didn't think there could be a worse place for women than the Desker tents, but Johor Road women were older and darker skinned. They wore dark, tattered and torn sarongs. Many were disfigured by scars, missing limbs and eyes.

"These poor women have only one thing they can sell and then only with the help and support of each other," Rose said. "Most of the men who guard them have been in prison and probably can't do anything else either. The cost of a woman here is thirty-three cents American or one Singapore dollar."

"I can't see any change here since I left the Singapore Police Department," Vicky said. She didn't look happy to be here either.

I wanted to be away from there so badly. I wanted never to have seen this and not to know people could treat each other so terribly. As we finally drove away, I was crying and hiding my face from the women on the streets and those in the car with me.

I realized I was on the top tier of this very same business. The sex trade. I hid my face, leaned against the car window and cried at the harsh, cruel lives inflicted on the women I had seen.

I grew more and more depressed in Singapore those last few days. I couldn't look at the audiences the same way I had earlier in my stay. These people lived here, they knew about Desker Road and maybe even about Johor Road and allowed it to exist. The men probably made some kind of jokes about those roads and what went on there. Some may have even paid for sex there. I was so thankful I would be leaving soon.

I knew of no way to help the women born or traded into slavery, women who lived and worked in the streets. The Prime Minister was beginning to inflict strict rules of personal conduct on the people of Singapore, in the form of fines for spitting on the sidewalk and graffiti on the buses, so perhaps some of the vice and prostitution would be cleaned up one day.

My decision to spend the first half of January in Bangkok and Katmandu, started a flurry of activity with Angela, Winston's wonderful secretary, my new friend. She took me to the small health department building to have a series of vaccinations for yellow fever, polio, small pox, malaria and some other things I didn't know people could get. They gave me documents to carry with me proving I had recently been inoculated and told me these were the papers to show the airline staff when I was asked. My arm was sore for a week.

Angela was full of good advice. "They will not let you on the airplane if you are wearing pants, Clarice. Be sure to wear a skirt but not too short." Angela looked at the skirt I was wearing and raised a fine dark eyebrow. "You want to wear very little makeup, also no false eyelashes. They don't want any foreign bar girls to come into the country. They have enough of their own -- and no T-shirts. They also have a rule about men having long hair. No man enters Thailand with "hippie hair." They have barbers at the Bangkok airport for those who have hair that reaches their shirt collar and if you won't cut it the police will put you right back on an airplane out of the country," she said nodding vigorously to stress her warnings.

In the next few days Vicky and I bought more gifts of gold and jade for Dreamy, Mitzi and my mother. We gave Rose and Ann all thirteen books of *The Forsythe Saga* that Mr. Lim had found somewhere. Maybe they could sell them back to the same people.

"I had my ticket changed. I only have to stay here for three more days then I can meet you in Bangkok," Vicky said while we were on the Chinese junk.

Margo and Anita had hired the boat so we could have a goodbye lunch the day before I was to leave Singapore. I guessed they were pretty glad to see me go. There had been a little drama but we ended up friends. We were moving slowly around the harbor, sails flapping, having a carefree day when Vicky dropped the little bomb of meeting me in Bangkok.

Looking at Anita, I could see her thinking, "Look who you got stuck with instead of my Margo." The wide eyes and innocent smile said it all.

Margo's profile showed a small smile. She turned full face toward me but lowered her eyes to the rice bowl before she turned away again. Margo slid her eyes back and looked at me like she was holding back a giggle. She really was a bitch, but a beautiful one.

Vicky was a lovely person but I was not happy about this unexpected complication. I did not want a relationship with her but it looked like she had made up her mind that I was hers.

It was amazing how fast she had tried to take over my life. When we ate she wanted to choose the menu and insisted that she serve me. She wanted to turn on my shower, set out my clothes, and would have brushed my teeth for me if I had let her.

Vicky wanted to plan all of my activities. The things she suggested were fun. Bougie Street, which was closed to traffic in the evening and off-limits to American sailors, was a great experience for a showgirl like me because it was all show and lots of sex.

Tables were arranged for the tourists and locals on Bougie St. to sit and talk with the beauties who served them tea or beer. The gorgeous transvestite prostitutes of many nationalities, dressed in feathers, silk, jewels and showing acres of smooth skin, waited to attract the sailors from many countries who didn't quite know they were being serviced by men. There were often brawls and sometimes riots when a man, there for the first time, felt the truth while groping between slender feminine legs and found a penis. Many sailors had been found face down in the water of the klongs when the morning street cleaners arrived.

Vicky was fun but I didn't like the constant pressure of intimacy with her. She was too close and I didn't know how to tell her to move back. I couldn't point to anything she had done to hurt me but everything irritated me. I felt like she was trying to swallow my life.

It had been so much easier at the Largo. Dreamy and I had broken up after eight years together and I was suddenly single. None of the women I worked with had known me as a single lesbian and the five or six straight dancers in our show were after me. I had to be careful. There were little kisses on the back of my neck, patting my rear when we were in the hall, caressing my breast when I was naked coming off stage.

I decided it was because they knew me. I seemed safe and they knew me. Knew I could not hurt them in any way. I must have seemed like just the right person to try out having sex with a woman. The jealousy each felt toward the others kept all of them off me.

I was curled up to a pillow on my side in the television room after my first show when Dana, a beautiful little blonde with only a pink silk G-string covering her, hopped on the couch, threw her leg over me and started grinding against my hip while reaching for my breast. Kenya, a six foot tall and muscular dancer who had been there for about a year, reached over, grabbed

Dana's blonde hair, held her above the couch then threw her to the floor.

"If anybody gets that ass it's gonna be me," Kenya growled.

That was much better. That was protection. Kenya never made a move on me and I don't think she wanted to, but when she was around, no one else did either. She wasn't always there so I still had to be careful. I wasn't interested in any of them.

It was too soon. I was still in love with Dreamy. I had been alone for over a year as I sat on the junk in Singapore but my heart was broken and I didn't trust. That was hard on me. I didn't trust anymore.

I was ready to leave Singapore. My four big suitcases and the new one, for all the dresses I'd had made, were packed. The battered red leather makeup case I had carried since my dancing career began now held all my new jade and gold jewelry was the last thing closed.

I wore a knee-length navy blue skirt, matching jacket with a white blouse and pearls. I was trying to look like my mother without her makeup. It succeeded, and I was allowed to board the plane to Bangkok after showing airline officials physical proof of current vaccinations, my valid passport, a plane ticket out of Thailand to Katmandu in ten days and a wallet full of American money to support myself while in both cities.

Not everyone had heard of the airline rules or didn't believe they would actually be enforced on Americans.

"Sirs, will you step over here please," said the polite Thai Airline official to the young men who sported pony-tails or loose fly away hair to their shoulders. They wore puka shell necklaces, shorts, tank tops and leather sandals and looked like they would go directly to the beach when they got off the plane.

Four young men were taken out of line and escorted away. We waited for twenty minutes after all the passengers who looked prim and proper had boarded. No one with the airline seemed hurried or ruffled. They acted like this delay happened every day.

Two men who eventually took seats on the plane looked like business-men. They were freshly barbered and clean shaven. They were dressed in long pants, shirts with collars, and shoes instead of the jean shorts, beaded necklaces and sandals they had worn in the airport. I wasn't sure they were the same men until I heard them.

"What the fuck, man. I haven't looked like this since high school. Look at this fuckin' baby-skin. Half my face is fuckin' white. Shit, man. Look at my hair. I look like a fuckin' mortician. I'm gonna sue 'em. I'm gonna sue, man," said the adorable boy in the baby blue shirt who was tearing at his Thai silk tie.

"Tim won't let 'em cut his hair. He won't ever let 'em. How's he gonna get to Bangkok?" said the one that really did look worse this way. With all that hair off his face you could see the weak chin and pitted complexion the beard had been hiding.

I was waiting for a taxi outside the Bangkok airport when I heard them whining. They looked transformed. They couldn't wait to shed the new clothes and get grimy again but they knew better than to do it before they reached their hotel in the city.

Chapter Twenty-Three

Bangkok, Thailand, January 1969

Clarice, the ocelot kitten, was about eight weeks old, soft gold with black markings, and teeth like needles that easily pierced my skin as she bit my arm. She was the first ocelot I had ever met. Adamo and Eva said they had named her after me but they didn't say why. They planned to train her and to make her part of their act.

Lily de Saigon was their agent also and she had told me, in one of her infrequent letters, to go see the show they were headlining in Bangkok as she might be able to book me there sometime in the future.

Ning's was large enough to support a cast of nine dancers plus a featured act. It was dark and loud, the atmosphere sexually charged as masculine eyes jumped up and down the bar to see who they could grab next. Everyone looked available for purchase, including the delicate boy bartenders who wore eye makeup and dressed in identical hot pink and lavender silk shirts.

Evening-gowned hostesses sat close to their exclusively male customers at small round tables, hands occupied under the deep purple tablecloths. Waitresses hung over tables whispering into young ears, lapping and tickling them with pointed tongues.

I could feel the eyes of the dancer on stage focus on me for a moment as I walked in and sat down at a back table, then drift off me and back to the door. Her eyes seemed riveted on the entrance door to see a good mark first and catch his attention before the other girls moved in and took him away.

No one approached my table to ask if I wanted a drink, which I did. I felt out of place and wanted something to do with my hands that didn't include smoking. Just breathing in there gave me enough smoke for several cigarettes.

I had on a peacock blue gown from New York with a matching wrap and matching greenish-blue fire opal earrings and a wide cuff bracelet. I was a bit overdressed for Los Angeles but not here.

The hostesses, waitresses and dancer on stage took one look at me, sitting in their club alone, showing more cleavage than any of them could muster, and their eyes flashed "foreign whore, foreign whore."

Adamo and Eva put on a wonderful show. It was mostly for themselves because no one was looking at them except me. I would never want to work here, but it was a nice thought on Lily's part. It would be like working with live sex acts going on beside you. They must have been receiving a good salary for the week but it was not the place for me.

When Adamo and Eva came out to the main showroom and stood by my table the atmosphere relaxed so fast it was almost a physical jolt. Two waitresses arrived at the same time like puppies bounding across the room with tails wagging. Hostesses smiled, their eyes tucked the daggers away, faces softening. I felt the room temperature actually change.

Smiling and sweet as pie, the little puppy servers asked what I wanted to drink.

"Don't think about it now. We are taking this dangerous woman away," Eva said as she put her arm in mine and swept me out of the club.

They took me out to dinner and up to their hotel room to see their new baby Clarice. Eva tucked a towel around me and another one over my lap so baby nails would not ruin my dress. All of a sudden they could speak English, they could smile, were thoughtful. They were even funny.

I had a beautiful room at the Siam InterContinental Hotel. They served pancakes for breakfast, my first since New York four months ago. I could eat all I wanted. Bangkok was full of young military men from the United States enjoying their scheduled rest time away from the war in Vietnam. They were filling up on the necessities they had longed for: pancakes, booze and pussy.

Eva thought I was spending too much for my big hotel room with the breath-catching view of Bangkok's orange and brilliant green temple roofs.

"Stay at Ed's house, chou, chou," she cooed.

I didn't know why she was talking like that but it was so much better than the silence and cold stares she had given me in Singapore. I didn't want to break the spell by asking her what had changed. She may have realized I wasn't after her man, like most of the women she met.

Adamo was so talented and beautiful it was easy to see women, little girls and even celebrities or royalty of both sexes throwing themselves at him. Eva was a good dancer and had a lovely body but she wasn't especially pretty. She had a hard job in front of her, trying to keep the others off of Adamo. A lesbian might be her only worry-free friend, and even then she couldn't be sure. I had known dancers who said they only liked girls, and then they would fall for some weird drummer or saxophone player.

When Eva insisted on introducing us I learned that Ed was a good-looking blond American who managed several clubs in Bangkok. He loved Eva's suggestion that we stay with him.

"Hey, I'm always open to female strangers taking up residence in my house for a few days. I've got a couple of airline stewardesses coming early next week but until then consider it home," he said.

I called Vicky in Singapore and asked what she thought. She was coming anyway and I sure was not going to stay at Ed's house alone. Vicky was more than willing, she was thrilled. When she arrived at the airport we went to his beautiful 200 year-old Thai house, with a swimming pool and shaded patios, and stayed for five days.

Ed was wonderful to us. I am sure he was a lonely guy. He didn't have a girlfriend that we ever saw, although he had access to lots of women. It seemed all the people in his life were work-related.

He took us out to the clubs he managed, showed us off and left us alone to be tourists in the day-time. I couldn't figure out his angle, but I kept looking for it. After all I had experienced in the last few months I thought I should finally become suspicious.

The one I should have been worried about was Vicky. She wouldn't keep her hands off my breasts. Her arm slipped around me as we slept in the double bed in Ed's guest room.

This was a girl who said she was straight but was more aggressive than anyone who ever had chased me. I don't like having sex with straight girls. Because it's their first time having sex with a woman, they think it's more important than it is. They get needy, jealous and possessive.

Vicky's silky hand slipped between my legs and I stopped pushing her away. My body gave in to her but my mind was not willing to go further into a relationship.

Bangkok was temples, flowers and beauty everywhere. I couldn't look at a table, a shop window, or a person without seeing the loveliness of Thailand. Female dancers, children and teenagers, costumed in gold and tiny mirrors, could be seen performing on the streets in front of the statues of Buddha. They draped necklaces made of red and white flowers around the hands and neck of the Buddha, in thanks for good fortune and prayed for healthy families.

The floating market was a culture all its own. I could have looked at it forever but I didn't want to participate. I saw young men and boys pee into the brown river from their open-sided living rooms which faced onto the river as naked children a few houses downriver stood in the water washed themselves and brushed their teeth while women washed clothes in the water flowing past their homes farther down river.

Flat-bottom boats filled with baskets of red, orange and yellow vegetables, fruit, or tourists floated by as men and women in wide flat-topped straw hats rowed along the river highway, crossing from side to side, in no particular order, shouting about the good quality of their food and selling it wherever they could.

Few pedestrian bridges crossed the river. The people who lived there had little canoes tied under the house which they used like cars. Stilts held the front part of their homes over the water.

Vicky and I went into light and colorful temples, dark temples full of smokey incense, a temple with an emerald Buddha, that was really made of jade, and one with a long reclining Buddha with mother of pearl toe prints.

We moved to a hotel when the airline stewardesses came into town. In a way I was sorry to leave Ed. We had been treated like princesses by his staff. He had been a real nice friend. We talked about me working in one of his clubs but I was excited to be on my way back to Paris and the Crazy Horse for a year.

A year seemed like a long time to be away from home. I was already missing Los Angeles and my friends. I missed the sense of independence I felt there. I could drive without fear and I knew where I was going.

A few days later, it was time to leave Bangkok. I was ready to part with Vicky.

"I have to go to Spain because I can't change my ticket but I will join you in Paris as fast as I can, sweetheart," she said as she hugged me tightly to her, licked my ear and pinched my nipple.

Oh, no.

Chapter Twenty-Four

Katmandu, Nepal

The Bombay airport was so tightly packed no one seemed to notice there was a family of five, a women and her little girls, living, cooking, and sleeping on the floor of the ladies' bathroom. Cooking their mid-afternoon meal over the small fire of sticks and trash burning on the white tile, a bit of clothing stored under the wash basin, they looked like permanent residents.

I was saddened and depressed by their situation. Never would I have thought it possible. However, it was the cleanest part of the airport and the only place there was a little space between people.

On second thought it didn't seem so bad if you looked at it through their eyes. It might have been the safest place for them. Who knew how many men were living in the waiting room, waiting to take advantage of the women and children in the early hours of the morning. Women in India had to cope with the constant crush of men who walked streets and halls aggressively brushing or squeezing breasts and buttocks as if it were their right.

Katmandu's airport was not large enough to accept jets so the plane we flew in used propellers to lift us above the Himalayan Mountains. Fifteen passengers filled the plane. The seats were small; the windows were tiny. I was inside a silver toy that could fall and kill us all.

The cockpit was so small the pilots kept the door open to the rest of the plane. They looked at the passengers over their shoulders, proudly pointing out the magnificent sight of sunshine sparkling on snow-white mountain tops, telling us the name of each peak.

Air crisp and clear, clean and frigid reached my lungs and they expanded toward it. I was starved for air. The brown, smoggy air of Los Angeles and the heavy, watery air of Singapore and Bangkok had made me feel that breathing could be harmful to my health. I had tried to take in as little air as possible each time I breathed.

That first blast of Nepalese air set the pattern of my time there. The moment I put my foot onto Nepal my back straightened. My shoulders went back and down. My chest lifted. I raised my head, took a deep cleansing breath, and started to sing. I didn't care that my voice sounded like me and not like Barbra Streisand. I sang.

> *On a clear day rise and look around you*
> *And you'll see who you are*

A tall, grey-haired fellow passenger, protecting a large briefcase with both arms, asked me where I was staying. I had no idea where to stay. I'd just wanted to go to Nepal. He recommended the Annapurna Hotel as we stood inside the tiny airport waiting for our visas to be approved.

"Annapurna is the second best hotel in the country. Take good care of you there. Give you breakfast, lunch and dinner and it's more authentic Nepalese than the Soalte which is owned by one of the royal family. He's trying to make that one look like Monaco," he said loudly, to make sure I could hear him over my singing.

The rosy beige and black tiger-striped taxi quickly took me past the waiting, tall, brightly painted rickshaws and off to the Annapurna. I sang at full volume as we slowly traveled the narrow unpaved streets, backseat windows open wide to let more air inside.

Every mysteriously dark little shop looked like the one I wanted to spend hours in exploring the treasures I could see calling me inside. Some of the metal things hanging outside were so unusual I couldn't tell what they were or how they could be used.

A very formal Nepalese gentleman, wearing a brilliant white starched turban, who stood behind the reception desk said, "Yes Madam, we have a wonderful room for you. You'll have all your meals here and a guard will stand outside your room all the night in case you will be needing something. Please don't eat outside of the hotel, Madam and be sure to take the flashlight from your room desk if you go out in the evening. As you will see there are no streetlights. That will be fifteen dollars per night."

I was alone and it felt wonderful. Vicky had been holding onto me with an iron grip since the moment we met. It was exhausting. Four fleecy white wool blankets covered my bed. The weight was almost enough to keep me pinned there all night but, I thought about dinner and crawled across the mattress to get up. All this room was mine.

Guests were seated in a square dining room at simple tables and straight chairs. A thin Nepalese man with slicked back hair played a grand piano that was set upon a dais against the far wall. English show tunes accompanied the waiters as they gracefully weaved between tables, serving rice and some kind of meatless curried stew of vegetables, a sticky Indian dessert and tea. I found out I was ravenous after my short nap. Everyone ate the same thing, just like a family.

A lone, silver-haired woman with a big smile asked if she could share my table. She introduced herself as Elaine Durbin.

"I'm a tourist too," she said as she sat and delicately placed her napkin across her thighs. "I have been working in Afghanistan with USAID, Agency for International Development, for a year and this is my first vacation. It's so clean here in comparison. Don't you love it? I can't get over the piano. The manager told me this is the first piano ever in Nepal. It was carried up these mountains on the Sherpa's backs. I just love it."

I was surprised, at the same time relaxed and comfortable with Elaine. What an interesting life she was living. We moved into the hotel lobby and made plans at the reception desk to take an all day tour the next morning. It cost us each eighty cents American. I wondered what we could see for eighty cents.

We sat there talking about her work in Afghanistan, the people, local art, and lapis lazuli, until I had to go back to sleep. Elaine was running on local time but I was still a couple of time zones away.

In the morning, a white van with large windows, waited for us outside. Our guide, a middle-aged man in a western style suit, who said his name was Ashok, gave us his card and led us from the lobby.

Two stout, red-faced German men wearing red and yellow vests joined Elaine and me as we rode to the Tibetan Refugee center. The huge round stupa that contained ashes of the dead had huge exotic eyes painted on all four sides. They looked out upon the world emanating calm mystery to my unknowing eyes. The Germans didn't seem to mind my singing and Elaine joined my song once in a while.

I found out Nepal also had the deep cobalt blue lapis lazuli stone I loved. We shopped in the tiny stores around the prayer wheel circle that surrounded the stupa. Rings and necklaces in silver and gold, lapis, coral and turquoise came away with me.

I sang softly as I turned each prayer wheel going around the huge circle made of dozens of ancient dark brass prayer wheels that were about three feet high. It was mesmerizing. The local people, monks and civilians, walked round and round the circle repeating their meditation mantra, turning a small prayer wheel on a stick in one hand, using the other hand to turn the larger ones. Inside each wheel were hand-written prayers that went up to the gods with every turn. The people became their own prayer wheel, circling and sending up prayers to the gods that asked for love and protection for their families.

A man and his wife in Nepal. 1969.

The Stupa

It was at the Tibetan Center that I had the truest spiritual experience of my life. I looked at the cloudless blue sky, the turning wheels, snow on the highest mountain peaks of the world. I saw all people as one family. No matter what we call the divine spirit, we all pray for the same things. I felt I was one with the universe, mother, sister and daughter of all. I was still in that frame of mind the next day as we saw peasants in the surrounding villages between the small cities of Patan and Bhaktapur taking corn drying on the flat roofs of their small mud homes. The men and women were beautiful in a rustic sort of way. They looked like pictures I had seen of Peruvian people who live in the high mountains around Cusco and Machu Picchu, short and muscular with browned skin. The children's faces with round rosy cheeks and dark almond-shaped eyes were remarkably the same in both countries.

I took Polaroid photos of the curious boys and girls. Together we watched the little square pieces of paper develop into black and white pictures of them. They started calling out in high-pitched squeals.

"They want their mothers and friends to come see what magic the strange looking woman had made," Ashok said with his eyes down and an apologetic laugh.

A crowd of fifty or sixty people gathered around our group. The children tussled to get closer to the pictures as the men peered inside our van. Women in their long skirts and warm vests were as excited and full of wonder as their children. I used up three packages of Polaroid film and gave all the pictures to the parents.

Ashok smiled as he said, "This was the first time some of them have ever had a picture taken of themselves or their children. Those pictures will now become prized possessions and placed near the family altar."

We saw temples where Hindus and Moslems worshiped together.

Ashok said, "It is against the law in Nepal for anyone to tell a person what religion he must follow. All religions are equal in Nepal. We do not let anyone come into the country with the idea to be missionaries or change our religions to theirs.

"There are twenty six tourists in Nepal today so we are proud to have four of you. I will take you back to your hotel for lunch and to refresh and then we will go to see our 'Living Goddess' in Katmandu."

The little girl we went to visit, after our lamb curry, stood at her second story lavishly carved balcony to let us gawk up at her. She looked sad. She was about ten years-old. Elaine and I frowned at each other with questions too rude for us to ask but waiting for an explanation.

"The Living Goddess, called the Kumari, is usually three or four years-old when she is chosen for her beauty and serenity. She must come from the Brahman caste, the highest cast of Hindus," Ashok told us.

The little face, forehead painted red with a third eye in the middle, had thick black eyeliner, dark tilting eyebrows and brilliant red lips. She looked down at us, letting us gaze upon her for a few moments but had no expression of her own. Her eyes made direct contact with mine as she must have heard me humming. Ashok turned, waving his hand to quiet me, but the solemn little Living Goddess turned her back on us, went into her quarters and out of our sight.

"As soon as she starts to menstruate we will have to find a new Goddess. Perhaps soon now. She lives here and only goes out once a year, when the King comes to worship at her feet and guides her around the city streets in a golden chariot for all to see. While she is here she will receive no formal education and will be taken care of by the priests and nuns. Only her mother is allowed inside the quarters to visit.

"Very bad luck to marry a former Goddess. Some husbands have died within the first year," Ashok continued. "Often former Kumari have to go into prostitution as they know nothing of working or family life. I think it's a sad life, don't you? Would you like to give her a little offering so she can buy candy or sweets for the children who come to honor her?"

The Living Goddess

Elaine and I decided to visit the famous Yak and Yeti Bar, still doing business in what had been an old royal palace. Now it was dark and dirty, an empty hotel that echoed each step back to us. It was wonderful having another woman, older and more experienced, with me. I felt brave just peeking through the big carved wooden entrance doors, but Elaine went in like she was looking to buy the place.

Using our flashlights we could see the ballroom, paint peeling from the ceiling, with royal family portraits and shuttered windows high up on the wall where the king's women could look at the dancing guests while being protected from their view.

Boris, the huge Russian owner and bartender, had made the bar famous for his grand hospitality. Even after he died the bar's reputation was enough to draw tourists and some locals. The round open fireplace in the center of the huge room was about seven feet across. It was made of ancient-looking brown bricks a foot thick all the way around. The round hood above must have been antique copper. Twenty or more wooden arm chairs surrounded the fireplace.

A roaring fire was the only light available, warming the seven men who were relaxing around it, talking and drinking. Elaine and I sat in the big circle and ordered brandy from the white turbaned waiter. We needed to be warmed up too. I took in a deep breath, felt my shoulders relax, half-closed my eyes for a moment and continued to hum.

Three men in charcoal and dark blue western style suits stood in the doorway and were still while everyone in the room, except Elaine and I, rose and showed the newest arrivals respect by putting their palms together in front of their forehead, bowing their heads and remaining silent. A word or two in Nepalese said by the man in charcoal who stood in front of the others was enough to make the men sit again,

Elaine and I perked up at this. No one else had been noticed when they walked through the wide arched door. Certainly no one else had walked in like they expected applause, heads held high, and eyes looking down their noses, as they entered the room.

The gentleman who had spoken walked toward us and sat a seat away from Elaine. The youngest man, whose dark lustrous eyes and intense expression made him looked like a silent movie star, sat next to Elaine, handed her his personal card and introduced himself.

"Good evening. I hope you are enjoying your stay here in Nepal. I am the Ambassador to the United Nations for Nepal and this is Basundhara Shah, our king's brother."

I had already been warned in Singapore and was worried about princes and what they could do to women in their countries. We talked and drank warm brandy for a while when the invitation came.

"Would you like to see the hotel and casino I own? You won't see another like it in all of Nepal," the prince promised.

What are you going to do when you get an invitation like that? Elaine and I looked at one another trying to silently convey doubt but desire to take a look. We thought we were being careful when we refused to go in their vehicle. We took our own taxi to The Soaltee Hotel and Casino.

The red and black squares of the wall to wall carpet, roulette wheels, card dealers and low couches that held glamorous women all reminded me of Las Vegas. The prince must have been on a hunt for all the tourists in Katmandu so they could gamble at his tables.

The ambassador took us to the games and asked about our gambling experiences as if he was trying to prime the pump. He ordered drinks for us and encouraged us to look around.

"Would you like to see how the native Nepalese gamble?" the prince asked when it became obvious we would not gamble at the tables.

I left Elaine sitting with Mister Ambassador as the prince and I approached an unobtrusive door set in a far wall. He knocked twice, paused and then twice more. He whispered something and waited.

"Don't pay any attention to the smell. This is the way the local people play," he said as the door opened to the small smoke-filled room.

The tiny room was cloudy with hashish smoke. I could almost touch the smell of hashish; it was so strong. Four long white cotton cushions formed a square on the floor where six men sat relaxing. Two were dragging smoke from the hookah between them. They were all dressed in coarse white cotton and the cowrie shells they threw were also white.

In the middle of the square sat a stylish, tuxedoed man with a dare-devil smile aimed right at me. His large dark eyes drew me closer. I wanted to kiss his forehead, to hold his hand in mine and stroke his fingernails. What was happening to me? This guy really had something special.

"Brandy, meet the former Prime Minister of Bhutan, Lenny Dorji. He has just escaped with his life by running over the mountains back to Nepal with Shirley McLaine, your American movie star. He is our new blackjack dealer and will be at the table in thirty minutes," the prince told me.

I wanted to stay in the little room and get into the middle of the square but Prince Basundhara could see that all gambling had stopped. He took my arm and led me out to the blackjack table. He had a million dollar asset coming to deal cards there soon and seemed to want me in place.

I turned to look at Elaine who stood with purse in hand as if she was ready to leave and I walked toward her.

Feeling hypnotized, I let Elaine take my arm as we said our goodbyes to the prince, the ambassador and the bodyguard. She led me out to a waiting tiger-striped taxi and shoved me in. I sang as she glared at me.

"Are you crazy? I should know better than to go out with someone who looks like you. Redheads!"

My few days in Nepal passed too quickly. I could imagine myself staying there for weeks or months the next time I visited.

There had to be a next time. I still had so much to see and I had taken the Nepalese people and their country into my heart.

Mr. Ambassador, who had not let a day go by without calling me, took me to the airport and into the airplane.

"Go sit in the cockpit once you get up in the air. I just arranged it with the captain. See the mountains from the air and you will want to come back soon."

Chapter Twenty-Five

The Crazy Horse Saloon: Paris and Munich, 1969

Paris froze in January. When I arrived snow sparkled as Parisians stepped lightly along the Avenue des Champs-Élysées. Strings of tiny white bulbs, wrapped around the horse-chestnut tree trunks and branches, filled the trees and streets below with light.

Hotel Central, where I had stayed the previous September, was full except for one room on the third floor that measured seven feet by ten feet. There was just enough space for the narrow wooden shelf they had placed a thin mattress upon, a tray-sized table, a straight chair with one short leg and a small sink. The bathroom and shower were down the hall.

There were two great things about this so-called room that made it livable. First was the breakfast. Warm croissants, with butter and apricot jam and hot chocolate were included in the two dollar per night charge so it was like getting the room for free. Second was the large window that opened outward to give me an unobstructed view of the Parisian sky above flat Latin Quarter roofs with their clay chimney tops.

I didn't know how long I could stay in a space the size of a jail cell but I wanted to try. I could go on the list for the next large room that became vacant after I started getting paid. This room had no heater. I had to use my mink coat as a blanket. It was almost romantic, in a starving artist kind of way.

I wasn't starving but I might have been if I'd had to support myself on the money Bernardin was paying me. I was not earning a franc. He was in New York when I arrived in Paris and my act had yet to be conceived, choreographed, costumed or rehearsed.

After a twenty-six hour flight from Katmandu to Paris, which included a layover at the airport in Tehran, I pushed my suitcases under the bed shelf. I had my hair cut, my nails manicured, a facial and a massage. I had spent three months in the steamy jungles of Singapore and Thailand, then spaced out in the Himalayas. This seemed the best and fastest way to become westernized again and catch up with city life. I had to get ready for work.

My hotel was half a block away from the Sorbonne University and a block away from the labor union and student protests that turned into riots every evening on the Boulevard St. Michele. The *flik* parked their gray trucks at the corner of Rue des Ecole. Ten policemen wearing riot gear sat in each one, holding batons and shields in front of them, waiting for the chanting, marching and rock throwing students to emerge from the buildings and small streets that surrounded the university.

Many evenings I leaned out the hotel door and watched the police waiting for the signal to charge the protesters. Their expressions were grim and determined. Most of the police were not much older than the rioters.

Hotel residents had been warned and knew better than to go out at night but often someone fell into our little lobby with a bloody head or skinned up arms and legs from rough encounters with the *flik.*

The Paris riots had been going on since the spring of 1968 and things were changing for the students and workers. The government of Charles de Gaul was teetering toward its end but the educational system of France was trying to hold on to the old ways. The students wanted to learn in the modern way, not in the traditional French way that demanded memorization of facts and very little interaction with the teachers. In the few months I had been away from Paris I could see that skirts had become shorter and little boys on the Boulevard St Michele no longer wore short sleeved white shirts and short pants as school uniforms.

Bernardin started screaming as soon as he saw me when he returned from New York. "You cut your hair!! What happened to all that funny hair? I love that hair. No! I will get a wig for you and you will wear it for every show! Stupid, stupid. I will never forgive you for this." He screamed at me and Lily, my agent, until he choked on his own saliva, turned and swept into his office.

Twenty days later, I was still waiting for Bernardin to start working on my act. Lily said he didn't want to look at me "hairless." It was her fault, after all. She was the one who had insisted that I cut my hair, a second time. It was about two inches long on top and half an inch in the back. Lily had misunderstood in her excitement about obtaining the job for me that Bernardin had meant my hair was funny wonderful.

Thankfully, he decided, with Lily's encouragement that I needed money to live on. He began paying me fifty francs, or ten dollars, a day to rehearse so we started to dance.

The American choreographer, Victor Upshaw, who had created all the beautiful acts I had seen in at the Crazy Horse in September, and the show at the Lido in Paris, was home visiting his family in Los Angeles and would not be back in Paris for weeks. It was too long to wait so Bernardin decided to choreograph my act himself. He didn't know how to dance but claimed he was "an expert on all things striptease."

"Your new name is Ruth Capitol. I want it to sound very Ameri-Ken," Bernardin said from the showroom as he was looking up at me on stage in the pink and blue lights. His head swayed from one side to the other.

What a sadist! He wasn't going to call me that. He couldn't possibly call me that. He just wanted to play with me.

My new wig which M. Bernardin's loved almost as much as my hair.

"Oh, my God, M. Bernardin, nooooooo!" I pleaded with him, my hand against my heart.

"Oh, well, what could be better? What is more funny than Ruth?" he said, waggling his head from side to side as he paused to delay the revelation of the real name he had chosen.

"Well, perhaps Candy Capitol would be better. No?"

"Oh, yes!"

I loved it. I had chosen Candy as my nickname in the second grade but had decided to use a more adult name when I worked as an office clerk after high school. Now it would be my name again in a more glamorous world.

That day the soundmen recorded the music and my voice, as Bernardin had decided I would do an old fashioned, 1930's style striptease, chewing gum, doing big grinds and exaggerated slow bumps. During the act I was to tell the audience where I was from, who I was, and give a big bump. Bernardin wanted me to look at the audience and say "but I am a good girl," with wide innocent eyes toward the crowd and a big bump against the breast- high screen I was to stand behind while taking off my costume.

It wasn't complicated or fascinating but Bernardin loved it. It was his creation.

Black and silver, 1930s style platform shoes were made for my feet. A costume maker came to the club three times for fittings to be sure everything was just right. The wig maker talked to Bernardin for hours about colors and length, the style and texture the hair should be, then measured my head and neck length and circumference several times.

Never had I seen a club owner so invested in the acts he chose to appear on his stage. Bernardin was a perfectionist in the best sense of the word. He made everything perfect. Maybe the Ziegfeld Follies had been produced this way but it was completely new to me. It felt like the very best way. Perhaps Bernardin really was an expert in everything 'striptease'.

Burlesque dancers in the 1930's and 40's must have been Amazons. The grinds Bernardin wanted me to do were low down, knees bent and feet spread wide apart. It required a tremendous amount of strength to rehearse this act four hours a day.

I had thought my legs were strong from dancing for seven years but I was weak in the knees and my thighs felt like they were made of jello after the first afternoon of rehearsal. These were not the 1960's graceful, polite dance steps that grinds had become in California. They were the "get down and let me do ya'' kind of grinds that girls were arrested for in carnival shows and burlesque theatres across the dust bowl and Bible belt of the southern United States in the 1930s.

The shoes were so funny looking, with thick four-inch heels and rounded toes on inch- high platforms. They were perfect for the period costume. Every time I looked at them I laughed, but they were wonderfully comfortable, not at all like the pointy stiletto pumps I had worn to dance in other clubs. I was rehearsing in them and learning how to take off the costume Bernardin had designed with its elastic sleeves of velvet and fringe. It was all black velvet and satin ribbon fringe, with mirrors on the G-string and velvet collar around my neck.

My act at the Crazy Horse would be seven minutes long and I would perform it once each night of the week. All fourteen of the girls danced in the finale so I was rehearsing that also. The week before my act opened, every dancer had to come in for a few two hours sessions to work with me as Sophia Palladium, one of our stars and the dance captain, led me through the routine of *Hey Big Spender* from the movie *Sweet Charity*.

Opening night at the Crazy was spectacular. The audience was full of American tourists, even two uniformed American sailors. They loved my act. I smiled, I flirted, I laughed and looked deeply into the sailors eyes. I chewed the Juicy Fruit gum energetically and searched the audience for my boyfriend. The lights changed my skin color from pale rose pink to sky blue, then back to powder pink. The red wig was just the right color to glow like a hot coal, bright and vibrant in the blue light.

Having fun learning how to be a Crazy Horse dancer.

This advertisement ran for several weeks in Une Semaine de Paris Pariscope.

Candy Capitol outside the Crazy Horse Saloon.

German Publicity

"I'm from Los Angeles, but I'm a good girl."

Two long-term residents from my hotel, a female psychiatrist from Wisconsin who was visiting family in Romania, and a linguist from University of Chicago who was going to the Ivory Coast in Africa to study soon, came to see the show. Afterward they met me at the stage door and took me off to celebrate in grand fashion with champagne and French pastries on the Avenue des Champs Elyese. I was happy.

I had watched the entire show several nights during the rehearsal weeks and loved it more and more. As I knew the girls better and saw first-hand the reaction of the audience to them, I appreciated all the work that had been done to make this club the best in the world. Then, things became even more exciting for me.

On February 12th Bernardin told me I was going with him to Munich, West Germany the following week to perform my new act live on a famous, weekly television show called *Nightclub*. I was to be the first live striptease act on television in the world. He was pretty excited but he would never admit it. He wanted people to think of him as too sophisticated to be moved that easily.

"Of course they want to have a Crazy Horse girl. Where else are they going to find girls like mine?" he said proudly, as though speaking of the famous white, Viennese, Lipizzaner dancing horses.

We arrived at The Four Seasons Hotel in Munich the day before the show was to air. I had a beautiful large room, which overlooked the famous Maximilianstrasse. There were down pillows and a deep featherbed just for me. The bathroom alone was larger than my room in Paris. Made of white marble, a bathtub long enough to lie down and drown in, was all mine. I had never heard of the Four Seasons chain of hotels but I knew it was the most beautiful, luxurious hotel I had ever been in. I wished Dreamy had been there to share it with me. She would have made it even more wonderful.

Bernardin took me out to dinner and club crawling through Munich the evening we arrived. I found out he loved to explore other clubs, looking for dancers to steal and to compare the clubs to his own.

We didn't see one dancer that Bernardin wanted to interview.

"These girls look like they should still be on the farms. Look at that belly, and she moves like a little cow, too," he sniped.

"That girl's pretty," I said as I nodded toward a pale dancer with large blue eyes.

"You think a dancer needs to be pretty?" Bernardin began to wave his arms around, pointing at two of the prettier but dull girls we had seen dance, to emphasize his point. "No, she does not. No. She needs something special about her that comes from inside, some flair, a spark, life! She needs grace and a sense of tease. Tease is in the mind. Remember that when you get back to The Crazy Horse. A dancer must use her brain as much as her body. The audience can tell when the mind is not working and they start to talk to each other or go to the bathroom. Think about that tomorrow, when you will have at least two million people watching you, because you are a Crazy Horse dancer."

I was shaky and scared to death I would trip on my panel or fall or make some awful mistake on German live television. I couldn't eat but I wanted as much wine as Bernardin would buy without me asking for more.

A morning rehearsal was called for the full cast of the show. The producers sent a long Mercedes Benz to transport us to the set. It was my first limousine and the only one I had seen in Europe. We did need the help of a driver. My huge wig box, the costume bag and black prop trunk were heavy and took up a lot of space. I wished the ride was longer.

Well-known singers, musicians and comics who had appeared all over Europe were to perform on the show that was set up to look like a real nightclub. We would have a live audience of European movie and television stars sitting at tables drinking champagne who would also be seen on camera, which would be exciting for the audience at home. I didn't know who any of the European or German stars were and I was glad. It would only have added to my insecurity to know how famous the people were.

My striptease was to be the last act. This was the answer to the West German public who had been demanding striptease on television. The last spot is always considered the star position and I was embarrassed that place was mine among all these veteran showstoppers. The famous singers, musicians and comics must have felt I didn't belong there either, as they did not acknowledge my presence in any way. Not a glance.

I had an almost paralyzing attack of shyness that was not helped by the way I looked. Nerves and not being able to keep any food down caused my stomach to inflate like a tire. By late afternoon I was afraid to eat anything to make it stick out further.

The nipple-sized bra Bernardin ordered made for the show itched my tender skin and looked ridiculous. When I had it on all I wanted to do was scratch and tear the little thing off. I was afraid I might actually scratch on camera.

The floor length white fox coat Bernardin had brought, and insisted that I wear, made me look like a teddy bear with a red hat but it was warm and I was freezing in the German winter with just a mini-mini dress on underneath the fur.

"*Achtung*! *Achtung!* We are ready now!" the assistant director shouted into the large sound stage, calling us to order. He reminded me of a drill-sergeant with his greying crew-cut, military bearing and harsh voice.

Carlheinz Hollmann, tall and handsome, walked onto the set dressed in a tuxedo. His brushed back hair was so shiny it looked like black patent leather. He had recently been cast as the new host of *Nightclub*. This was to be Hollmann's debut and his guarded glances to the right and left made me think he was nervous too.

If only Victor Upshaw had been able to choreograph my act I know I would have been more comfortable and had more confidence. Now I had to make this show glamorous and sexy through the force of my own personality. This was my test run and would be the largest audience I had ever danced for.

The front tables of the in-house audience were at least forty feet away from the floor where we would perform. Keeping the entertainers so far from the live people made it hard to develop any heat, any rapport, but it had to be done. The bulky lights and cameras had to have their own space and could not be seen on the television screen.

The performers were given a small space to move in and had to keep within those confines. Singers and some dancers were just fine with those rigid rules but a stripper has to be able to look into the eyes of both the men and women watching her and bring something out of them, so they feel a part of them is gone when she leaves the stage. Not much chance of that when there is so much cold space between them.

I decided to play to the camera which was closer to me and would hold the larger audience. As I watched the singer who was to perform before me, I could see that's what he was doing. It looked good. The celebrities would probably be more interested in themselves, the stars around them and drinking champagne, than looking at my show.

Rehearsal didn't go well. The music was fuzzy. My voice sounded like it was coming from an echo chamber because it wasn't live as the other performers were. Bernardin wanted the act performed to the tape he had made at the Crazy Horse.

The stout, silver-haired director was frustrated as all the sound equipment had to be set up differently for my act which took extra time and effort. The tape had been edited at the Crazy in Paris to make my voice a bit deeper than the real me. It was sexier and more fun.

"*Gott hilf mir*, is there no one who can do the sound for this one act in less than half a day?" the director growled.

The wide smile that Dreamy and Lillian had taught me to use in Texas finally calmed the director. It made things easier once he was feeling friendly. The smile won me patience from the director and kindness from the lighting team, but to work it had to be sincere.

"This show, and working at the Crazy Horse will be the highlight of your dancing career Candy. Try to enjoy it," said Bernardin when he came to see me in the Green Room a few minutes before the show started and looked at my face. "Give them the smile Ameri-Ken," he called as he was on his way out the door to a table in the audience.

This was scary but I had been through worse. It was better than having the dental students feet on my neck and chest in Houston, or being forced almost naked into the Mediterranean Sea off a tiny raft half a mile from shore for a photo shoot in Israel. Better than stranded in a frozen car with the temperature at minus twenty-seven degrees in Minnesota.

I thought about all those things and more that had turned out all right so maybe this could be great. I felt better after giving myself a pep talk and applied more lipstick. I had already chewed most of it off.

Wearing the black and silver four-inch platform heels and the high red wig I was close to six feet tall for the first time in my life. It felt good. I felt strong now. The costume of black ribbon fringe and velvet, trimmed in silver, flowed and flared around my ankles as I walked toward the set of Nightclub to watch the handsome Irish tenor who was on before me.

"Meine Damen und Herren!" Carlheinz Hollmann announced, sounding like a circus ringmaster. "We proudly present, from the world-famous Crazy Horse Saloon in Paris, France, striptease on television for the very first time. At your request, here is the newest member of the Crazy Horse show, Miss Candy Capitol, performing a parody of the nineteen-thirties American striptease."

The music was loud and clear when the black curtain parted. Standing posed as directed for four full seconds so the home viewers could get a good look at me, my shape and the costume, I flashed what I hoped was a one thousand watt smile toward the camera and the eighty people in the temporary nightclub set, held my head high, and with arms out gracefully began to parade across the floor.

My thoughts were: *tummy in, back straight, shoulders back and down, smile. Wow, those people are really far away. Never mind them. Look at the camera. There's someone out there who will love you. Draw them in to you.* But I hoped I looked like I was thinking *Look at me darlings. I'm having so much fun and I want you to have a wonderful time with me. Like these long legs? Yummm! Want to touch? Come here. Come here to me. Oh, but not too close. Not yet, baby. Look at this.*

I was having fun. It was the truth. The entertainer in me kicked started when the spirit of 1930's type music, dancing and teasing took over my thoughts. My physical conversation with the audience became looser, more relaxed. Juicy.

Then it was over. My five-minute act on live German television ended as I received enthusiastic applause from the celebrity audience. They had their part to play too.

A wrap party on the set started immediately after the show stopped broadcasting. A waiter brought a bottle of French brut champagne to my dressing room, poured me a glass and left. It was the first time I had a full bottle all my own. I was so relieved the show was over and there had been no mishap, I wanted to drink every drop.

Dressed in the peacock blue silk evening gown I had worn in New York City, I walked out to join Bernardin and the other performers. He looked proud to be himself and in this company, although I could not tell if he had been satisfied with my performance. I didn't know if I was completely happy with it either but I had done the best I could.

Bernardin and I knew it had been at least one- hundred percent better than any of the German strippers we had seen at the clubs. The questions I had were: should he have chosen a better dancer with a more established act from his club? And why had he chosen me? I was sure all the other Crazy Horse dancers had asked themselves why Bernardin had asked me to represent his club but it hadn't occurred to me until then to wonder why. Sophia had told me he liked his newest dancer best until the next one came along, so I thought that was the answer.

Everyone, celebrity audience members and performers alike, were being interviewed by the press and radio commentators for the next day's reviews and for sound bites to publicize the show. There were almost more photographers now than audience members. They wandered around the stage and faux nightclub sections. Flashbulbs exploded, popping in every direction as the champagne flowed.

When we returned to Paris the clipping service the Crazy Horse retained sent us reviews of the program from papers all around the world. Some reviewers loved my show, thought I was funny and sexy, while others thought I danced like a flea but they all agreed striptease on television was necessary.

In Costume

Chapter Twenty-Six

How to Live in Paris

Juggling newspaper and television interviews and photography sessions for several magazine layouts during the month of February was just part of being a dancer at the Crazy Horse. All fourteen girls had busy schedules during the day in an attempt to keep the people of Europe interested in our entire show and the individual dancers. It was the first time I'd had to think about keeping to a publicity schedule and always looking picture perfect since my first days of dancing on the road with Lillian McCardle in Texas.

I felt like a starlet but was treated like a real star by the public and the media. We were all treated like true artists. The only difference between me and the other dancers was that they expected it. Coming from Los Angeles where a stripper was still thought of as 'a little dirty, probably a prostitute,' the reception here was surprisingly warm.

The other dancers didn't think it unusual to be followed along the street by photographers and fans who asked for autographs. They accepted the flowers and fan mail we received at our makeup tables each night as a normal occurrence and would have been surprised or worried if there were no letters or cards.

Bernardin had ordered beautifully posed, bare-breasted pictures of Sophia Palladium, Bonita Super and me, made into black and white king- sized postcards. They were for sale in the small souvenir store in the lobby that featured Crazy Horse items. I loved being a sexy French postcard, like the ones I had read about in Victorian era mystery novels. It was such a funny way to think of myself.

After a few drinks and seeing the girls up close, an enamored tourist might want to buy a nice souvenir on the way out the door. An audience member could purchase a belt buckle with the Crazy Horse name in wild pink, a set of twelve picture slides showing the interior and exterior of the Crazy Horse Saloon or a fancy silk scarf with the club name.

Because I didn't speak more than twenty words of French those first months, I couldn't easily tell if there was any jealousy or back-stabbing going on in the dressing room. Occasionally I could feel some tension, hear a raised voice or see another girl look at me with venom in her eyes. We assessed our looks and each other constantly, asking ourselves *is her skin as smooth looking as mine without the body makeup? Do I look as creamy-soft as she does? I think she's getting lines around her mouth, am I? Is that cellulite in the back of her legs? Are my boobs sagging like hers?*

That would be true of any room that held fourteen actively competitive beautiful young women who sat looking at each other, most with only a G-string on, seven nights a week. Each wanted to be better than the other. We all wanted the audience to love us best, the boss to like us most.

The last day in March, right after my show Bernardin had his secretary, Agate, call me into his dimly lit, beautifully furnished, salon. This was the room where he often entertained movie stars, politicians, writers and other high profile guests. They wanted to meet their favorite dancers in person just like the rest of the audience.

A few of us had met Italian film director Federico Fellini in the lounge earlier in the month. He had two tall blondes with him who were magnificently beautiful women, but it looked like he was casting for more accessories. It was obvious Fellini thought he was the most gorgeous person in the room in his dark suit, soft camel hair overcoat resting on his shoulders, and couldn't be bothered with us once he had seen us. Fellini reminded me of mobster Tony Boots in Cleveland. They had the same taste in wardrobe and held the attitude of being the most important person they had ever met.

This night I put on a long black dress, simple but with a deep v-neckline, and strolled into Bernardin's lounge as requested.

"Miss Clarice, Paris has only made you more beautiful," said Richard Lim from Singapore, as he thrust an arrangement of at least three dozen red roses toward me.

I stared at Lim while hugging the roses close to my chest. Had it only been three months since I had last seen him in Singapore? It seemed so much longer and was definitely in another world. He had wanted me to stay and become his "little wife" or "second wife." I would not have been interested in becoming his first wife much less his mistress. Instead of having that conversation again I had left Singapore a few days early.

Now that he was here in Paris, what was I going to do with him? I had to think fast. Dinner or a day-trip to see the French country-side with him would be fine. He was a very nice man but I needed to find a way to divert his attention.

Bernardin had let Lim come backstage as a professional courtesy, I guessed - one club owner to another. By now, Bernardin knew I was a lesbian from dressing room gossip, probably passed on by the blonde and dutiful dancer, Lova Moor, his current lover.

My head turned to the corner where Bernardin sat looking at us with a small expectant smile and bright eyes. Had he let this scene come about for his own amusement? What did he hope to see? Whatever he wanted, he was not going to witness any drama of unrequited love or tearing of hair in his lounge that night. It was obvious he knew nothing of formal Singaporean manners and how understated a Singaporean man could be.

"I will wait for you after the show," said Lim. He turned to shake Bernardin's hand and left.

Bernardin looked surprised and disappointed. Most people like to stay in the lounge and drink or hear stories about the dancers. From the way Lim had looked at me I thought he was there to see if I had changed my mind about living in Singapore.

During his one-week stay, Lim took me out to dinner a few times at fancy French restaurants. He was extraordinarily wealthy so I let him buy me anything he wanted because it made him so happy. He loved ladies shoes and French perfume. I had to be careful about mentioning things like tables or chairs if I thought they were pretty because I could wind up with four of anything delivered to my hotel. By then he knew he wasn't going to be thanked with sex so I wasn't worried.

His hotel arranged for a car and driver to take us to Versailles for the day. I had never seen anything like the formal gardens or the ancient furniture and paintings except in real museums. I couldn't understand why the beds were so short until the guide told us people thought it wasn't healthy to sleep lying down so everyone slept sitting up.

In my agent's office I thought of something that might solve my problem and make Mr. Lim feel his trip had been worth the trouble.

"Lily, we should show Mr. Lim some pictures of dancers you could send to Singapore to work at the Tropicana. Now that they have had one exotic dancer I think they would love to have more. Don't you think so Mr. Lim? Do you have any pretty blondes with long hair and legs that could pass the police tribunal?" I asked Lily.

Freddy Yu had been the exclusive agent for the Tropicana for years. He was the one who chose the acts from around the world to work there. That was about to change.

Lim went back to Singapore a happy man. I had been his first encounter with a western dancer and he liked our style. During the meeting with Lily we arranged for several European dancers to work at his group of clubs in the Tropicana. Lim would have many chances to obtain a second wife which would deflect his attention away from me.

After seeing Versailles I could hardly wait for my mother, Beverly, and sister Michele to arrive so I could take them there. I was already writing to them about their visit. I wanted to know how long they could stay and where else they would be able to travel but Beverly was such a secretive woman I couldn't find out much from her. All I knew was they would be in Paris during the summer when my fourteen year old sister was out of school.

Even though it had been twenty-four years since the end of World War II, my mother wanted very much to meet with the families, in Rotterdam, Holland, to whom she had sent CARE packages during the war. Beverly had worked in the doll department of the Emporium, in downtown San Francisco, for a year and sent three hundred Story Book character dolls to their village the Christmas of 1943. The father of the family was a milk man and delivered the pretty little dolls in the empty milk bottles on the porch. Beverly had also sent impossible to find sewing needles and even fine fabric for a wedding dress. The families still corresponded.

Beverly also wanted to visit London where her mother had been a concert hall singer before immigrating to America in 1910 to become a Hollywood actress. She wanted to walk into the Mayfair theaters and visit Covent Garden where her mother had performed. I had always wished I knew more about my grandmother. I didn't even know her last name, only her stage name Rose Keeler.

Paris is a city made for women. Everything is centered around a sensual woman's needs and desires. I was surprised at how much I loved to look in the shop windows. Lim bought me a pair of Roman type gold leather sandals. I had never imagined spending that much for shoes in my life. The shops drew me in off the street and I thought I could spend all my savings if I ever went there by myself.

The beautifully designed shoes, gowns of all shades made of the softest materials, Italian leather handbags, stores just for perfume, the whisper-thin silk lingerie, heavy gold and diamond jewelry, made my mouth water. I wanted to touch everything, smell everything I could on the Champs Elysees, but even touching could be expensive because then I had to have it.

Once inside the shops, I was tempted to buy everything which would have been a disaster. I didn't know exactly what I was going to do when I went back to the States but I was sure whatever it was would cost a lot of money.

At the end of February, 1969, United States President Richard Nixon came to Paris for a visit with French President De Gaulle. Protesters in the Latin Quarter, marching against the war in Vietnam, were louder and the streets more crowded than ever. Every Frenchman knew that when Nixon was in Paris the American press would make any local disturbance an international event. Thousands of protesters marched down the freezing Boulevard St. Michele shouting *"Aba les flik,"* down with the cops.

Guests from Los Angeles came to visit me in March and April. As with Richard Lim, I was again the tour guide. Dick McInnes, a publicity agent and leg-man for television gossip columnist Rona Barrett, and a good friend of mine from Hollywood, stayed for a week at my hotel. I took him every place in Paris I knew. I loved being able to return the kindness he had shown me when I stayed with him for a couple of weeks after breaking up with Dreamy. Like me, McInnes hadn't been to Europe before and was entranced.

We went to Notre Dame and the Arc de Triumph at the top of the Champs Elysees. I took him to the Eiffel Tower. It was rather chilly but so clear you could see forever. Being there felt magical. We were up so high and I imagined that all the people down on the streets and in the houses were doing interesting French things.

The funniest thing I saw McInnes do was on the first stage of the Eiffel Tower. Seeing him holding onto the top of his head with one hand, his other grasping the back wall of the lovely restaurant on that level, was hysterical. Who knew he wore a toupee and was afraid it would fly off any second and that he was terrified of heights? My poor McInnes. We had a wonderful time though. He took me to see Jacque Brel perform *Man of La Mancha* in French which neither of us understood. We sat in box seats and were so proud to be there.

I was tired though. It was hard trying to keep up with the day and night schedules at The Crazy Horse while being followed by photographers, looking perfect every moment in case someone might see me, entertaining guests and planning for a family visit. To help cope with the constant pressure I learned to drink in Paris.

I discovered alcohol of pear at the Crazy Horse, a clear distilled spirit, something like vodka, with a refreshing pear aftertaste. That and champagne on a regular basis helped keep up my spirits at night and into the morning hours. I drank wine with lunch and dinner as most French people do. I had none with breakfast, though some Parisians are fond of drinking a light rose` with their morning baguette.

Vicky Noon was due to arrive in early April. A big double room with bath became available for six dollars a day and I moved in. It would be much easier to have a female guest that way. It made me nervous though. I was afraid she would cling to me as she had in Bangkok. I didn't want that from her but I thought it would be nice to see her for a few days.

Wrong! Wrong! Wrong! Vicky was there for three days, every one of which seemed a year long, and I was already dying for her to leave. I was miserable. She was angry with me for not loving her.

The last two days had started with me waking up about nine a.m. in time to watch Vicky take more sleeping pills.

"No, please don't take any more pills," I yelled in her ear while trying to push the hand that held a water glass away from her mouth. As she moved toward the door I pleaded with her to stay with me. "Vicky, stay in the room. You can't go downstairs like that again. If you want to eat breakfast you have to look like you're awake."

"You don't love me," Vicky bellowed as she opened the door and stumbled down the stairs toward the breakfast area near the reception desk, while barefooted, dressed only in a light silk robe. "You never loved me. But I loovvvveeee yoouuuu."

Now she started to play, thinking she was cute, going down the stairs backward while hanging on to the handrail and leering up at me. How had she been a police-woman for three years in

Singapore and then worked at Scotland Yard in London? How had she hidden this part of herself so well? She was actually ill and trying to keep me hostage to her sickness.

Picture taken in 1969 for an Italian magazine article about a day in the life of Candy Capitol, dancer at the Crazy Horse Saloon

I tried to hold my anger inside but it was an impossible task. I was so embarrassed in front of the hotel owner, the staff and the other residents. Why couldn't she be like a normal Singaporean woman, quiet, self-contained, with her eyes down and her mouth shut?

But no, here she was. Loud, her emotions played out for all to see and hear, and drugged out of her mind.

The hot chocolate and croissants were delivered to Vicky quickly, perhaps in the hope that she would leave the table soon. That seemed impossible though as she waved the bottom of her robe like a little hanky and half of her face fell into the large chocolate cup.

"Umm yumm, umm yumm," Vicky murmured, her eyes closed as she lapped up the sweet drink .

I began to think Vicky was playing me for a fool and decided to leave her sitting there by herself.

"You left me there, almost naked and sick. You left me," Vicky accused loudly while brushing away chocolate and tears, as she entered my room and threw herself on the unmade bed.

I didn't have to worry about an answer as she was already asleep. She was still in Paris many days later. I couldn't get her to leave. I began to think she would never go. It came to me that she would only leave when she ran out of money so I started accepting her offers of paying for lunch, taxis and anything else. Finally, she left Paris for Spain.

Victor Upshaw, American, black and gay, the Crazy's own choreographer, had returned to Paris from his hometown of Los Angeles. He had lived and worked in Paris for eight years. The Crazy buzzed with new activity. The finale, the last and very special number, with all fourteen dancers performing to *Hey, Big Spender* from the movie *Sweet Charity* was rehearsed and smoothed. All the little kinks that come about in a girl's act when the choreographer is absent were straightened out and everyone was happy again. It seemed that the whole show took a collective sigh of relief and regained confidence.

Paris 1969
Crazy Horse Dancers

I wanted Victor to re-choreograph my act, give me a few interesting steps, but he didn't want to make Bernardin feel bad. The parody of the 1930 striptease needed something extra but I didn't know what. Victor refused to help me.

"Babe, you know Bernardin by now. He always has to be right. Please, don't put me in this position," he said.

I didn't think to say I would pay him myself for a few hours of his time, so the act stayed just as it was. It was good, but it could have been better, and I wanted my act to be great. My mother was coming to Paris and would see me dance. She had never seen me strip, but if there was any place for her to see me this was it.

When I started dancing in 1961 I told my family I was doing the bookkeeping for a chorus line and had to travel with them. That lasted almost two years until my mother asked me during a telephone call why I hadn't thought about working in the chorus line.

"Honey, don't you think you could be a dancer too? You have nice long legs and all those dancing lessons should help," my mother said innocently.

She must have figured it out and wanted to manipulate me gently into telling her I was a stripper. I was so relieved I didn't have to lie to her anymore. I had always told my mother everything. She was my best friend until I met Dreamy. I had felt guilty and a little resentful that Dreamy didn't want me to tell her anything about my exciting new career. Any woman whose mother had been married five times and a bar room singer in her youth should understand that life and love can take you interesting places. I told her almost everything.

In early April I saw my face taking up a whole page and looking happily insane in three weekly magazines, including *Semaine de Paris Pariscope*. They told locals and tourists where to go to plays, local events and movies in Paris during the week. I felt dizzy and had to hold onto a nearby bicycle rack on Boulevard St. Michele to steady myself. Everyone in Paris read at least one of the little magazines each and every week. I thought I was an instant celebrity.

However, the only person I was aware of who recognized me was Siegfried, of Siegfried and Roy, who was performing his magic act in the Lido show.

I could see him coming as he dashed from the opposite side of the Avenue des Champs Elysees, ran up to me and put his arms around me, hugging me in a generous welcoming gesture. Blond, fit and entirely camera ready, he looked as happy as a man could.

"You're the new dancer at the Crazy Horse. I saw your show last night," he said with a wide theatrical smile. "This is marvelous. We should meet at the Lido Bar after the show some night soon. You should meet Roy."

I was thrilled. Could this nice man be a friend of mine in Paris? This was not another pick-up allowed because of loneliness. He was for real, another performer on the road. We agreed to meet at the Lido Bar after our shows. We did meet and had fun together but they were busy with their animals and rigorous training and work out schedules. They were very nice to me but not close.

All of Paris saw my face at least once a week for a month, until Bernardin needed to change his advertisement. He loved my face. He thought I looked amusing, almost exotic, with pale freckles and wide blue eyes compared to the chic, sharp Parisian features.

"I found you an apartment, and it's so funny cute," Lily called to say. "My friend has a place on Rue Clare, across the Seine about six blocks from the Crazy Horse. It's on a special little street." She was excited for me to see it right away.

I had been looking for a couple of weeks and couldn't find an affordable place that was habitable. The rooms were miniscule and dark, or had no windows at all, and there were few elevators in any of the old buildings. I had been asked to look at some places for two hundred a month that were dirty and even dangerous. I couldn't find the nerve to step into some of them.

When I had left Hollywood, six months before, I was paying seventy-five dollars a month for a nice apartment. Two-hundred dollars for a ruin was quite a leap. They say location is everything in real estate and I could see that now. This was Paris. I worried about not being able to find a nice clean place for my mother and sister when they arrived in July.

"Come and see the street, then we'll look at the apartment if you like it," Lily encouraged.

As soon as I saw the apartment building I realized she knew I would fall in love with the street and was counting on that before she let me know the apartment was on the seventh floor and there was no elevator. Once I climbed up the seven flights and could focus on something other than trying to breathe, I saw that the kitchen had a small sink, a two-ring hot plate and a bathtub with a piece of plywood over it to use as counter space. The toilet room was in the hall and I would share it with the other apartment on that level.

The living room and bedroom had big windows and clean blue carpets. Both rooms were large and airy. This was a much better living space than I had been offered before and there was even a telephone in the living room, so I took it for one twenty a month. Now I was fitting in. With a few things from Moneprix, where one could buy anything from a toothbrush to a couch, I could make this a cute place.

Living at the hotel had become a sad experience for me. I would make what I thought were friends, would know them for three or four days and then never see or hear from them. I was getting depressed again. I wouldn't be exposed to this sadness if I lived in an apartment. I would save money on the hotel and taxis, and I could walk home. Paris was safe enough to walk alone even after two a.m. if I had to.

We were still having riots in Paris when President Charles De Gaulle, the leader of France for almost ten years, resigned in late April. My taxi driver waving an open bottle of wine out the window drove on the sidewalk as there was no room for cars in the street. People were out of their apartments, dancing and drinking, celebrating their election success in the streets of Paris. The De Gaulle government had fallen. The students and workers wanted full participation in business and government and saw this time as their moment of victory.

On stage at the Crazy Horse.

Chapter Twenty-Seven

Mama and the Man on the Moon

"Wake up, wake up. Open the door. I'm back. Let me in," I could hear Vicky yelling happily in front of my apartment door at the top of seven staircases.

Bonita Super woke up too. Both of us still had our stage makeup on and wanted more sleep after a night of working, bar-hopping and making love. I put my finger over my lips, asking her not to say anything yet. Bonita crinkled her brow in silent question.

"It's Vicky, from Singapore," I whispered.

Hoping that Vicky would think I wasn't home and leave, we were quiet as she screamed louder. It was only eight a.m. and she knew me well enough to be sure I would sleep until at least ten.

"I'm going to stay here until you get up, you know." Her voice became deeper with suspicion. "I'll bet you have a woman in there with you. Which one is it?" Vicky demanded.

Four long irritating hours passed as Vicky stayed at the top of the stairs and shouted to us every few minutes. There was no real food in the apartment, just a peach, some pate de fois gras and crackers. Bonita and I dressed but couldn't go downstairs for breakfast or even speak except in gestures and whispers. We just kept looking at each other, raising our shoulders and shaking our heads in wonder at this stubborn woman's persistence. When would she leave?

Bonita knew Vicky from her last visit to Paris and understood that we were not lovers or even friends any longer. But she didn't want Vicky to know she was there and had been with me all night. Bonita knew Vicky would tell anyone she could about making this scene. Judging from her lack of expertise this may have been the first time Bonita had tried to make love to a woman and she didn't want anyone else to know about it.

"Open up in there! This is the police. Open the door!" a man's voice said loudly as he banged on the door hard enough to rattle the glasses on the table.

Even though he was speaking in French, and I was scared, I could understand that much. How he must have hated each of the seven flights upstairs to settle this fit of lesbian jealousy that Vicky had somehow dragged him into. I couldn't think of what she might have told him to get him up there.

The loud banging on the door and the policeman yelling non-stop in French, caused Bonita to look at me with a stony stare.

"A necklace, you have stolen her necklace?" Bonita asked in astonishment.

"Noooo!" I put my hand on my heart as if to swear this was true. "She gave me a necklace the first time she made love to me. It was the piece of jade every young Chinese person receives from family when they leave home. It's for good luck. She put it on my neck and wouldn't take it back," I whispered gesturing to make Bonita understand. "She wants it now?"

Shaking her head, Bonita glared at me. She had been bored and irritable for a while, waiting for Vicky to leave but now she was mad. I knew she was hungry. She was angry that she couldn't get out of the room and had to pee in a cup and empty it into the kitchen sink. Now she was involved in a police investigation because of me.

I ran into the bedroom and grabbed the necklace. It was a beautifully carved, two inch long rectangle of light green jade on a 24 carat gold chain.

It was pretty but I was more than happy to give it back to Vicky. It was a special piece. She should never have given to me in the first place. Pushing the necklace under the front door, out into the hall, I was anxious for this farce to end. It was noon and we hadn't been able to have breakfast yet.

"You must open the door." The policeman's voice came through the door loudly. I was sure people in the other apartments could hear him and that his voice carried down seven flights all the way out to the street.

Looking at Bonita and opening the door to face the police and Vicky Noon was such a hard thing to do. I was embarrassed and furious at the same time. It was obvious Bonita would never speak to me again and maybe even thought I had actually stolen the necklace.

"I knew it! You have a woman with you," Vicky accused. She whirled around, looking back only to throw the necklace in my face, and ran down the stairs where her luggage must have been with the porter by the front door.

The policeman stood there assessing the situation. Bonita had last night's makeup on and the same evening wear with the deeply scoop-necked blouse she had worn to show off her magnificent breasts the night before.

As he questioned Bonita, the policeman seemed bewildered, then I could see it dawning on him. He seemed to have figured out what Vicky wanted all along. He raised one eyebrow while looking me up and down, then left. I understood what he was thinking. We didn't look our best but even so Bonita was spectacular. About three floors down the staircase he started whistling.

A few weeks passed and then my mother Beverly, and sister Michele were getting ready to make the grand tour of Ireland and England, then come to Paris and stay with me for a few weeks.

"I already feel guilty about leaving your dad all by himself in Boston for the whole summer. He's so happy we're able to make this trip though, it seems ungrateful for me to feel bad," my mom said during one of our frequent telephone conversations.

This trip to Europe was something my mother had always longed for. They were going to visit my dad's cousin in Ireland also. I guessed the whole family in Boston was pretty excited about that.

My dad's four brothers and two sisters had been acting cool toward my mother for wanting to leave Jack alone for the summer and take his daughter off to foreign places. But when she had the insight to include a visit to relatives in Ireland into the itinerary, the siblings acted as though she was making a holy pilgrimage and it was absolutely the right thing to do. Jack's mother and father had never been back to "the old sod" since arriving at Ellis Island. None of his sisters or brothers had made the effort to go either.

Funny Girl, starring Barbra Streisand, was showing on the Champs Elysees. I saw it every afternoon for a week. It was so relaxing, so wonderful to hear the English language spoken beautifully, without a French accent. *The Lion in Winter*, with Katherine Hepburn and Peter O'Toole was my next favorite. I saw it over and over waiting for Hepburn to say, "When pigs fly!"

Vicky went back to London but started calling me every few days.

"You have been such a big influence in my life," she said. "I'm a nude model now for photographers. I smoke pot every day and at night I go out looking for birds. It's very popular to be Asian in Britain now. Everyone wants a Chinese or Japanese girlfriend. We're cool."

I wasn't sure if she wanted me to rush over to London and rescue her from " a life of evil" or if she was bragging that she could live a fast life in the big city. Whatever she had in mind it didn't work. I was happy the melodrama with her was over and had no desire to start it up again.

The pianist who worked at the Crazy took me out to a dinner before the show, which he promised would delight and surprise. It was eye-popping and delicious. Leroy, who had to be at least 6'4", a mountain of muscle and belly, had been a star on the Morehouse College football team. He had received his Bachelors and Masters degrees there. Chez Haynes was a Mississippi soul food restaurant in the working class area of Pigalle.

"Hi y'all, glad to see ya'. Just come right on in and have a seat. Make yourself comfortable," said Leroy as he was tying on a clean white apron.

We weren't the only ones there at six in the evening. While Europeans dine late, Leroy knew his American customers would be there early.

We had mammoth-sized plates of barbequed ribs, corn bread, potato salad, corn-on-the-cobb, Iberia hot peppers and sweet potato pie for dessert. No tiny French-sized portions here. The Saint-Emilion Bordeaux accompanied the meal perfectly. It was my new favorite wine. If it was good enough for Leroy it was good enough for me.

I had searched for a Mexican restaurant ever since arriving in January but didn't have any luck finding one. I missed the El Carmen Cafe, in Los Angeles, like I missed my mother's kitchen. Spanish food was not the same as Mexican and why eat it in France? Now I had Chez Haynes, a homey place I would return to often.

A sweet July came at last. My mom and sister arrived from Ireland where they had spent part of their ten-week trip. They flew in on a fabulous day. The weather was warm, the air fragrant from bakeries and flower stalls in every block.

"Did you really say the seventh floor?" Beverly questioned me as we reached Rue Clare and my new apartment.

When we stepped out of the taxi, the fruit and vegetable stalls caught her attention and she turned away from me to browse among them.

"Come here, my queen, look at this. Good for tonight," the potato seller called to her with shaking jowls, holding out some of his produce.

"Princessa, come help your mother. Get some of these beautiful tomatoes for her. Want strawberries ?" the wrinkled Spanish fruit seller called.

It was a good day. Beverly and Michele bought apricots, some purple grapes, a peach and three boxes of strawberries. They were happy and that's what I wanted.

"I'm willing to climb seven flights, up and down, to live on this street a while," she said when we had reached the fourth floor.

I had tried to get a good place, an interesting place, for Beverly and the street market atmosphere had won her over. The fact that we had two bakeries within a block of the building was a big part of her joy in the location. The block seemed to exist in another, earlier age which my mother had been part of in early Hollywood.

Each morning she descended seven flights with the string bag she bought as soon as she saw it, and made her way to the bakery line. She was a round woman with silvery hair in a bun at the top of her head, soft blue eyes and a sweet open expression on her face.

Beverly shopped for bread just like the locals who bought it fresh early each morning and late afternoon. All the French words she learned in Paris were acquired while in line at the bakery, shopping at the fruit stalls, and eating in restaurants. She also hoped if she didn't speak, just pointed to what she wanted, she could pass for French.

We went on bus tours to the palaces of Versailles and Chantilly, but mostly we stayed in Paris, walking the streets or taking the Metro everywhere they wanted to go. I hoped to make the five weeks they would be in Paris momentous, something they could only do because they were there with me.

Michele was so proud she could order her own beer in Paris and drink it in public. That was something she could brag about for years to her American cousins. There was no age limit for drinking alcohol in Paris, so the fresh-faced fourteen year-old with huge green eyes and long chestnut curls drank beer on the Champs Elysees or wine at dinner, swirling the liquid in her glass as she had seen on television, so everyone in the place would notice the "little girl" drinking like a grown-up.

The Sunday before we were to leave for London, Dreamy called at seven a.m. Paris time. Beverly shook me awake. She had already been down to see the baker and his tiny wife who she adored because the lady was so friendly.

"Brandy, I'm coming over in a few weeks if it's alright with you," Dreamy said.

I could tell she was upset, but she didn't say what was wrong.

"I'm staying with Dick McInnes now. He said I can stay with him for a while if I'm going to go to Paris. Otherwise, I have to find a place of my own because I'm not living with Mitzi anymore."

"Oh, Dreamy. Yes, of course, come here to me. What happened, honey?" I asked, trying to sound concerned for her pain yet unable to conceal my happiness. My wish had just come true. I was thrilled and full of questions as to how it had happened.

"I can't tell you now. I want to be with you but I'm still afraid to travel across the water. You know I've always been afraid to leave the United States. I'll fly to London if you meet me there and fly with me to Paris. Just come and get me and take me there. I think I'll be able to do it that way," Dreamy said, dread and fear in her voice.

It sounded like she was trying not to breathe, but I couldn't be sure because there was so much static and noise on the phone. Did she think London and Paris were as close as Burbank and Glendale? Didn't she realize we were talking about flying to another country, going through immigration and customs twice in one day, to get her to Paris? No, how could she?

"Don't be afraid, Dreamy. You let me know when, and I'll be there waiting for you to get off the plane."

This was wonderful. Not quite like taking a cab to pick someone up at the airport but as good as it could be, considering the circumstances. Beverly and Michele would be gone by that time and Dreamy would be with me if she agreed to walk up seven flights of stairs. I had not moved into this apartment with her heart problems and newly diagnosed arthritis in mind.

I took Michele to the Crazy Horse to see a rehearsal since she wouldn't be able to go to an evening show. More dancers had joined the ensemble to take the place of girls going on vacation so we had to work them into the *Big Spender* finale.

A young, African woman from Mali named Zaboo Maiga had joined our cast. She was a rebel. We could see that immediately from the way she looked at us through half-closed distrustful eyes. Sophia, the dance captain, rolled her eyes toward Prima Symphony, head of the four-girl ballet corps. Prima nodded back, raised her eyebrows and sighed as if to say, "This should be fun to watch."

Zaboo wouldn't learn the choreography Victor created for her. She didn't want to wear the costume Bernardin had designed for her. She was late to rehearsals and shrugged when she was reminded to be on time, which put Bernardin into a fit of temper.

"No! You will not go on my stage and do whatever you feel like doing at that moment. This is my show, and I don't care if you think you are the best dancer in France. You will do it my way or you will not dance for me," Bernardin threatened.

He stood in the showroom glaring at her, as she posed on his stage, in all her black, sweaty, muscular beauty.

"I dance as I please," said Zaboo with her head high, her black eyes closed to slits, not backing down.

"Very well, you shall not dance. You will not move your feet at all. You will stand there and move only as Victor shows you. You will not have a costume. So, we shall see who does what on my stage. Victor, rehearse the finale once more. That she will learn to do, or she can leave now. Begin."

I glanced over to see if my sister was still in the back of the show room. She was there, sitting on a low, blue-velvet stool, listening intently. She couldn't tell what was being said but the body language spoke for itself. Her immense green eyes were focused on Zaboo as were most of the eyes in the room. Michele was holding on to the table with one hand, her icy club soda in the other, as she leaned forward in anticipation.

Zaboo shrugged one shoulder slowly, and smiled with her brilliant white teeth parted as if ready to bite into someone. She was closest to me. I took a step back. She looked at me and winked so no one else could see it. My heart fluttered. I stood straighter. Suddenly the air sparkled and what I breathed in felt effervescent. I remembered having had that exquisite moment of instant sexual attraction before. Things just became complicated.

Michele was excited as we left the Crazy Horse. She skipped most of the six blocks to the Seine and back to Rue Clare. She could talk of nothing but the finale.

"Did I see the dancers pubic hair through that G-string thingie? That plastic thing? It really looked yuckie. You looked kinda good though in that big wig. I like the color, and the boots. Wow! I never saw anything like those before. Tell me about that dancer who the owner was so mad at. She was the best of all."

I loved the finale. It was so artistic and all Bernardin. The almost nonexistent costumes the dancers wore, the see-through clear plastic G-strings, my red wig were all his idea. Bernardin had fallen in love with my wig and insisted all the dancers wear a bright green or blue wig for the finale. I agreed with my sister, the black, thigh-high, soft leather boots handmade for each dancer's feet and legs were the sexiest things I had ever worn.

True to his word, four days later Bernardin put Zaboo on the thirty-six inch circular disc embedded in the stage floor that was usually used to balance or turn props, and made her stand on it her entire act.

"She can move her hips, her knees, her arms, her shoulders and breasts, all that, but if she lifts one foot off that disc she is gone," our choreographer Victor told me in confidence. "It doesn't matter. She's sexy as hell and the audience will be riveted to her crotch. It's a simple countdown of break-away G-strings. She starts by taking off a red one with the number ten and gets down to a white G-string with a red zero which she throws high in the air over the audience as the spotlight follows it and the stage goes black. Sexy as hell, I'm telling you. I'm just sorry I can't claim credit for it. It's all her. You'll see tonight," he said.

The dancers were dying to see how Bernardin and Zaboo had come together and made an act out of nothing but force of personality and charisma. The beat of drums, tom-toms, congas, bongos, snare drums, high-hats and more filled the Crazy Horse. It was all Zaboo needed to mesmerize us with loose limbs and fierce energy.

Glistening black skin, hot sweat running down defined muscles, Zaboo slowly turned round and round on the silver circle. Each red G-string had a number. As she took one off, and the numbers decreased, I could feel the audience holding its breath. They wanted to see those few square inches of her body the G-strings covered so much they stopped smoking, stopped drinking, stopped blinking.

Sweat flew, drops glittered in the pink spotlight, a red zero on a white background rose into the air. Black.

The act was four minutes long. Through the peep-holes backstage we could see Bernardin standing at the bar listening to the conversations around him, until the audience stopped talking to watch the next act. His stance and triumphant smile at the sound of applause told me he thought this was how he had planned it all along.

It was Zaboo's night. She knew she was the winner. We all knew that.

July 20, 1969

Sophia Palladium, Capsula Popo and I had been toasting Neil Armstrong for an hour in a little club near the Crazy Horse. With the piano player, we sang *Fly Me to the Moon*, *Moon River*, *Moon Over Miami* and all the popular sing-along moon songs on that one spectacular night. We drank Calvados, French apple brandy, and sang our hearts out.

"We need the moon. We need some air, the hell with singing. Let's go look at the moon. Maybe we can see them up there," Capsula enthused.

"To Neil Armstrong, the man on the moon!" we screamed, running down the street next to the Seine.

When I got home around three a.m., still tipsy, I tried to get Beverly and Michele out of bed to share the moment with me.

"We'll see it in the morning newspaper, honey. Let us sleep now," my mother complained. "Turn off that radio and go to bed."

I was able to catch a scratchy *Voice of America*, broadcast coming in from Luxemburg, on my shortwave radio. I wanted to hear the actual moment of Armstrong climbing down the ladder and placing his foot on the surface of the moon. This was the beginning of all those dreams in the science fiction stories my mother and I had read when I was a child, coming true. This was the real thing. Why didn't they want to fill themselves up with the moment?

I was sitting alone on the floor of the living room drinking champagne. It was about five a.m. when Neil Armstrong made his way out of the capsule, down the white ladder, ever so slowly, and then the extra-long final leap onto the moon.

"Amen," I breathed.

Later that day Beverly, Michele and I gawked at the huge screens erected along the Champs Elysees with a hundred thousand Parisians crowded around us. We watched Armstrong and the crew in the spaceship. The events of earlier that morning were available to the world.

I saw men and women crying, holding children on their shoulders for a better look at the screens. Some were biting their nails, brows raised high on their foreheads, looking nervous and fearful. They were probably hoping and praying, as I was, that the astronauts would be able to get back home to earth.

My mother and sister had a few adventures and stories of their own to tell about Paris. On a warm summer evening as we were leaving Chez Haynes, Beverly got her rear-end pinched in

Pigalle by no one knows who. It made her laugh. She was glad that hers was the one pinched in the tradition of Pigalle instead of her younger daughter's.

Beverly could hardly get Michele out of the apartment after I gave her the pocket book of *The Chosen* by Chaim Potok. This was the first book she had ever read for pleasure and she couldn't get enough of it. Michele wanted to read this book about teenagers who were Jewish, as she had always wanted to be.

"Why did you have to choose this moment to start to read?" my mother questioned. "In a family of readaholics you had to decide to become one now?"

All of Beverly's complaining did her no good. Michele lay in bed and read day and night to the end of the book and wanted a sequel.

One early morning Beverly was alone, feeding the birds while sitting on a bench near the Eiffel Tower. A loud American mother and daughter who were scaring the birds away strolled by and stopped to stare at her.

"Is she cute or what? This will be my perfect French picture. I feel so close to the real people here," the mother trilled.

They tried to speak a word or two in French, gesturing to ask Beverly if they could take her picture. Beverly lowered her eyes with false modesty, nodded and murmured something she thought would sound Frenchy, and allowed her picture to be taken.

"I can hear myself being talked about by those midwesterners, when they share their pictures, as "that sweet-looking old French woman who was feeding the birds," she chuckled while telling us the story.

"Yes, instead of that devious, well-trained actress from Hollywood," I countered with a knowing grin.

Beverly and Michele saw my show before they left Paris for London.

Bernardin said, "Yes, you can let the little girl come to see the show with her mother, but she cannot drink alcohol. I do not like to see the children drink."

Both my mom and sister knew Bonita and Sophia as I had taken them all to lunch at the Pub Renault on the Champs Elysees. They were anxious to see the show, especially Zaboo's act, as Michele had been raving about her for days.

They loved every minute of our show: the four girl ballet numbers, the black-light puppet masters from Czechoslovakia that M. Bernardin had helped escape to the west and all the dancers, even me.

"Zaboo was going round and round on that little circle thingy and when she got down to the zero G-string she threw it right at me. I had my hands up to catch it but this huge hairy guy threw his arm right in front of my face and grabbed it. He almost sat on my lap, the big pig!" Michele told me after the show.

Bernardin had been generous with my family. He gave them complimentary entre, champagne for Beverly and cokes for Michele, plus a special tour of the dressing rooms and his celebrity lounge.

I was in a celebratory mood and relieved in a way. It was the first time my mom had seen me strip on stage. Things had gone well. My mother wasn't offended by any of the acts and, most importantly, she liked mine. They were leaving to spend a week in London then return to Boston and I wanted their time with me to end on a high note.

My mother and sister wanted to take me to London and I wanted to go with them. England was part of the dream trip my mom and I started planning when I was twelve, after my first baby-sitting job.

Before she left the apartment for the last time, while Michele was out of sight, taking their luggage down seven flights of stairs, Beverly showed me a sealed envelope.

"I'm not taking this home with me because I don't want your father to see it. So I am leaving it with you. It's my birth certificate. I don't want you to open it. I'm going to put it in the bookcase here," Beverly said as she slipped the envelope into a book.

What a mysterious woman my mother was. Didn't she know her oldest child at all? I was dying to rip open the envelope right then, but now it would have to wait until after the London trip.

There were so many contradicting thoughts swirling around inside my head as I shopped for English detective books and American record albums in London. I had to tour London with my family, go to Stonehenge and Cambridge, get back to Paris, open that envelope and have a short affair with Zaboo before Dreamy arrived.

In late August, I returned to Paris from a beautiful week in London with my mom and sister Michele. The French were coming back to Paris from their warm Italian and Spanish holidays. Hordes of summer tourists from the United States, Great Britain and all places around the globe were packing to go back home to school or work. Paris was becoming herself again, the reigning beauty of Europe: calm, chic, self-involved.

Immediately upon returning to my apartment in Paris I opened the envelope my mother had left in the bookcase. It was a birth certificate, but was it really hers? The name on it was Clara King. Whose name was that? Looking further down I saw Mother – Hebrew, Father – Rumanian. They were the right first names, Rose and Samuel, but why would they lie about their nationalities?

Who was King? I had many questions that would have to wait for answers but I knew that Cuba in Tel Aviv had been on the right track. Something was hidden in this birth certificate business. I would coax answers from Beverly, the mystery woman, while face to face the next time I was in Boston with her.

The apartment seemed cold and empty now. I had been so happy with my mom and sister, my two love girls, there. While they were with me I dreamed I was a senior, graduating from high school for the seventeenth time. Why was I graduating so many times? It felt so real it stuck in my mind, not like other dreams that fade from memory a moment after waking.

Chapter Twenty-Eight

Zaboo: The Best Dancer in Paris

Things seemed the same when I returned to the Crazy Horse after being in London for a week; Zaboo was not allowed to lift her feet on stage, Bonita ignored me, and Sophia was still madly in love with her sexy Italian, Roberto.

Each of the Crazy Horse dancers wore a light coat of beige body makeup on stage. It covered up blemishes and tan lines but it also made them seem even more alike. The body makeup was mandatory for every dancer except Zaboo and me. Bernardin had been told by several people that they liked the whiteness of my skin, as I was the only dancer who became pink or blue with the change of lights.

The first night back at work I carefully timed my departure from the club. Zaboo and I walked down the hall to the side door exit at exactly the same moment. We were alone, as our showers after the show didn't take as long as the painted girls.

I hadn't figured out what to say when I got this far, but I knew it should be something casual.

"Going home?" I asked.

"I never go home after the work," Zaboo said in a voice used to command while raising an eyebrow. "Jean-Claude will take me to eat and then to dance. Come with us. He won't bother you, but he'll pay for everything," she promised with a grin.

Amazed at how two words had already taken me so much closer to my quest, I said, "Thank you." We left the club together and stepped into the maroon and black Citroen waiting at the curb.

"This is Candy," Zaboo announced to the skinny man who was the driver as we entered the car.

We drove to a brightly lit Senegalese restaurant that was packed tightly with more than two hundred patrons eating dinner and drinking wine at two in the morning. What sounded like African music to my uneducated ear accompanied the diners as they smiled and laughed, kissed each other, chewed heartily and drank voraciously in the warm and relaxed atmosphere.

We were taken to a red leather booth that was set on a dais along the farthest wall from the entrance. Ours had a little reserved sign on the white tablecloth. I could see everyone and they could all see us if they wanted to look. Jean Claude and I were the two Caucasian people there, so some African customers did glance at us.

"Welcome, I am Doudou, the owner. My name means 'sweet'." His lips puckered up as he said his name slowly, as if to kiss the air, then burst out in deep melodious laughter. "Any friend of Zaboo's is a friend of mine," said the tall, heavy-set black man. Doudou smiled, showing each of his healthy square white teeth, radiating kindness and charm.

We drank French wine, ate what Jean Claude said were typical Senegalese dishes of baked chicken in a spicy onion and lemon sauce and had banana flambé with ice cream for dessert. I was in heaven.

Jean Claude, a small and wiry Frenchman about fifty years-old with thinning dull grey hair, turned out to be a 'computer architect' who taught his subject at the Beaux Arte University. He spoke some English so we were able to communicate more than Zaboo and I could.

Even while speaking to someone else, Jean Claude kept his eyes on Zaboo's face. She ordered the food for all of us as he nodded in agreement. While we drank, he observed her. When she spoke to me, trying to tell me about the food and the people there, he drank her in as well when he translated Zaboo's words. It was easy to see he was obsessed with her.

When I tried to contribute money for the bill tears welled up in Jean Claude's eyes.

"Oh, no! I must pay for everything. She must have it so," he whispered while leaning far back into the booth, his shoulders rounded and head down.

I understood now why Zaboo had been able to seem so cavalier about keeping her job at the Crazy Horse. Jean Claude took care of all her financial needs, yet during the meal she hardly spoke to him. She did not look at him.

We danced to African and American music at the disco Jean Claude drove us to. I mainly watched Zaboo dance while trying to stay as close to her as I could. Men drew near, wanting to steal her away from me. They danced up from behind, brushing and thrusting their pelvises against her hips, but she would have none of them.

Zaboo danced for me that night. She wanted me to see what the Crazy Horse and Bernardin were missing by not letting her dance as she could. Spectacular was the only word I had for her dancing. She made up exciting, complicated double-time combinations and executed them so easily, so gracefully, always ending on precisely the right beat. It made her seem beautiful to me which she was not when she was still.

Full busted and muscular, at five foot five it was her attitude of dominance and queenly bearing that told you about her personality. We were the only women dancing together. It felt quite daring.

It was sad that she couldn't - that she wouldn't - take direction. If Zaboo had accepted Victor's choreography for a week, then started dancing her own steps, Bernardin would never have known. He would have congratulated Victor for his genius, and admired himself for how Zaboo was dancing better every evening.

Jean Claude dropped me off on Rue Clare after six in the morning. Tired but happy I walked past the fruit and vegetable peddlers as they filled their little stalls with fresh produce. They were ready for their day to start while I was almost done with my night. I hadn't had so much fun since arriving in Europe.

The next night Zaboo and I left work together again, stepping out the side exit and into the waiting Citroen. We ate at Doudou's then danced for hours. I tried to keep up with Zaboo's dancing but it was impossible for me.

"Drop Candy off at my house tonight," Zaboo told Jean Claude while winking at me. This moment was the first I had heard of her decision. I had been thinking about just that all night. We let it seem like it was something Zaboo and I had already agreed upon.

Leaving Jean Claude in the car with barely a goodbye, Zaboo led me up a flight of stairs, into a one bedroom apartment that was much nicer than mine. Her's had a larger kitchen and a private bathroom.

"Come here, come here, mmmm,uhmmmm," she sighed as she kissed my lips.

We were already in the bedroom. Zaboo was pulling my sweater off. I was trying to get her skirt unzipped. We were a little drunk, yet we were managing to take our clothes off. That was one of the things we did best.

Zaboo explored between my legs with her fingers. She found me wet and wanting her there. Her tongue found the best part. She stopped her journey of my body only after she was sure I could not climax once more. She stayed there while her hands fondled other parts of my torso, buttocks and thighs.

"Once? One time only? My last girl, three, four, five times," Zaboo complained, looking through my legs up to my face.

"Well, honey, lay back and by the time I'm finished you can have another try," I teased as I moved to a better position to kiss her stomach, wanting to open her tightly closed thighs. Her skin was satin smooth, with incredibly solid, hard muscle underneath.

"No! Not there!" she commanded. She threw the blankets off the bed and stood up. Moving away from me she left the room.

What was going on? If not there, where? Did she have a special place on her body that was more sensitive to her than the vagina and clitoris, as I had heard other women speak about? She wanted to make love but was not ready to receive love. I couldn't figure it out, but that was the way Zaboo wanted it. Try as I might I couldn't get her to loosen up, and that was how it stayed throughout the few weeks of our love-making.

She and Jean Claude took me to the late-night spots of Paris. Most Parisians would never have seen them, and I loved it. I felt safe with them and wanted to repay her somehow. Paying Jean Claude would have been against the rules. To return her kindnesses I bought her a Dunlop gold cigarette lighter and another time gave her a golden necklace I had brought from Tel Aviv, and a few other little things which she accepted with grace.

A couple of weeks into our nightly forays, we were once again at Doudou's. As Zaboo exited the ladies room, she either bumped into a young waitress in a short purple velvet skirt with and high black leather boots or touched the girl's boyfriend. I never found out. But the girl was not happy. She started screaming at Zaboo, "You're a shit, you're a shit!" Doudou's muscular bouncer took the waitress outside and talked to her, then left her on the dark street corner by herself.

"Fuckin' village vas!" the girl screamed in a mix of English and French as she stuck her head back in the glass door, her lips curling up in disgust and anger.

Zaboo jumped up and ran toward the waitress at the door. Jean Claude and I ran after Zaboo, trying to catch her. We didn't get there in time. Three customers from the restaurant were outside ahead of us. They jumped on Zaboo, hitting her in the abdomen and ribs. One held her arms so she couldn't defend herself. Maybe that was the boyfriend. It was crazy.

By the time we reached the street Zaboo was backed up against a brick wall and the girl in black boots had pulled out a small knife hidden somewhere in her clothing. In an instant she had put the knife deep into Zaboo's nostril then pulled up and out. The knife easily cut through the tender skin. Blood was everywhere.

"Merde! Merde!" Zaboo screamed, swiping at the blood dripping off her chin, her tongue catching some. "Get back here you fuckin' whore !" she yelled after the waitress who was running down the street.

Doudou's bouncer arrived to help Jean Claude steer Zaboo into the Citroen. We took her to an emergency hospital to receive treatment.

On the way there I held her hand next to my mouth, kissing her fingers gently. "You're going to be fine my darling. It's alright. It's going to be alright," I murmured in a soft persuasive voice, trying to calm her.

Zaboo, her face and chest covered with blood, veins filled with adrenalin, wouldn't be comforted. She was anxious to return to Doudou's as soon as she was free of us.

"Go back, go back. I need to find that bitch. Don't let her get away, " Zaboo wailed in frustration.

When we arrived at the emergency clinic, attendants put her on a gurney in a small room and left us to wait. Zaboo jumped off the rolling bed, blood running into her mouth and down her cheek as she started thrashing through the cupboards and drawers.

"Scissors, scissors or a knife. Where are they?" she mumbled.

The doctor, whose wrinkled watery eyes had probably seen every kind of injury there was, entered the room after Zaboo had found two pairs of sharply pointed scissors. Zaboo hid them in her pocket. The doctor shot a sedative into her arm, retrieved the scissors from Zaboo's pocket, cleaned her face and neck of blood and furious tears, and put four stiches in her left nostril. The coarse black catgut stuck out of Zaboo's nose and lay on her cheek like long whiskers.

"These can be taken out in seven days. Try to stay relaxed and do not play with them," the doctor advised.

I knew Zaboo would have to present herself to Bernardin. That was not an enviable task. She would be yanked off the stage for a week. There was no way he would let her on his stage with stitches sticking out of her nose, but we knew he would complain and try to make her feel stupid for months. Bernardin had a strong, sadistic streak which he did not bother to hide.

We took Zaboo home first that night. Together Jean Claude and I put her to bed. She went to sleep immediately. Then he drove me to Rue Clare.

"What really happened back there, Jean Claude?" I asked. "There had to be more to it than a little bump against the chair."

"Yes, they have a history, those two. The waitress is from Mali, too. She's from Bamako, the capitol. She is proud that her family is modern, that they did not cut her when she was a child. She called Zaboo a 'village girl' which in their culture means she had her clitoris cut out, probably with a piece of glass or the edge of a sharp stone, and her vagina sewn closed except for a small hole to release the blood of womanhood. They both think it's a terrible insult to be called a village girl, so it is," Jean Claude answered. "Do you understand me?"

I was stunned to silence. This was the first time I had heard of female genital mutilation. I understood the words and kind of what he said had been done, but couldn't understand why mothers would allow that to happen to their little girls. My beautiful Zaboo, no wonder she hid that part of herself from me.

After worrying about it during the next few days I decided it must be sexual insecurity and the drive for power of African men. They must feel if they are married to mutilated women they can control them easier than men with wives who are able to feel physical passion.

Strange things were happening all around Paris in 1969. A few days after Zaboo's bloody fight, as I was leaving a crepe restaurant near the Arc de Triumph, a terrified young boy knocked me back into the restaurant window. I tumbled onto the sidewalk in front of the doorway as he ran around the corner and down the little street. Fifteen or sixteen teenaged boys and young men, all dressed in black, charged around the corner chasing the youngster.

A quick change of focus turned the crowd's attention to me, the lone female on the street who was struggling to get up from the sidewalk. Long-haired boys, two carrying French flags, surrounded me.

"USA, out of Vietnam! Yankee go home! Yankee go home!" they yelled over me.

I tried to inch back toward the door of the restaurant, but they wouldn't let me move. Pressing forward they grabbed at my hair and my purse. I considered trying to run but I knew these boys would have delighted in chasing me around like cats after a mouse, so I stayed still.

"Get out of here, you garbage!" the crepe-maker wearing a white apron yelled from the restaurant doorway. He had a heavy copper pot in his hand.

With the other hand he grabbed for the back of my jacket collar and pulled me toward him and finally through the door as the boys kept yelling "USA, out of Vietnam!" A few of the customers had stood to support the chef. Others were backing away, turning to look for an exit door at the rear of the restaurant.

The young men in black wanted to yell, run, jump around and vandalize. They wanted to run up and down the Champs Elysees shouting slogans, to join others like themselves who were rioting against the war in Vietnam and to be seen on the television news broadcasts. They wanted to fight with more than one American woman in a tiny street. They took off to get some real satisfaction.

I sat down at the little bar for a moment to catch my breath and thanked the chef. He wouldn't hear of me walking toward the Champs Elysees to the Crazy Horse, so he called a taxi and sent me safely off to work.

I didn't see Zaboo for the week she was healing. She didn't pick up the telephone when I called. I was sure Jean Claude was there taking care of her with loving devotion, probably crawling on his knees to present her with a glass of wine or a cold compress. It was obvious he loved every moment he could be in her service.

When Zaboo came back to work, she looked the same as always. No scab or scar was noticeable as makeup was able to cover whatever was there. But things were different between us and because we spoke in French and gestures I wasn't able to discuss it. I would not ask Jean Claude or anyone else I knew to help me with this very personal dilemma.

Occasionally, we would go out dancing but we never slept together again. She seemed embarrassed or just put off by the whole fight experience. She might have thought I could understand the words that had been screamed at Doudou's. Perhaps Jean Claude told her I was curious about the fight and that he had told me she was a cut woman. I never found out. She had Jean Claude to take care of her. The best dancer I had seen in Paris was back, but still was not allowed to move her feet on stage.

Chapter Twenty-Nine

Dreamy: The Dream Unfulfilled

October was cool and sunny, a perfect time to fall in love with Paris. I was famous, and Dreamy was with me. She was mine again. I loved her. How could I have been happier? What more could I want?

Dreamy had been kept busy on the flight from Los Angeles to London by the two Indian children who shared the seats in her row as they played their games and read books to her. She said all their questions about Hollywood and the movies had kept her mind off her fears.

"How am I going to do this every day?" Dreamy asked on the third floor landing of the seven story walkup, already out of breath. "Why did you do this to me?" she moaned as we reached the fifth floor. Dreamy was only thirty-five. I thought, if my fifty-five year-old diabetic mother could do it, Dreamy would easily be able to climb the stairs once she realized this was the way European people lived.

This was the same reaction everyone had when they first came to my apartment so I wasn't surprised. Once she got up the seven flights of stairs I knew she would like the view and how I had fixed the little table by the living room window with flowers.

When we got up to my apartment and were comfortable, Dreamy said, "I couldn't take it anymore," when trying to explain the breakup with Mitzi. "If I spoke to another woman, young or old, Mitzi wanted to kill her. She accused me of still being in love with you and never stopped nagging me about it. I'm so tired of her. She must have been right though, because here I am, and I'm glad." She took my hand in hers and kissed each finger.

Dreamy had always been sweet and affectionate with me. I had missed her familiar touch. I looked for any little clue about how she saw our future together. Would she stay with me now that she had overcome her fear of leaving the United States? Was this a break from Mitzi or a break with Mitzi? I thought I wanted Dreamy because I had wanted her for so long, but I wasn't sure. It would take a few days of being together again to start figuring that out.

I had changed in the last two years. I drank much more now. While still living in Los Angeles, the year after our split, I had started sneaking red wine or vodka into the Largo as most of the girls did. I drank pink champagne in Israel and vodka in Singapore but in Paris I learned how to drink with the heavy hitters. Mostly I drank alcohol of pear or wine. Lots of wine.

I liked my women feminine and beautiful now, not the slightest bit masculine or controlling, but you can't always get what you want.

What would happen when I wanted to express my own opinions, not just agree with Dreamy? I had a few of my own by now. They had come from my personal experience, not Dreamy's, and I would not give them up easily.

We had no television and Dreamy didn't read much. There wasn't even a couch to lounge on in the living room, just the blue blow-up chair I had used as a stage prop in Singapore. We had to go downstairs and walk the streets or take the metro to find something to eat or to do. I hadn't thought about that when agreeing that she come to Paris. Dreamy had no idea what she was letting herself in for, although I had written letters to her and my mother almost every day for the last twelve months explaining the scene.

Born and raised in Louisiana, Dreamy loved French food. As the days passed she grew to love Paris as well. We ate strawberry crepes, steak tar-tare, white fish basted in butter, Greek-French musaka, Vietnamese-French wok, Chinese-French sweet and sour. The French are famous for their small portions and the satisfaction they produce. We ate and ate and ate.

Happy to be together again, we were more like friends than lovers. That was disappointing to both of us although we didn't speak of it.

We tried to have sex once. Dreamy kissed me deeply and I was willing. More than willing, I wanted to show off in a way. Wanted to show her she wasn't the only woman I'd had and there were things she hadn't taught me that I knew. I wanted to be better in bed than Mitzi but I didn't know if I was.

There were thoughts buzzing around the little bedroom that did not make for good loving. It wasn't the passionate reunion of lovers who had been apart for two years that we both hoped for, so we didn't do it again. We never even talked about it. I was too self-conscious to bring it up and that hope shriveled.

After the first few weeks Dreamy began to grumble loudly and often about the apartment. "How could you get a place like this? This is awful. You can make it up those stairs but how can you expect me to?"

"I don't like being supported anymore," Dreamy would say with a sigh. "I feel guilty about the high cost of everything and all the money you're spending on me. I miss the work I was doing in photography. I had hoped there was a chance I might have an actual career."

By mid-November I had heard that so many times I said, "Well, why don't you go to Los Angeles and see if you can get your job back, if that would make you happy?"

Again, she had manipulated me into saying the words that would break us apart. I had come to rely on her company and her advice again.

"Yes, it would make me feel better. I'll find a place and you can join me there when this contract is over in January. That's a good idea, honey," she said.

I heard the little crack of a twig that breaks under your foot in the park. It was my heart. Then, for the first time in ten years, I felt nothing for Dreamy but friendship, a deep, caring friendship, but no passionate love, no desperate sadness, no intense joy of being in her presence, and no tears ready to fall. I felt nothing but the freedom from hurt that I had wanted to feel for two years.

"No," I said looking directly into her green eyes. "You go back to Mitzi. She'll take good care of you. You are her whole life and I think you miss that feeling of being the adored one, the pampered one. Mitzi gives you that. I don't. I'll share my life with you but I could never again make you my entire life. I just learned that. Call her. She'll take you back in a minute," I encouraged, without rancor.

Dreamy's beautiful eyes filled with tears.

I left the apartment, and walked the few blocks to the Seine, so she could have some privacy to make her telephone call. She seemed relieved and sad at the same time, but I wasn't sure. She could have been embarrassed that I was right.

I was depressed. I felt grateful to Dreamy for holding my hand and leading me into the world of burlesque. It was a high-paying, glamorous life, if you were aware of the possible downside of pills and liquor and occasionally being surrounded by gangsters and pimps. You had to be careful about the company you kept.

Burlesque and striptease had also given me a great deal of enjoyment. I spent my working hours with beautiful talented women and met people from all parts of the world.

I loved being a lesbian. I never wanted to make love with men again, after having women who were anxious to please and tantalize me with their soft, sweet bodies. Dreamy had opened that door for me as well. Even though we had been together for seven years, since the first day of 1960, something was missing now. The decade was almost over and so were we.

Dreamy left Paris two days after Thanksgiving. It was obvious she could hardly wait to go. By then I was ready for her to leave. I wasn't angry with her. I was just finished.

It was time for me to go home, too. I needed Los Angeles, and friends who spoke English, sunny weather in November, furniture in my living room, a toilet in my apartment. I wanted meatloaf, baked potatoes, salted butter, and the ocean. I felt like cooking for the first time in my life. I needed libraries, dollar bills and American toilet paper instead of the puce- purple crepe paper the French used.

I was ready for something new and interesting. A dream of graduating from high school for the seventeenth time had come into my sleep many times in the last few weeks. I finally figured out I was telling myself I needed to change. I knew I could change into something else. I had done it many times. But what was my next move?

First, I needed to get out of the contracts to perform in Geneva, Switzerland and Barcelona, Spain which Lily had booked for me the following year. I was done with Europe for a while.

My hands started cramping making it hard to lift my thumbs off my palms. The brain is a great and mysterious thing. It can move your world if you understand the tools it is giving you. The thumbs were doing their best to stay down on the palms of my hands. I couldn't lift them, except when I was on stage.

"You need a doctor's certificate stating that you are not well enough to perform, for the clubs to cancel your contracts, Candy," Bernard Hilda growled at me during our meeting in his office at 33 Avenue des Champs-Élysées

. "How can you do this to us after all the work and publicity we have done for you during the last year to make you an international star? My time and efforts are all wasted."

"Did you show me any of that publicity? I don't remember it," I mumbled, my eyes down. We both knew he had relied on the Crazy Horse to do the best publicity for me.

"That doesn't make any difference." Hilda whipped his head around pointing a finger at my face as he continued to rant. "I am going to choose the doctor that examines you. In fact, I'll send you to my brother and let him see what he thinks of you and your depression. You won't be able to wrap him around your finger with your little helpless act." He wrinkled his nose to emphasize the point and ran a plump hand through his greying hair.

Two days later I was in Dr. Hilda's sparsely furnished white and pale gray office, near the Paris opera house. He was as round as his brother but had the kind and intelligent brown eyes of a Labrador retriever. I was still nervous. What if I wasn't able to convince him? Would he be able to see how much I needed to go home?

My face was bare. I hadn't put on any makeup. Without the help of eyebrow pencil, lipstick, blush and the blue sapphire stud earrings that made my eyes look brighter, I felt pale and hoped I looked as weak as I felt.

"You have worked the last ten months with eight days off, is that right, Candy?" Dr. Hilda asked as he felt the muscles in my neck and shoulders.

I nodded yes.

"Let's look at your hands," he said.

When he had finished the physical examination of the tension in my muscles and the reaction of my limbs to the awful rubber hammer, Dr. Hilda invited me to sit in his office. He wanted to talk about my experiences in Paris, that all my friends were in Los Angeles, and my mother was in Boston. Dr. Hilda watched the tears slowly roll down my cheeks. I couldn't help it.

Dr. Hilda looked at my face and monitored my breathing while he called my agent, his brother Bernard, on the telephone.

"Bernard, this girl is on the edge of a nervous breakdown. I have examined her for two hours and I can see that she is in a deep depression." His plump fingers beat out an order to his brother on the desk between us. "She has to rest and go home to live with her mother for a while. I had no idea you were such a beast. Do you treat all your clients like this? I am writing Miss Capitol a letter stating my findings. You send copies of my letter or call to get her out of these contracts. She needs rest and care."

Relieved, I nodded. Dr. Hilda was right. I was tired and I needed to go back to Los Angeles. Perhaps if I had kept traveling, had been constantly stimulated by new places, and not hoped to make friends in Paris, I might have lasted longer on the road. Each time I thought I had made a friend, they would leave Paris to continue their vacation or business elsewhere and I would never hear from them again. People I had hoped would be friends were mere acquaintances and that was not enough for me. I had been away from home too long.

I could hear Bernard yelling at his brother on the phone from the other side of the desk.

"What does she look like? Does she have any makeup or lipstick on her face? Does it look like she is trying to fake it? I think she's faking," Bernard said. I heard a deep sigh, then "Ah well, what can you do? Have her bring the letter to my office tomorrow."

His voice was calmer. He was cooling down and trying to accept the fact that he would not have ten percent or more of my salary next year or any year in the future.

Sitting in the Crazy Horse dressing room that evening, drinking an alcohol of pear, I wondered what I would do at home. Which college did I want to go to? How much was the tuition? I would need to buy another car. I wondered if I could I go back to work at the Largo. Should I really go live in Boston with my mother? I hadn't lived with her for ten years, but we had had a good time together in Paris. Of course who wouldn't have had a good time in Paris? I decided to have another drink while putting on my stage makeup and think it over.

I still had to get through December, the Christmas holidays, and the first few months of 1970 before my contract at the Crazy Horse would be completed. My new acquaintance John Buchanan, who was the director of the American Express office in Paris, told me if I left Paris in March instead of January, after living out of the United States for eighteen months, I wouldn't have to pay income taxes on the money I had made working abroad.

I had to ask Bernardin if I could stay a few extra months. I was pleased and surprised that he agreed so readily. It would be hard to stay two whole months longer but I had been convinced it would be worth it in the long run. I had made good money and had very few tax write-offs.

Our choreographer, Victor, had gone to California to be with his family for the holidays as he did every year, and things were becoming tense in the dressing room again without his calming influence. At first it was just little things, like a missing eyeliner brush or a drink accidently spilled on my wig but when a small part in a movie, as a flag carrying, partially nude patriot was offered to me because I was a Crazy Horse dancer one of the other girls couldn't keep her anger from spilling all over me.

"Why would they offer it to you? You're no good for French movies. You look like an American, you act like an American and that is disgusting for French," Vicky Toboggan sneered at me.

She had wanted the part. When she heard there was one being offered to someone at the Crazy Horse she was wild with anticipation, absolutely sure that she would get it. Then Vicky found out the part was mine and started following me around asking insulting questions in front of the other girls.

"How did you get this? Who do you know to fuck?" Vicky asked.

Vicky was about five foot eight, with dark hair and eyes, but it seemed the movie director wanted a redhead with blue eyes. She couldn't do much about that and was frustrated.

Vicky found out the scenes were going to be shot in a theatre near Montmartre and came to the set. She wandered around, tried to rub the director's back while he was telling the lighting man what to do, talked loudly to anyone who would glance her way and made a pest of herself.

We were in a small theatre with lighting cables and sound equipment all over the floor. I had on cute silver panties and waved a French flag while walking in circles on the stage, shouting political slogans in French that didn't make any sense to me. I was confused and couldn't figure out how to do it.

"So, why is she in the movie and not me?" I heard Vicky asking the director in the sultry, manipulating whisper that felt like she had her tongue in your ear.

I wondered why I was chosen, too. It was not a good fit for me.

"I'm sorry, but why is she here?" I decided to ask the director.

"Oh, thank God. I thought she was a friend of yours. That's what she said when she walked in. Paul, walk this lovely girl off the set and outside. This is a closed set." As he turned away from the assistant director and focused his attention back on me, he said, "She doesn't seem to have a good effect on you, my little dear. Now, let's see if you can actually do this."

After that experience there was no getting along with Vicky. Our choreographer, Victor Upshaw, might have been able to calm her but he wasn't there.

Just before the Christmas and New Year's holidays in December, Bernardin decided to have a "Phryne '70" contest to bring attention to the Crazy Horse. He named the contest after the Greek courtesan who in ancient times had illegally posed for a nude statue of Aphrodite, Goddess of Love.

Twelve famous authors, who had recently won recognition for their writing from the French government and been in all the French newspapers, were invited to judge the contest. The authors sat together at fancy tables with flowers. They were to decide which of the fourteen dancers currently at the Crazy Horse had the most beautiful body.

We dancers didn't like the idea. There was no way anyone could come out a real winner. We were all conceited and wanted to win just for the pride of it. There was not even a real prize. Most of us agreed it was another example of Bernardin's sadism, his desire to pit us against one another and see what would happen.

On December 18th the invited audience consisted of more than two hundred famous French painters, sculptors, movie stars and journalists. Also in attendance were diplomats from the German, Swiss and Italian embassies, plus some well-known hotel and restaurant owners. All were drinking fine wine and spirits at the Crazy Horse's little tables.

The lights were low and there was more than the usual excitement among the dancers. This was Bernardin's holiday fete for those who had brought large parties into the Crazy Horse that year. The hope was that they would bring more and larger groups next year.

"This is the order you will go on stage tonight," Sophia said. "We start with Prima. Remember, you step onto the silver disc, get into your statue pose and do not move. The curtain will open. You go around three times and the curtains close. First time you wear the short white silk drape that covers your breasts and the G-string. After all the girls have one go-round, we start with Prima once again but no drape this time, just the G-string. Relax into your statue position once again, go around three times and you're finished. We don't know how long it will take them to make a decision so go to the celebrity lounge, have a champagne, and we all wait together."

The band played as Phryne '70 was about to start. We who were standing backstage waiting to go on, heard the announcer thank the audience for attending and introduce Prima Symphony. She was a dancer in the four and five girl routines between the striptease acts, and did not have a solo performance.

Prima in all her tall, long limbed beauty stood barefoot on the disc as it went around three times. The curtain closed and she hopped off, passing the next girl in the semi-darkness as she exited the stage.

Each girl looked beautiful as she turned in the spotlight, on the silver disc, looking like a distant goddess, arms straight down at her sides, eyes blank.

The audience was silent.

I was number nine in line. I didn't want to stand in exactly the same pose as any of the other girls. Sophia had not said we all had to stand the same. I held my hands clasped behind me, resting on my lower back, my face looking slightly to the right, my right knee bent and in front of the other as I had seen dancers pose in paintings.

"Miss Candy Capitol!" was announced. The curtains opened.

Looking at the handsome audience of well-dressed powerful men and women, all looking at me, made me feel good. I smiled. I forgot I probably wasn't supposed to, although it had never been mentioned. So I kept smiling. They were such a pleasure to look at.

Wild applause broke out across the whole club. I went around on the disc three times. The applause did not stop. What was going on?

Bonita Super was on the disc when Sophia grabbed my arm.

"What happened out there?" she said

"I don't know," I said, and we both turned to ask the next girl in line.

"You did something you shouldn't have done. What was it? Did you move? We're all supposed to stand still, no dancing," said our little Italian darling, Rosa Fumeto.

No one else received any applause on the first turn.

Prima did her next three turns on the disc, nude except for a small silver G-string. A few hands clapped. This time she stayed backstage to see what the rest of the girls did on the disc instead of going to the dressing room or for champagne in the lounge.

The second time on the disc we were to go around three times again. Each dancer before me took their turn and waited backstage afterward. I knew they were waiting to see what happened when I went on stage. I would have done the same thing. They were curious and intensely competitive.

By the time it was my turn again, I knew what I had done the first time. Smile. I probably should have kept my face serious and lifeless as all the rest had, but I couldn't. From the moment I had begun my career as a dancer it had been pounded into my head to smile on stage. Was it wrong? Was I cheating? I didn't have time to think about it. I just did what was natural for me again.

The audience showed their appreciation of my smile with loud applause, yelling and whistling. It sounded like the audience, of mostly older men, wanted to look at someone who was alive, joyous and upbeat.

The other dancers were bitterly offended. Standing naked and flat-footed, some with fists clenched, thirteen women looked like they wanted to spit at me and beat the smile off my face. Their eyes assured me they would prefer to do it sooner rather than later.

Bernardin had no need to spend time wondering who his judges would choose to win the title of Miss Phryne '70. It was obvious, though I was not happy about it. I had lost the good wishes and any affection the other dancers ever held for me.

The prize was a white, plaster- of-Paris torso of Aphrodite. I was ready to take the newspaper pictures with it when the short, dark and extremely hairy artist who seemed to have led the applause danced up to me like a pixie.

"zzzz zzzzzzzzzz zzzzzzz have to bite you," I thought he said.

Before I knew what was happening he grabbed my arms, pulled my almost nude body toward him, stretched up and bit my neck.

"Yeeeccccckkkkkkk!!" I screamed as I pushed him away from me, into the circle of judge-artists ready and waiting to have their picture taken on stage with the contest winner.

"Oh, darling, don't be mad. You're not hurt, are you?" One of the other dark suited, older artists leaned toward me and explained quietly, "He must do this to keep up the reputation. He bites all he loves. The little one is famous for this biting," he said with a tolerant chuckle while nodding his head. "Is funny, no?"

The next morning, the newspaper pictures taken of Miss Phryne '70 showed an angry, non-smiling, Miss and seven confused artists who didn't know which way to look toward the cameras. What a catastrophe.

Candy and the authors. Candy's not happy.

Christmas and a snowy, cold winter alone in Paris was awful to think about. There was nothing to do in my apartment except lie in bed and read or sleep. I started singing some of my feelings to myself each time I walked down the stairs, crossed the Seine toward the Crazy Horse, then as I climbed back up the seven flights after work.

"*Everything passes with time. Don't worry this will be gone someday.*

Everything passes with time and I must be on my way."

It wasn't poetry or song but similar to a mantra, it was necessary. I needed to boost my spirits somehow and this helped.

Even then I knew I would return to Paris, which would always be the most beautiful city in the world.

There had been rumors for the last few weeks that a great new act would start on New Year's Eve. For the first time, Bernardin would display a lesbian act in his show. It would star Sophia, who had been in his show for years and was his most trusted dancer.

There was also a new dancer who would be Sophia's partner. Silky La Mer, a small-featured and delicately-boned, nineteen year-old blonde who Bernardin had discovered in Vienna, had joined our show at the Crazy Horse. Everyone thought their act would be a wild success.

On the night the new act opened, when the waiters came in to deliver the dancer's drinks, they told us that men and women in the audience groaned, clutched their friends and partners, and ordered more to drink when the act was over. It was as if they too had achieved orgasm and needed strength to carry on.

I watched the act almost every night and heard the groaning too. It was extraordinary and daring because it truly did look as if the two beautiful young women were making love. The choreography suggested and implied this was a fairy-tale sex scene taking place in a 19th century brothel. The rich lavender of the chaise lounge, tiny peach-colored lace and seed pearl costumes, the subtle lighting and perfectly matched and styled blonde wigs all enhanced the effect.

Silky sat on the chaise as Sophia licked the inside of her creamy thigh. Moving up the tender flesh of the abdomen, kissing as she went, Sophia sucked a nipple as her fingers lightly touched her lover's pelvis. Silky arched her back, raised her knees and spread her legs, giving Sophia full access to every part of her body. Sophia completed a slow, graceful, balletic cartwheel over the chaise kissing Silky's mouth while her feet were pointed straight up to the ceiling.

Their soft blonde wigs and the pale pink lighting made the dancers look like angels as one writhed on the deep lavender velvet chaise-longue as if in sexual ecstasy while the other danced around, beside, and over her.

This was the reason audiences came to the Crazy Horse Saloon. There was always the opportunity to see something original and exceptionally beautiful. There was no comparison to the frumpy sadistic act I had seen months earlier at the lesbian club El et Lui. Hollywood club owners would drool with longing to present this exact lesbian number.

Paris was cold and rainy when I took nine pieces of luggage and went home to Los Angeles. I had given away almost everything else collected in my twenty months away from home.

Chapter Thirty

Los Angeles, 1970

Dreamy and Mitzi met me at the airport in the 1965 dark green Volkswagen I had named Perky, because she perk/perk/perked along just like an old-fashioned coffee pot. They had been exercising her and returned her to me now.

I felt awkward and I could see they did too. Mitzi and I were super polite to each other. After they had left me in the parking lot of the motel where they had arranged for me to spend the night I knew Mitzi would measure and count every syllable I said five times, searching for some kind of insult.

"Boobie, you look so tired. Poor thing you must be exhausted," Mitzi said.

I just smiled, nodded and acted tired. Mitzi had gained at least forty pounds while I was gone.

Dreamy stood between us like a prize bull who didn't know which foot to put down next.

As I had returned to Los Angeles in the evening, I was surprised when I opened the Hollywood motel door the next morning. The sun was so strong it pushed me back into the room. I fell against the wall and squinted out the open door. The sun's reflection off the dazzling white stucco buildings, electric green palm trees and red Spanish-style roof tiles glared back at me.

No weak French trickle of light here. In Los Angeles the sun is forceful and hits the earth in a different way than it does in Europe. It beats down upon tender skin, stealing its moisture. It reaches into windows fading each color, heats to burning every car it touches, and melts the black top around the slides and swings of playgrounds.

Everything I planned to do on my first day back in Hollywood had to wait until I had breakfast at El Carmen Café on Third Street, near Crescent Heights. I had been day-dreaming about the reunion with my favorite restaurant ever since I stepped onto the plane a year and a half ago and took off to Rome.

El Carmen was a family-style Mexican restaurant. Clean white walls, green leather booths and high wooden backs was the total gesture toward creating a Mexican atmosphere. Unlike the nearby competition where all the waitresses wore old-fashioned costumes and green plants hung from wooden beams, El Carmen's food was unquestionably the best in town.

The *chile con queso* plate which included the best refried beans in the world, corn tortillas and tongue-tingling salsa, had called to me all the way to Singapore and Paris. I would have gone there directly from the airport but El Carmen closed at nine p.m.

I was very happy with the large one bedroom apartment I found on Franklin near Gower, in the center of Hollywood. It was furnished comfortably, and had a full sized gas stove and refrigerator. There was even a small dining room. I had a bathtub, a private toilet, an elevator to take me from my reserved underground parking place to the second floor. In Europe this was luxury living, but it was available to the American lower middle class in Los Angeles for eighty-five dollars a month.

I had a strong urge to cook meatloaf and spray Windex. I wanted to wax the wooden floors and decorate the living room. This was a brand new part of me. The rooftops of Paris were no longer the first thing I would see in the morning. I wouldn't hear the fruit and vegetable vendors seven floors below and I would miss them. But I had all of Hollywood just a few blocks away and a car to take me to the beach in Malibu. I could go anywhere and understand what was going on around me. I could listen to real American rock and roll and not have to settle for the bland French imitation.

I did go to Boston after a while and stayed for several months although I kept my sweet apartment in Los Angeles. Just as Dr. Hilda had said, it was healing and restful to be with my mom and dad and the sixty-seven Irish cousins. My dad's Boston brothers and sisters and all their children lived in the houses built on five acres of land in the suburbs their father had bought to make a family compound in 1925. Our house was a mile or so away but still felt close.

Attending the Massachusetts Institute of Technology for one semester kept me busy. With the help of my family I realized it wouldn't be hard to fit into school now. Driving into Boston taught me a little about the city but I knew I was a Southern California girl all along and would return to Los Angeles when the semester ended.

It seemed like all of striptease had changed while I was in Paris. The Largo had changed although some of the girls I had worked with were still there. They were no longer wearing G-strings or flesh colored panties to suggest nudity. The dancers were totally, gloriously nude.

The audience could see everything. At the Largo the emphasis was no longer on dancing, beautiful music, costumes or story as it had been just two years before when we were still in a burlesque frame of mind. Now it was all nudity, bare-ass and hairy.

The police had a new ordinance that all the patrons' chairs had to be nailed to the floor close to their table. I couldn't figure that out until someone told me about something called "lap dancing" where the dancers sit on or near a man's lap for money.

Diane Lewis and Joni Carson didn't seem to mind taking off that one last little piece of costume. The pay was better. Early in the third and last song of their act everything had to be off except the jewelry and shoes.

There was more free style Go-Go type dancing and less structured striptease choreography at the Largo. The Pink Pussycat owners, Alice and Harry Schiller, had reorganized also. Their club was similar to the Largo but they had added a six foot two, gorgeous blonde female impersonator, Lady Diana, and a male-female simulated sex act to their show.

There were clubs that only had Go-Go dancers. Fringed knee or thigh-high boots and mini-skirts that ended above the crotch were the norm. The girls worked for an hourly wage and collected tips from men who happily hung five and ten dollar bills onto a garter or the elastic of a tiny pantie for a little extra attention from a big pair of breasts.

In some clubs the dancers, waiting for their turn, sat on straight chairs at the back of the small stages in their little robes while the girl who was "up" danced to three songs from the jukebox. She then went back to her chair, where the audience could still see her every move, and covered herself with a short wrap, while the next girl went to the front of the stage to dance or in some cases just walk around. Some clubs showed pornographic movies on each side of the stage so dancing didn't matter much.

The dancers were always on stage so it was hard work. Flirting and lining up your next big spender even when sitting was not easy with this type of competition. No moments of privacy to scratch or rest between dance spots. However, if she was in the right club, a girl could make more than one hundred a night in tips plus her seven dollars an hour.

Some places the girls rented out tiny flashlights, at five dollars a minute, so the audience could do vaginal exams while the girls stood or sat on the bar with legs spread, G-strings moved to the side. No touching was allowed.

Costumes were different too. Most everything could be purchased at a fancy lingerie shop or at Fredrick's on Hollywood Blvd. Now mass production was the norm, rather than personal taste and custom-fit, but it was inexpensive and flashy. It was easier to put together a show than it had been, and more girls were drawn to perform nude on stage.

A good thing was that dancers no longer needed agents to work at the strip clubs in town. The American Guild of Variety

Artists had lost its tight hold on nightclubs in Los Angeles and was concentrating its efforts in Las Vegas.

"Why pay an agent to find a gig, Brandy? Come back to the Largo. Let's talk to Chuck," Diane Lewis persuaded. "We have the same set up and it would be fun. Of course, Joni is the star now... and I am the co-star."

I heard her. She was really saying, "Just because you've been to Paris, don't think you can come back here and lord it over us. I have won my place and you're not going to take it."

Diane was right. She had worked very hard to win and keep her place at the Largo. I didn't want to take anything from her, nor could I have taken anything. No one in Los Angeles knew or cared about what happened at the Crazy Horse. If I was planning to return to the Largo, it would be as Brandy Wilde, hometown girl, not Candy Capitol, one of the most famous strippers in Europe.

I hesitated at the thought of dancing completely nude at the Largo, even though it was still the best club in Los Angeles. Nude was different in Paris, with the see-through clear plastic G-strings that didn't make me feel completely naked.

After talking to Joni and Diane I realized that all the clubs only hired dancers who would work nude. I had started off my striptease career that way with a roadshow in Texas, so why not? But I hoped I could find something better soon.

I needed to work while I was going to school. I felt like Virginia Mayo in that 1952 movie where she plays a stripper, "*She's Working Her Way Through College*". Virginia's character worried every minute of the movie that someone from her school would find out that she was a stripper but I wasn't worried about that. Another big difference was Virginia had much more clothing on at the end of her act than I would have in mine.

I called Chuck Landis.

"Brandy, you ready to come back to work? I got a place for ya next Tuesday, but I gotta know now."

Chuck had always been economical with words. I guessed that he still gave his dancers their one week notice on Tuesdays. He must have had someone he wanted to let go right away.

"That would be great, Chuck. Did Diane call you already?" I asked.

"None a-you call me unless you want a job. Be here early, like always." I noted the cynicism in his voice before the receiver of his phone clunked into the holder, breaking our connection.

Of course no one called him. He had no telephone manners, but he had given me a job and that was much better than merely being polite. I was thrilled.

Chuck Landis on the Sunset Strip and Bernardin in Paris were similar in many ways. Both were middle-aged, Jewish burlesque club owners with two sons, who wanted everything to be perfect. The main difference between the two men became evident once I was back in Los Angeles. Chuck was shy and left the girls alone. He had a rich family life and ran a great business. Bernardin kept mistresses like the European millionaire he was. He made it a point to keep control and assert his superiority by insulting everyone who worked for him at the club which he had made into the world's best and most famous striptease venue. The Crazy Horse Saloon was his life.

I had to admit being back at the Largo was fun. It had always been fun and felt like I was returning home now. I could join the formal language and the slang of the Largo, knew the politics, how to do the sneaky things like bring in my own alcohol and not get caught. I knew enough to recognize venom when I saw it and not get bitten. All that had been hard for me to see in Paris.

"Come here, you," Bett Casey murmured in her sweet Alabama girl accent. She was as pretty as ever. Her round breasts, dark eyes and full lips were just as inviting. Her brown hair was still worn short and straight in a little cap style.

She circled my waist with a slender arm, drew me close to her body and kissed me on the lips. She had a confident demeanor as if to say, "There's nothing life can throw at me that I can't handle!" She was the right person to meet again at this phase of my life.

"I've missed you, baby," Bett whispered in my ear. "Come home with me tonight. We'll have a little celebration, just us."

I remembered her "little celebrations." The first time we worked together at the Largo Bett had taken me home with her. She dressed me in a long, rose colored, draped silk nightgown with a tight bodice and neckline that showed every bit of cleavage I had. It must have belonged to a movie star in the 1940's. The silk flowed and folded softly against my body like a movie costume. We drank champagne while she pinned gardenias in my hair, decorated me from ear lobes to toes with jewels and made sweet wonderful love to me. Bett was unforgettable.

This engagement at the Largo was starting off just as it had ended two years before, with beautiful women kissing me, stroking me and trying to get me alone so they could do more. The only difference was that this time I appreciated it.

Chapter Thirty-One

A New Act

*H*enry Mudd bought Bett a house in Westwood for her thirty-second birthday in June, 1972.

"I can't wait to get in there again. Let's go see if they're really going to move their stuff out tomorrow," Bett said on a Friday night. She wanted to spy, to watch the current tenants carry their boxes to the truck - as if that could let her start the remodeling sooner.

Henry had been her lover for almost a year and Bett no longer had other paying customers. At sixty, he was an elegant six foot five, grey-haired multi-multi-millionaire who was kind and good-tempered. He had inherited copper mines in Arizona and Cyprus and had grown them into a huge corporation. Although he had a wife and four other mistresses, he was extremely generous with Bett. He had already bought her a Mercedes 450 SL because he couldn't stand the thought of her driving a leased Ford sedan.

She fell crazy in love with him and did her best to keep jealousy from getting in the way of their happiness, but it was hard for her sometimes. Judging from what Bett had said around the dressing room, before she stopped dancing, no one had ever treated her with so much love and respect. To Bett respect was very important.

The only little problem was Henry's second wife. Henry and Bett thought she knew nothing about what he was doing when he was away from her, but was that possible? As he literally stood above most crowds, people were bound to see him and report back to his wife that he had been seen escorting several fancy blondes, redheads and brunettes. He took "his girls" out to restaurants, plays, clubs, and generally did whatever he wanted to do even though he was a well- known society figure who founded the Harvey Mudd College for mining and engineering in the Claremont College complex in Pomona.

All of his mistresses made it a point to wear evening gowns when out with Henry and that was becoming rare in the early 1970's. The general consensus among the girls seemed to be: "If a man is going to pay me several thousand dollars a week to engage my services, I should look special for him." This attitude seemed to work. Henry looked like he was in a continual state of bliss, blue eyes misty and a little smile on his lips.

Henry's very first mistress was the personality packed, red-headed, Ricki. She had taught Henry, who was in his fifties at the time, to have fun with sex. She told him he could have as much sex and as many women as he could afford to buy. Ricki was growing older, and had told Bett she wanted a life where she was not on-call to any man except her chubby little husband. Henry bought a Beverly Hills duplex for Ricki as a "Goodbye to our sexual days" present and all former and present mistresses remained friends.

"Brandy, what would you think about moving into the new house with Bett?" Henry asked on a July afternoon in 1972. "Now that she's not dancing she feels a little lonesome when I'm not there." The three of us were drinking champagne in the main dining room of the beautiful Scandia restaurant, while waiting for our brunch to be served.

Bett nodded like she, the poor little lonesome thing, thought it was a good idea. It was obvious to me they had spoken about it and Bett had chosen who, of all her girlfriends, she could stand to live with. I had my own life and had never been judgmental of hers.

"You know I am paying the mortgage," Henry said gently. "You'll have your own bedroom and bath, and I'll pay all your college expenses. Would that be alright with you?"

I could hardly believe what he was saying. It would be so wonderful for me but would I be taking advantage of a friendship?

He made it seem that I would really be doing him a big favor because having a nice friend living with her would mean so much to Bett. He was such a sweet and innocent man at that time. I loved him too.

"Bett, are you sure you want someone living with you? Don't you want your privacy?" I asked as our brunch order was set down before us.

"You know, in the last few weeks I found out I don't need much privacy. I miss having friends around. We could have so much fun decorating the house and traveling. Henry likes to travel with one or two girls when he takes his wife to Hawaii or somewhere. So, you could go with me, if you wanted to. I'm not going to hang around all day and night by myself to be with him for just one hour a day," she said persuasively.

Henry nodded in agreement while enjoying his eggs benedict.

I had always called Bett the "steamroller" because when she was involved in something, she carried her friends right along with her. This new way of life sounded like jet-setting to me, so glamorous and exciting. I didn't know anything about it, and Bett didn't seem to either. She seemed a little unsure of herself, which was completely foreign to anything I had ever seen from Bett.

I slowly let Henry talk me into living with Bett by nodding and listening carefully to everything he said. His love of higher education and his desire to help others obtain it was a mainstay in his life. Living with Bett would solve my immediate problems of where to live and how to pay my college tuition. I could see all the pros, and only one con against saying yes to his proposition immediately.

"There's no demand for sex included with this offer, Brandy" Bett said, her eyes looking straight into mine. "Henry knows you're a lesbian and that's fine with him."

I looked at Henry for reassurance that what Bett had said was true. He was still paying attention to the conversation and smiled sweetly and nodded yes. He was used to paying for- and getting- whatever he wanted.

Once the absence of a sex requirement was out in the open, I happily agreed to the arrangement. I didn't want there to be any misunderstanding that I had asked for this opportunity or that I was willing to pay for it with sex. To make walking around money I would work part-time at the Largo while I attended school full time. It felt like the perfect solution.

Loving the house was easy. It had three large bedrooms, rose gardens in the front and back-yards, and a sweet blue and white breakfast room with bay windows beside the open kitchen. The formal dining room and enormous front parlor which over- looked beautiful tree- lined Eastborne Street sealed my love for Bett's new home.

Bett started decorating the house with color and texture be- fore we moved in. Trying to choose materials from tiny swatches didn't work for us. When we finished the living room it had a purple-pink woolen wall-to-wall carpet, red flocked wall paper on one wall and an orange and tan striped couch. I could see Henry block his eyes against the onslaught of mismatched colors every time he walked in the front door.

In a few weeks there were no longer three bedrooms. The smallest of the three had been split to enlarge the bedroom where Bett would entertain Henry and to make her walk-in closet larg- er. closet was now 8' x 16' including the built-ins which suited Bett just fine.

The walls beside and behind the bed were covered in the same heavy, delicious pink velvet as her king sized bedspread and draperies. The room felt like it pumped pure estrogen. It was my favorite room in the house.

My much smaller but beautiful bedroom was done in the same heavy velvet, but leaf green, which suited my coloring and taste. The shadow of the golden angel Moroni, on top of the

Mormon Temple, came in through the window and stretched across my bed.

Henry set a weekly schedule so he could see each girl as often as he wished and still have time for his wife. He spent time with Bett on Wednesday evenings and on Saturday afternoons. For this she received two thousand dollars a week plus her house payment, a maid who came in three days a week, a no-limit credit card for clothing, the remodeling of her house and whatever presents Henry wanted to give her.

Bett thought all the girls received the same amount of money but the only people who knew for sure were Henry and his accountant. Bett was not demanding, but the other girls, who were more used to the free-flowing dollars, probably were.

I couldn't figure out how Henry managed his time. Certainly, he had to make some time for his wife, but when? Did he schedule her in for the remaining three nights and three afternoons? Did she know her schedule as the others knew theirs?

Sometimes I was invited out to dinner or to a show with Bett and Henry. So there I was, a full-time student at Los Angeles City College, and a part-time stripper, living in the lap of luxury.

To keep herself busy Bett bought all her clothes and mine too, on Rodeo Drive. But how many dresses, gowns and shoes could she wear? She was a very creative person yet she had nothing to do but take care of Henry for a few hours twice a week. She did need extra bodies to dress. She was trying to bribe me into wearing prints while she knew I liked solid colors. When the price of gowns started reaching four thousand dollars at Worley's on Rodeo Drive, I began to wonder if that might be a strain on Henry's wallet, considering that he was supporting six women now.

I needn't have worried. Anything Bett spent was fine as long as it was legal. He was serious about his girls not using illegal drugs of any kind.

Bett had choreographed my new French act and it was a great hit with the Largo audiences. I loved it too. Bett had made a moveable light pole prop out of a tall floor lamp. She also found *In the Old Fashioned Way* sung by Charles Aznavour, the most famous and beloved French cabaret singer of the time. I was to play the street walker looking for love, and paying customers.

In my new act, the black satin hat with a huge rhinestone pin in the front was the first thing I took off. My hair fell to my shoulders in a bright red surprise. Attached to the long gown of black silk crepe was a heavy rhinestone necklace that covered my shoulders and part of my back that stayed on when the dress came off and throughout the entire act. The black lace corselet, a vintage beauty, held my waist in tight. The music was French, a little more sophisticated than the music I had started dancing to. The full and sheer black silk and lace penoir I slipped on as I whipped off the corselet was soft and billowed out behind me as I danced. Made of delicate transparent silk, it felt sensual on my body, like the softest skin, sweet to my touch.

Bett had done a great job with my choreography. She had been a teacher at an Arthur Murray's dance studio in Alabama before becoming a stripper. The act felt French - almost.

"I'd like to write a book about your life," said the pretty, dark- eyed young woman who brought my dinner plate to the table at El Carmen. Her dark brown hair was long and straight. She was wearing strings of blue and brown hippie beads with several very white human teeth thrown into the mix.

I smiled, and laughed at her terrific pick up line. I wondered if she meant it like that. Any way she meant it, it was a great icebreaker. No female had ever said something so funny and original to me. She was cute, too.

"You'll have to stand in line. Truman Capote has already asked for my story," I teased.

She looked so interested in what I was saying I kept on talking.

"I met him in a bar last year when he squeezed up next to me, put his hand on mine and said, "Tell me your story. I know I love it."

"I didn't know who he was at first but he was so little and cute I let him sit down. He was kind of unsteady on his feet, and we talked for a few minutes. I recognized him mid- conversation and was flattered he was taking such an interest in me. He was funny but he asked the most intimate questions. I didn't mind his asking and told him where I had been and what I was doing."

"I knew you had a story. I can see it. Write it down or let me do it." he said.

"The guy he was with got nervous at that and started pulling on him to leave. But Truman already had my number."

It was about 3:30 in the afternoon at my favorite restaurant. I was the only customer. I always ate early when I was dancing that night. My first agent, Lillian McCardle, had said, "The audience can see a pork chop through a beaded gown, so always eat early." I kept true to my first lessons, hard won in the makeshift burlesque venues of a decade before.

"This is my grandmother's restaurant. I come here after school sometimes to help out. Montserrat," she said, introducing herself and offering her hand for me to shake.

"I'm Brandy." I put my hand in hers.

"Yes, I know. You're famous here. The cooks and bus boys fight each other to peep through the little window in the kitchen door just to watch you eat with whatever gorgeous girlfriend you come in with. They call you the 'Red lesbian.' They're all jealous of how many women you have, and how they look at you."

Montserrat smiled and her face became beautiful right in front of me. I had never seen a smile change a face so radically. Seeing the perfect white teeth and energy that came into her eyes with that smile, dimples flashing, was amazing. It changed my reaction to her, made what she was saying more fun. The way she looked at me made me feel I was important to her.

She sat in the booth with me for a few minutes then left for an appointment. I glanced at the kitchen door. In its narrow window, two faces with shocked expressions looked back at me. This time I had been talking and laughing with the boss's granddaughter. The look on their faces asked me if I was going to try to corrupt her. They already knew the answer.

I took Montserrat to Lloyd's, her first gay bar. It was so much fun watching her. She couldn't take her eyes off the men dancing with men and women dancing together, kissing and fondling each other on the small dance floor. She seemed entranced by the freedom they were enjoying. Same-sex dancing in clubs had been illegal in California just months before.

In the spring of 1973 Go-Go dancing was more popular than burlesque and business at the Club Largo was slow. We were in the middle of a recession and public nudity was no longer rare. Chuck had tried everything to bring in audiences, like letting women in free and later no cover charge at all, but nothing had worked.

He even made Candy Barr come in from Texas to complete the six month contract she'd had with him years earlier before her arrest and imprisonment for marijuana possession while she was visiting friends in Dallas. Mickey Cohen, known to the Los Angeles police as a member of the Mafia, had been Candy's lover then and a frequent member of the Largo audience. Candy's arrest was all over the Los Angeles newspapers. The articles included rumors that the Largo was under investigation for alleged Mafia connections. It was romantic and daring for striptease audiences to be in such famous company. The club was full then and Chuck was happy. I guess he thought that might happen again.

When Candy arrived, she was naturally the star of the show. Her name went up on the marquee and she was given one of the two private dressing rooms.

Candy was resentful about being dragged back to Hollywood. It showed in her act and her attitude. It was no longer the unusually fast, original and 'bounce off the walls' act it had been before her time in prison. Her costumes were plain and pale next to the other acts in our show and so was her face as she wore no makeup other than lipstick. She didn't smile. She looked bored. Candy was telling Chuck to go screw himself in every way she could.

After a month of disappointed audiences and poor newspaper reviews Chuck let Candy leave the Largo for good. Joni Carson returned to her place as the star and Diane was the co-star again.

Candy had been living with our former star Joni and her husband while in Hollywood, at the request of Chuck Landis. He felt she needed a sort of caretaker. I can't imagine Joni felt very good about that. Joni realized Candy did need someone to take care of her once she had Candy installed in one of the upstairs bedrooms, but she couldn't ask Candy to leave.

"I'm so relieved now that she's gone," Joni said the night Candy left for Las Vegas. "She wandered around the house humming and singing about how she needed a knife to kill someone and bury him in the desert. I didn't understand it but I didn't want to ask her about it either. She said she had found God and became a gospel singer in prison but I don't believe a word of it."

Most of the girls were glad Candy Barr was gone. She was her wild self in the dressing rooms, smoking pot and drinking bourbon from the bottle, but she wasn't friendly. She didn't share. Among the Largo dancers her reputation for having sex with two girls at the same time on the dressing room carpet lingered, but Candy no longer performed in that way either. Pepper Daily had fallen in love with Candy, who had given Pepper her stage name, and was heartbroken when she left the Largo.

There were now dozens of Go-Go clubs in Los Angeles. The music was faster and more modern than traditional burlesque torch songs and instrumental blues. Go-Go customers were younger than striptease audiences, and they usually drank beer instead of scotch and bourbon highballs. It was casual and seemed more like background atmosphere instead of a show.

Some nights we only had a dozen people for the first show and one or two customers for the last few hours of the evening. We still had to dance, no matter how many people were in the audience. Some of my very best shows were given to that one person, so they wouldn't feel discounted.

One evening I picked up the telephone in the dressing room and heard the club manager say, "Tell the girls, Chuck wants everyone in his office after the show." It was the first time that had ever happened.

"Oh, my God, what's going to happen now?" and "Oh, shit!" were the main reactions when they heard what the call was about.

Chuck sat behind his big desk while we dancers stood in a ragged semi-circle around it.

"You know business has been slow for a long time. So, I'm going to close the Largo next week. I'm sorry. I know this is going to cause you trouble, but it can't be helped. That's all," Chuck said as he stood up to let us know he meant for us to leave his office immediately.

"But....but...." is all that Twinkie Reyes got out before the manager, who was losing his job too, lightly took Twinkie's arm to lead her out of the office and into the corridor. The rest of us followed -- like sheep in shock -- as Chuck quickly shut the door.

I started walking to my car and saw Joni and Diane talking on the street. They were feeling the same way I was. No one wanted to leave the property now that it was slipping away from us. I had worked at the Largo for five years with just a few interruptions. All my friends were there. It had been the perfect place for a lesbian stripper; no mixing, no harassment from the owner and lots of beautiful women. I missed it already.

I was carrying twelve units, four classes, at Los Angeles City College, but decided I should try to find a job at the Pink Pussy Cat on Santa Monica Blvd. Alice Schiller, the owner was nice and I still needed money for girls and car insurance, all the things that make life fun.

It was hard keeping school hours and work hours without making a few mistakes. The first History of Religion class with Ms. Fuchs I showed up late and still drunk at 10 a.m. and could hardly stay awake. That only happened once but I felt terrible about it.

"I'm going up to Canada. Not going to be much work around here now and Canada is just opening up, so the money is great," Kitten said to me as we were packing our gowns and panels into their long dress carriers. "You should try it. Let me give you the agent's address and telephone number. Call him and find out what he can do for you."

I talked it over with Henry and Bett one evening when they took Montserrat and me out to dinner. I didn't want it to seem like I was shrugging off my obligation to them. We were at a trendy new restaurant called Gatsby's, we three women in Grecian style evening gowns, Henry ordering drinks.

"What do you mean you can't tell the difference between vodkas? I can taste the difference between Stolichnaya, Vyberova and Smirnoff any time," Montserrat boasted.

Within minutes we each had three bottles of cold vodka, labels covered, in front of us and a tray of square shot glasses. Why we needed twelve bottles to do this I had no idea, but that's the way Henry liked to do things.

A waiter stood ready to pour and we began to drink. Bett didn't guess right at all even after many tastes, neither did Henry. Montserrat won the contest as she guessed correctly twice. I don't remember what I guessed. I only came back to my senses after my nap when dinner was almost over.

When I did call Bill Duckworth, the agent in Ottawa, he sounded excited.

"From the Crazy Horse? Man oh man! They'll go nuts in Quebec. Anything from France and they go ape shit! Send me the French publicity and the stuff in English too and I'll put it into a collage up here and send it out to club owners right away.

Maybe you can come up for the whole summer if you send it to me quick enough. I can probably get you a grand a week plus lodging. You could do a week in several little cities around Quebec Province for most of the summer. Sound good?" he asked.

It sounded wonderful. I wouldn't have to dance at all during the school year. That would be a new experience for me. I had worked almost every day since leaving high school. Concentrating on college was what I wanted most and it was fun. I was searching for a new profession to prepare for the rest of my life and I could see Montserrat in my arms.

Afterword

(In alphabetical order)

Barr, Candy

Candy returned to the Largo in 1972, several years after she was released from prison where she had served three years for possession of two marijuana cigarettes. She still owed Chuck Landis, owner of the Club Largo, several months of work on a play-or-pay contract. She was one of the most famous burlesque performers in the world but she was no longer glamorous and her act was less than thrilling. Candy retired from show business in the early 1970's. In the early 1980's Candy Barr was acknowledged in the magazine *Texas Monthly* as one of history's "Perfect Texans" along with Lady Bird Johnson. She lived in her hometown of Edna, Texas. Candy Barr died at the age of 70 while in Texas. Pneumonia was listed as the cause of her death in 2005.

Bernardin, Alain

Bernardin married Lova Moor in 1984. He owned and directed the Crazy Horse Saloon in Paris from 1951 until his death in 1994. The Crazy Horse became famous, under his direction, for being the finest striptease club in the world. He committed suicide in his office with a shotgun. Bernardin's children sold The Crazy Horse Saloon but the show continues. A version of the current show is now performed at the MGM Grand in Las Vegas, Nevada.

Bertolino, Mario

Bertolino had an international opera career that lasted 52 years.

Carson, Joni

Joni starred in a show on the Las Vegas Strip for several months then went on tour around the United States. She became a real estate broker and married another broker she met in class. Together they bought eighteen apartment buildings and had a property management company of their own.

Casey, Bett

Bett sold her house in Westwood. She bought a large bus and travels around the United States with her husband and a series of rescued Greyhound dogs. Henry Mudd left Bett an irrevocable trust fund to help support her for as long as she lives. She is a devout fundamental Christian, involved with helping others in her church.

Coralie Jr.

Coralie was still blonde and beautiful in her 80's when I visited her Burbank agency in 2011. She is now an agent for entertainers who perform on cruise ships and in clubs as well as actors.

Crazy Horse Saloon

Alan Bernardin started the Crazy Horse in Paris in 1951. He made all the decisions for over forty years. It became the most famous striptease club in the world. There were many imitations but no other club reached the same level. The waiters were the most handsome, dancers the best and most beautiful in the world, drinks were of the highest quality spirits. He decided what story the acts would tell, the dancers names, the costumes, music, makeup, hair styles, choreography and props. It was one man's vision, carried out to perfection, by an entrepreneur who made it his entire life. After M. Bernardin died in 1994 a corporation took over the operation of the club and things changed.

Currier, Althea

Althea now lives in Southern California near her son, his wife and three of her grandchildren. She also has two daughters. Althea became a member of the Church of Latter Day Saints when she married her second husband. She is active in their efforts to help others.

Dobritch, Alexander

Was the owner of Dobritch International Circus until 1968. He remarried Rusty Allen. He jumped or was pushed from the 15th floor window of a room at the Mint Hotel in downtown Las Vegas. The write-up in New York Variety newspaper reported he owed $1.6 million to casinos in Las Vegas.

Flanagan, Dreamy and Mitzi Pransky

Dreamy and Mitzi were together for 42 years. They stayed in the same apartment that Dreamy and I lived in before our breakup. Once she found out she could travel outside the United States, Dreamy took Mitzi to Europe many times. Dreamy worked at Northrop, helping to put satellites in space for twenty years. She retired at 65. She lived ten more years, dying of a mysterious, painful disease in July, 2010. Mitzi and I took care of her to the end. Dreamy remained my close and dear friend all of her life. Mitzi's health declined after Dreamy died. She never recovered from Dreamy's death and died thirteen months later in August of 2011.

Fontes, Montserrat

Montserrat was a very successful high school and university teacher for over 30 years. She has written three published novels. We met in 1972 at her family's Mexican food restaurant, El Carmen Cafe. Later she would tell me the first time she looked at me she thought, "I have found you." Montserrat said she decided to spend the rest of her life with me at that moment, but first we had to meet. We were friends for a while when I realized how much I loved her. We bought our dream-home in 1976 and continue to live there. We have been together for over forty years. Without her help and support this book would never have been written. Monsy was a dear friend of Dreamy's and Mitzi's, helping me to care for them in their waning days.

Gillis, Beverly and Jack

My mother, Beverly and father, Jack, moved to Oregon when Michele, their youngest daughter graduated from high school. Beverly died at 71, still a woman of mystery. There are many questions that Michele and I still want answers to. Jack died two years later.

Hills, Beverly

Known as Miss Beverly Hills, she was in several movies, including *Breakfast at Tiffany's* and *Kissing Cousins* with Elvis Presley. She appeared on the Red Skelton television show over 30 times. Beverly moved to Hawaii and became a minister, known in the islands as Rev Bev. She marries couples from around the world near her home at the ocean's edge.

Lewis, Diane

After leaving the Largo, Diane starred on the Strip in Las Vegas, Nevada. She danced in the United States and Canada. Diane bought a home in the Boston area. She worked in one of Boston's roughest areas, called the Combat Zone, as a dancer, then bartender until she was 65 years old. Her mother died in 2008 and left Diane a millionaire.

Moor, Lova

Lova worked as a dancer at the Crazy Horse Saloon for many years before marrying Alain Bernardin, the owner and director in 1984. She became one of the choreographers when she no longer danced there. Lova became a singer and acted in at least three movies. She also introduced a perfume, called Lova Moor Woman.

Mudd, Henry

Henry was a well-known and respected mining engineer who owned copper mines in Arizona, Cyprus and Peru. He died at 77 from two types of leukemia. Henry cofounded Harvey Mudd College in the Claremont Complex of Colleges in Pomona, California. He married one of his six lovers in an effort to protect the trust funds and property he had given each of his "girls." Henry's children sued the estate to nullify the trust funds. The trial was televised in Los Angeles. His children lost their bid to change Henry's will.

Noon, Vicky

Vicky visited Los Angeles with an English man and his wife who was her lover. They stayed at the Beverly Hilton Hotel and loved Beverly Hills which was the only part of Los Angeles they wanted to see. When I visited Paris in 1982, I was told by the owner of the Vietnamese-French restaurant we often went to that Vicky had returned once to eat there with her husband and two children while on vacation from London.

Palladium, Sophia

Sophia married Roberto, her long- time lover. They opened an Italian restaurant together and bought a home in the suburbs of Paris. She remained with the Crazy Horse as a choreographer for more than twenty years when her dancing career was over. She now lives in Nice.

Stacher, Joseph

I met Joe in 1968 in Israel. He treated me with kindness, respect and generosity. Joe was arrested for income tax evasion in 1964. The United States government wanted to deport him to Poland but it was against the law to send a person to a communist-controlled country. Joe was able to take advantage of the Israeli "Law of Return" available to Jews from all countries. He immigrated to Israel in 1965 and obtained citizenship there. Joe died at seventy-five under mysterious circumstances in a Munich, Germany hotel room in February, 1977. Buried secretly, his grave plate was altered to hide the gravesite. In 2011 I read in *Tough Jews* by Rich Cohen that Joe Stacher had been the coordinator between the Jewish Mafia and the Irish Mafia in New York City, bringing them together to form Murder Inc. in the 1920's and 1930's.

Upshaw, Victor

Victor was a choreographer in Europe for twenty-five years. He died in 1990. He choreographed many shows at the Crazy Horse in Paris, in Las Vegas, Spain and Lebanon, and several French films.

Wilde, Brandy

I returned to the United States in April 1970, and for several months lived with my family in the Boston area. I attended MIT for a semester but decided I really was a California girl. Montserrat and I bought a home in 1976, the same year I earned a Bachelor of Arts degree in Speech and Language Pathology. In 1991 I obtained a Master of Arts degree in Health Science while going to school in the evening and working for the Los Angeles

County Health Department Alcohol and Drug Programs Office. Most of my years working for L.A. County were in the Sexually Transmitted Disease Programs Office as a Surveillance Branch Manager/ Public Health Investigator. I worked in the sex trade to the end of my career. Montserrat and I have traveled to more than sixty countries together including France, Israel, Singapore and Nepal.

Zaboo

Zaboo returned to Mali after dancing in Europe for many years. She was the subject of a documentary film made in Gao, Mali in 2003. I have not been able to find the film nor have I been able to locate Zaboo. The written summary about the documentary describes it to be about Zaboo's life. It states she was arrested upon returning to Mali. She was tortured mentally and physically. It also states that after her career as a famous dancer in many European capitals, she is currently homeless, living and begging on the streets of Gao, Mali but retains her queenly attitude. My search to find her is ongoing.

First visit back to the Crazy Horse in 1982, dressed in shamrock green sequins

About the Author

Brandy Wilde was born in Long Beach, California and raised in San Francisco and other Navy towns. Brandy is a member of the Screen Actors Guild and has appeared in several major motion pictures and national commercials. Her favorite role was with Arnold Schwarzenegger and Jeff Bridges in *Stay Hungry*.

As a striptease artist, Brandy receive many recognitions:

- featured performer at the finest striptease club in Los Angeles at the Club Largo
- the first striptease act in Singapore

- the first American to be hired as a dancer at the Crazy Horse Saloon in Paris, the most famous striptease club in the world. She was renamed Candy Capitol.
- the first winner of the Miss Phryne contest in Paris. The contest celebrated "Aphrodite in the Spring."
- the first dancer to star in a live striptease act on international television in Munich, Germany.

The owner of the Crazy Horse Saloon wrote a song for her act entitled *I am a Good Girl* which was immortalized in the 2010 movie *Burlesque,* sung by Christina Aguilera. Cher was the co-star.

English portrait artist Sadie Lee came to her home in Los Angeles to paint her portrait for the British Petroleum sponsored "Queens of Burlesque" exhibit at the National Portrait Gallery in London.

Brandy received a Lambda Literary Foundation scholarship to attend the Emerging Writers Retreat in Los Angeles

Following her career in Striptease, Brandy earned a Bachelor's degree in Speech and Language Pathology and a Master of Arts degree in Health Science from California State University-Los Angeles. She worked for the Los Angeles County Health Dept. Alcohol and Drug Programs Office then transferred to the Sexually Transmitted Disease Programs Office where she was responsible for monitoring all laboratories in Los Angeles County that test for sexually transmitted diseases.

She and her partner of forty-one years live in southern California with their two dogs, two cats and a rescued desert tortoise.

www.ingramcontent.com/pod-product-compliance
Lightning Source LLC
LaVergne TN
LVHW051108080426
835510LV00018B/1952